Law and Society
Recent Scholarship

Edited by Eric Rise

A Series from LFB Scholarly

Equal Educational Opportunity
Brown's Elusive Mandate

Mary F. Ehrlander

LFB Scholarly Publishing LLC
New York 2002

Library of Congress Cataloging-in-Publication Data

Ehrlander, Mary F.
  Equal educational opportunity : Brown's elusive mandate / Mary F. Ehrlander.
     p. cm. -- (Law and society)
Includes bibliographical references and index.
  ISBN 1-931202-45-1 (alk. paper)
  1. School integration--United States--Case studies. 2. School integration--Law and legislation--United States. I. Title. II. Law and society (New York, N.Y.)
  LC214.2 .E57 2002
  379.2'6'0973--dc21

2002008583

ISBN 1-931202-45-1

Printed on acid-free 250-year-life paper.

Manufactured in the United States of America.

Table of Contents

Acknowledgements

I would like to thank my dissertation committee members, Professors David M. O'Brien, Henry Abraham, Edmund Moomaw, and A.E. Dick Howard at the University of Virginia for their encouragement and assistance. I particularly wish to thank Professor O'Brien, whose expert insight, guidance, and support throughout the course of my research and during the writing process have been invaluable.

I also want to express my heartfelt gratitude to my husband, Lars, and our sons, Staffan, Wyatt, and Marcus, whose unwavering support, encouragement, and understanding contributed immeasurably to my ability to complete this project.

Finally, I would like to thank my assistant, Christian Hicks, for his meticulous editing and formatting as we have prepared the manuscript for publication.

Introduction

At the turn of the twentieth century, the Supreme Court's once extraordinary *Brown v. Board of Education of Topeka, Kansas* (1954) holding that *de jure* segregation in public schools violated the Constitution hardly raised an eyebrow. Chief Justice Warren's resounding declaration that "separate educational facilities are *inherently* unequal" rang with clarity and simple truth. The principle enunciated in the decision was in fact so fundamental to America's principles of equality and human dignity that one could only wonder what took the Court and society so long to recognize it. Yet, while the principle behind the Court's decision eventually gained widespread acceptance, that is, that dual school systems were unconstitutional, desegregation of America's schools proved very problematic. Socioeconomic issues rendered the goal of providing all children an equal educational opportunity perhaps even more challenging.

Following a decade of resistance to *Brown*, much progress was made in desegregating the nation's schools, especially in the South. Subsequently, however, demographic trends began to overwhelm school systems, and segregation grew in many areas of the country beginning in the 1970s. Desegregation orders often came to include elaborate busing plans aimed at integrating students living in segregated neighborhoods. By the 1980s, residential segregation had grown so widespread in many areas, that even the most ambitious busing plans did little more than transport children from predominantly minority neighborhoods to slightly less predominantly minority schools. In light of growing residential segregation, many educators, community leaders, and parents began to advocate a return to the community or neighborhood school concept, with increased attention focused on the special educational needs of America's predominantly poor and minority inner-city school children.

As the turn of the century approached, courts were releasing school district after school district from court supervision following decades of compliance with court orders to desegregate. Yet, despite apparent compliance with the court orders, many of which included costly remedial and other compensatory programs aimed at eliminating the vestiges of past discrimination, poor and minority children continued to achieve at significantly lower levels than white children. This persistent achievement gap called into question the effectiveness of educational programs designed to compensate children for their disadvantaged backgrounds. There was little evidence that they produced lasting results. Neither desegregation efforts nor compensatory education programs had succeeded in closing the achievement gap between minority and white students.

As schools became increasingly segregated, as minority children continued to achieve at unacceptably low rates, and as communities were reclaiming control over their school systems, the questions of what *Brown* had accomplished and whether the social and economic costs had been justified naturally arose. More importantly, what *could Brown* have accomplished, given the limitations of the judicial branch's power, issues of federalism and the tradition of local control in schools, and deeply rooted socioeconomic, historical, and political issues that divided Americans and rendered minorities weak in the political process? In the 1950s and '60s, the plaintiffs in the desegregation cases had no other option than to seek a judicial remedy for *de jure* racial segregation in public schools, given the political climate at the time. However, this study offers compelling evidence that while judicial decrees could end the dual school systems, they could not force indifferent and resistant communities to provide quality education for poor and minority youngsters, nor could they eradicate the socioeconomic factors that hindered their academic achievement.

Reevaluation of the desegregation and busing efforts promulgated by *Brown* must begin with examination of the wrong found and the remedy envisioned in the Court's decision. In *Brown v. Board of Education of Topeka, Kansas* (1954), which came to be known as *Brown 1*, the Supreme Court found that the official dual school systems operated in America's South and Midwest violated the equal protection clause of the Fourteenth Amendment. The Court postponed prescribing relief until the following year, when in *Brown v. Board of Education of Topeka, Kansas* (1955), commonly known as *Brown II*, it ordered school districts to establish unitary systems under the supervision of federal district courts. The Court originally called for desegregation, which later came to mean integration, and the requirement that school districts take affirmative action to promote racially integrated schools. *Brown*'s mandate expanded to the North and West, as the Court recognized that segregation in schools existed there, as well, not as the result of statutes, but owing to residential housing patterns which were reinforced by discriminatory practices on the part of school district and state officials.

Segregation in America's schools in the 1990s reflected deeper societal problems manifested in entrenched residential segregation, rather than statutorily or administratively formed dual school systems. Since the 1970s, the white student populations in the vast majority of large urban school districts had been decreasing. Ironically, by the 1980s, the South had the highest level of integrated schools, though segregation grew significantly in that region after 1988.[1] In the 1990s, the Northeast had the highest rate of segregated schools in the nation, with respect to both blacks and Hispanics,[2] but segregation of Hispanics was increasing most rapidly in the West.[3] Thus, the *Brown* mandate evolved, but the philosophy supporting the remedy was that educational isolation harmed poor and minority children, and that exposure of disadvantaged minority children to white middle class children and values would enhance their learning environments. The *means* was integration. The *end* was improved educational opportunity for black and other minority children.

At the turn of the twenty-first century, one of the greatest challenges facing public education was providing America's increasingly isolated poor and minority children the equal education opportunity promised them in *Brown v. Board of Education* and its progeny. The number of children below the poverty line was increasing, and growing residential segregation resulted in greater racial

---

[1] Gary Orfield, *The Growth of Segregation in American Schools: Changing Patterns of Separation and Poverty Since 1968* (Boston: Harvard Project on School Desegregation, 1993), 1.
[2] Ibid., 8.
[3] Ibid., 1.

isolation in schools. Approximately five hundred school systems remained under court supervision, but meaningful integration was no longer possible in many areas. Plaintiffs in certain prominent cases, such as those involving the Kansas City and Wilmington school systems, argued that the persistent achievement gap between white and minority students represented evidence of continued unconstitutional discrimination. However, the Supreme Court in the Kansas City case, followed by the district court in the Wilmington case rejected those arguments, which inferred a judicial mandate fundamentally different than the right to an equal educational opportunity enunciated by the Supreme Court in *Brown* and its progeny.

The Supreme Court indicated its willingness to begin releasing school districts from court supervision in the early 1990s with *Board of Education of Oklahoma City Public Schools v. Dowell* (1991) and *Freeman v. Pitts* (1992). In doing so, the Court acknowledged the limited mandate of *Brown* and its progeny, which was to eliminate *de jure* racial segregation and its vestiges from public schools.

Determination of the point at which the vestiges of past discrimination had been eradicated proved difficult and controversial, but the Court made it clear that no constitutional authority existed for court-ordered racial balancing in schools to counteract residential segregation resulting from private choices. Legal experts predicted that by the first decade of the twenty-first century, relatively few districts would remain under court supervision to desegregate.[4]

Thus, public education was at a crossroads in its obligation to provide quality service. As the vestiges of past unconstitutional discrimination were eradicated, and the legitimate role of the courts ended, individual states, communities and school systems were left to grapple with the challenges of providing an equal educational opportunity to poor and minority children. Having exhausted the resources of the judicial system to protect the rights of minority students, advocates for truly equitable and quality public schools systems would have to turn to political means to render school systems more accountable and responsive to the disadvantaged.

---

[4] Peter Schmidt, "Districts View Desegregation Within a New Light," *Education Week*, 13 December 1997, 10.

CHAPTER 1

The Legacy of Jim Crow

With the end of the Civil War and the passage of the Thirteenth, Fourteenth, and Fifteenth Amendments, (which abolished slavery, made all people born in the United States U.S. citizens and provided them equal protection of the laws, and prohibited states from denying the right of suffrage based on race, respectively), the future looked promising for African-Americans. The basis for optimism was short-lived, however. With the end of Reconstruction, deep-seated racial prejudices, no longer constrained by northern occupation forces, began to chip away at the freedoms enjoyed by former slaves. The Supreme Court, in several late nineteenth century opinions, dealt tremendous blows to the status of blacks by very narrowly construing their newly won constitutional protections.

In the 1873 Slaughterhouse Cases, the Supreme Court confirmed that the legislative intent of the Thirteenth and Fourteenth Amendments had been to protect former slaves from oppression. Then, the Court proceeded to destroy the protection it had affirmed, by declaring that the Fourteenth Amendment merely restricted states from abridging the privileges and immunities of United States citizenship, leaving the states free to deny whomever they pleased the rights of state citizenship.

A decade later, in the Civil Rights Cases (1883), the Court held that the Civil Rights Act of 1875, which forbid racial discrimination in public accommodations and transportation, was unconstitutional, because such discrimination was private, rather than public.   In a reaffirmation of the state action doctrine,[1] the Court held that neither it nor Congress could regulate the affairs of private individuals.   Near [1]the turn of the century, the Court in *Plessy v. Ferguson* provided a legal foundation for the Jim Crow laws which defined the southern way of life by the early twentieth century.   Segregation in public education was but one manifestation of a system designed to ensure the separation of the races.

In *Plessy v. Ferguson* (1896) the Supreme Court sustained an 1890 Louisiana law that called for equal but separate accommodations for white and colored railroad passengers.   In the landmark ruling, under which racial segregation was justified for the next half century, Justice Brown said that the Fourteenth Amendment meant to correct political, not social, inequalities and that it did not call for the commingling of the races where members of either race did not desire it.   Justice Brown said that separation did not imply the inferiority of one race and noted that separation of the races for various reasons, including education, had long been upheld as a right of the states.   The Court held that as long as laws requiring separation of the races were established for "reasonable" purposes, they were constitutional.   The Court noted that laws could not abolish social prejudices and opined that if blacks believed that separation implied inferiority, it was because they chose to do so.   The Constitution could not place two classes that were socially unequal on the same plane.

Justice John Harlan wrote a stinging and now famous dissent to the otherwise unanimous decision, wherein he proclaimed that the Constitution was colorblind and "neither knows nor tolerates classes among citizens." Justice Harlan predicted that the ruling would in time prove to be as pernicious as the Dred Scott case.[2]   He declared that race

---

[1] The Court first iterated the *state action doctrine* in United States v. Cruikshank (1875),), when it held that the types of lynchings which Congress attempted to prevent in the Civil Rights Act of 1870 usually consisted of *private* rather than *state* action, thereby denying a constitutional basis for the Act; the Fourteenth Amendment forbid only state action to deny equal protection.

[2] Dred Scott v. Sandford, 60 U.S. 393 (1857) held *inter alia* that Congress did not have the authority to restrict slavery in the territories, thus declaring unconstitutional the Missouri Compromise, and declared that Negroes could not be United States citizens or citizens of states. The decision met with vehement opposition; it sullied the prestige of the Court

hate should not be sanctioned by law and asked what could produce more hate than the implication that blacks were so inferior that they could not be allowed to sit beside whites. He condemned the ruling, pronouncing, "The thin disguise of 'equal' accommodations (will) not mislead anyone, nor atone for the wrong this day done."

The Court first implicitly endorsed Plessy in public education in *Gong Lum v. Rice* (1927). Gong Lum, a Chinese man, had challenged the fact that his daughter was forced to go to a "colored" school. The Court held that Chinese were "colored," applying Plessy to public education, and it reaffirmed the states' right to legislate in such matters. Chief Justice Taft wrote: "The right and power of the state to regulate the method of providing for the education of its youth at public expense is clear." A decade later, though, the NAACP achieved its first victory in its drive to abolish racial segregation.

The Court set a major precedent in Missouri ex. rel. *Gaines v. Canada* (1938), in striking down a portion of Missouri's law which denied blacks entrance to Missouri's law school, but provided funds for qualified black residents to attend law schools in other states. The Court held that each state must provide equal, if separate, school facilities. However, a decade later, in *Sipuel v. Board of Regents of the University of Oklahoma* (1948), the Court indicated that it would accept virtually any facilities for blacks as equal. In this case, rather than arguing that the facilities provided for colored students were far from equal, Thurgood Marshall, counsel for the NAACP, and later Supreme Court justice, challenged the constitutionality of the separate but equal doctrine for the first time. The plaintiff's brief declared:

> Segregation in public education helps to preserve a caste system which is based upon race and color. It is designed and intended to perpetuate the slave tradition. . . . Equality, even if the term be limited to a comparison of physical facilities, can never be achieved . . . the terms 'separate' and 'equal' can not be used conjunctively in a situation of this kind; there can be no separate equality.[3]

---

for decades to come, and it is regarded as having been a major catalyst for the Civil War.

[3] In Richard Kluger, *Simple Justice: The History of Brown v. Board of Education and Black America's Struggle for Equality* (New York: Alfred a. Knopf, 1976), 259.

The brief did not directly challenge the constitutionality of the *separate but equal* doctrine *per se*; Marshall challenged the doctrine as practiced in Oklahoma. However, the Court accepted the state's establishment of a roped off law school in the state capitol, served by three law professors, as compliance with the constitutional requirement to provide equal (if separate) educational facilities. Two years later, the NAACP convinced the Court to adopt a more critical view of the inequities between higher educational facilities for blacks and whites.

Sweatt v. Painter (1950) and *McLaurin v. Oklahoma State Regents for Higher Education* (1950) together marked a major milestone in the road toward *Brown*, when the Court for the first time considered intangible aspects of higher education in determining whether separate institutions were equal under the Fourteenth Amendment. In *Sweatt*, the Court considered such intangible qualities of law school as the prestige of the institution and the reputation of the faculty. The Court ruled that Mr. Sweatt could not receive an equal education at the newly established law school for colored students, because the prestige of that institution, a factor very important in the career opportunities of graduates of law schools, and that of the renowned University of Texas Law School were incomparable. In *McLaurin*, the Court considered another "intangible," the intellectual exchange among students so important to the quality of graduate education. George McLaurin, a black man in his 60s, had been forced to sit outside the classrooms for white students and had been required to sit in a segregated section of the library. The Court held, "Such restrictions impair and inhibit (McLaurin's) ability to study, to engage in discussions and exchange views with other students, and in general, to learn his profession. . . . State-imposed restrictions which produce such inequalities cannot be sustained." Having achieved significant victories in higher education, the NAACP decided it was time to attack racial segregation in public elementary and secondary schools.

The landmark case *Brown v. Board of Education* (1954) capped nearly a century of strictly enforced racial segregation in public schools in the South. The decision consolidated four lower court cases: *Briggs v. Elliott* (South Carolina), *Davis v. County School Board of Prince Edward County* (Virginia), *Belton v. Gebhart* (Delaware), and *Brown v. Board of Education of Topeka, Kansas*, all of which challenged particularly egregious disparities in the public education provided black and white children. The Court delivered its opinion in a companion District of Columbia case, *Bolling v. Sharpe*, the same day.

In litigating these cases, attorneys within the upper echelons of the NAACP had debated whether to adopt the strategy of equalization under *Plessy* or to challenge the *separate but equal* doctrine itself. As the four cases went to the Supreme Court, the NAACP chose to attack the *separate but equal* doctrine head-on and ask for reversal. The Court did not technically reverse *Plessy* in *Brown,* though the case is generally regarded as having had that effect. In *Brown* the Court established a special category for education, because it was absolutely essential to success in life. The Court ruled that separate was inherently unequal with regard to schools; thus, black students were being denied the equal protection under the law guaranteed in the Fourteenth Amendment. The Court came to the same conclusion in *Bolling v. Sharpe*, but based its holding on the Due Process Clause of the Fifth Amendment, because the Fourteenth Amendment applied only to the states.

Chief Justice Earl Warren had painstakingly endeavored to craft an opinion that would garner the support of all nine justices. The *Brown* (I) opinion has often been described as uninspired, bland, and simple, and its brevity cannot go unnoticed. Yet, the need for a single, unanimous opinion outweighed the desire for a more stirring or thorough treatise. Unanimity on such a divisive case was extremely rare, but it was essential to the effectiveness of the ruling. As J. Harvie Wilkinson wrote, "To speak with one voice was to speak with force and finality; to speak otherwise was but to lend comfort to any enemy already in prey."[4] Brevity was all but imperative. As Chief Justice Warren reasoned, each additional sentence would invite opposition or offense among the justices and insistence on writing separate opinions,[5] which would, in turn, invite resistance.

Brown relied on social science, and footnote eleven was perhaps the most remarkable part of the opinion. It listed seven works by contemporary social scientists who described the detrimental effects of racial segregation on children. Experts had testified that their research showed that segregation in schools damaged the personal and mental

---

[4] J. Harvie Wilkinson, III, *From Brown to Bakke: The Supreme Court and School Integration: 1954 -- 1978* (New York: Oxford University Press, 1979), 30.

[5] Ibid., 31.

development of Negro children. This reliance on social science invited derision from opponents of the decision and continued to draw criticism from court watchers who approved the results of *Brown*, but disagreed with the Court's role in "social engineering." Yet, public acceptance of the decision grew and by the end of the twentieth century, few questioned the justice in its central holding. Noting the public's acceptance of this new role for the court, Wilkinson wrote, "If the departure from appropriate process was so evident in *Brown*, never was the temptation greater to look the other way."[6]

Yet, the controversial reliance on social science, rather than on the text of the Constitution, historical evidence of original intent, or precedent gave opponents of the decision ample justification for rejecting it as social engineering. The Court had clearly expanded its traditional role in reaching the only just decision possible. The question remains whether the Court was within its jurisdiction to formulate a sweeping policy change when the legislative branch was unwilling or unable to do so. It is difficult to argue that nine appointed justices who are virtually free from political accountability should attempt to create broad social policy. Decades after the decision, advocates of judicial restraint, despite their support for desegregation policy, still found themselves unable to reconcile the Court's decision with constitutional principles. Yet, segregation was anathema to America's most basic democratic, libertarian, and egalitarian principles. Had the Court ruled otherwise, the reaction might have been equally or even more violent.

Most Americans in the 1990s accepted the Court's ruling that purposeful racial segregation in public education was unconstitutional. Continuing controversy surrounded the implementation of the decision and to what lengths courts could or should require school districts to go to effect racial *integration*. The judicial mandate that school districts provide an equal, and some courts went so far as to demand a *quality*, education proved unworkable. Political resistance to integration, as well as state and community indifference to inequities in public education, were insurmountable barriers to the implied goal of *Brown*, which was to provide all children with an opportunity to succeed in life.

The Court did not immediately announce the remedy for the constitutional violation in *Brown* I. It heard arguments regarding

---

[6] Ibid., 39.

implementation of the decision the following year. In *Brown v. Board* (II) (1955), the Court ordered school boards to develop plans for admitting children to school on a racially non-discriminatory basis, under the supervision of federal district courts. The courts were to be guided by "equitable principles." School districts were to act in "good faith" and make a "prompt and reasonable start" at compliance, after which courts could allow more time to effectively carry out the order. The courts and school districts were to move with "all deliberate speed." Like *Brown* (I), *Brown* (II) was unanimous.

Vehement resistance to the *Brown* decisions did not take place immediately. By 1957 many school boards, especially those in large cities had taken significant, voluntary steps to comply with the Supreme Court ruling. State officials in the upper south reacted temperately, as well. "From Texas through Virginia compliance was underway."[7]

Beneath the surface calm, however, the import of the *Brown* decision did not go unnoticed. Segregationists who dominated the rural areas, especially the "Black Belt," (Mississippi, Alabama, South Carolina, Georgia, Eastern Arkansas, Northern Louisiana, Northern Florida, and East Texas, where the concentration of blacks was highest,) were aghast. They feared that if they did not take action to stop the movement towards integration in the larger cities, it would soon spread, and there would be no stopping it. This mostly blue collar, rural whites generally felt most threatened by integration, because they were in direct competition with blacks for jobs, homes, and social prestige. They lived adjacent to or interspersed with blacks, so integration would be easiest to implement in their neighborhoods and would likely affect them first.[8]

Moderates, who tended to be urban, educated, more prosperous, and *more sensitive to outside opinion*, reacted much more calmly to court-ordered segregation. The majority of the moderates were not enthusiastic about integration, but they could accept it on a gradual basis. More importantly, they embraced constitutional principles and accepted the authority of the Supreme Court.[9]

---

[7] J.W. Peltason, *Fifty-Eight Lonely Men: Southern Federal Judges and School Desegregation* (New York: Harcourt, Brace & World, Inc. 1961), 32.
[8] Ibid., 32-33.
[9] Ibid., 34.

One of the most effective methods used by school boards to delay integration was the pupil-placement plan. Also called "freedom of choice plans," they called for automatic placement of children in the schools they had previously attended, (which meant that segregation continued,) although students could request a transfer to schools closer to their homes. Such requests resulted in exceedingly complex procedures to determine whether the students qualified for enrollment at the alternative schools. Pupil placement boards became adept at devising reasons why black students were not suited to attend the schools they requested. A significant advantage of such plans, in the eyes of segregationists, was that they put the burden of desegregating on individual black students, rather than on the school boards. The courts usually accepted the plans, probably because "bad faith" on the part of the school boards was difficult to prove.

The *Brown* decisions resulted in tense relations between the federal government (primarily the judiciary branch) and state and local government officials who were being pressured by their constituents. Once again, a fundamental aspect of the southern way of life had come under attack by "outsiders." Traditionalists rallied their forces, and segregationist hysteria swept through the South. Ironically, as the federal district court judges struggled to maintain order and induce at least minimal compliance in the years immediately following the *Brown* decisions, the Supreme Court was silent. For three years following *Brown (II)*, the Court did not hear a segregation case, and southern school districts grew increasingly defiant.

A major victory for the segregationist cause came with the 1957 signing of the "Southern Manifesto" by 101 southern U.S. Congressmen. Declaring the decision in *Brown* "contrary to the Constitution," the signers vowed to use "all lawful means" to bring about a reversal and to prevent its implementation. The Manifesto urged southerners to refrain from disorder and lawlessness during "this trying period."[10] The only southern senators who did not sign the Southern Manifesto were Estes Kefauver and Albert Gore of Tennessee and Lyndon Johnson of Texas.[11]

The segregationist cause was further bolstered by the fact that neither the executive nor the legislative branch of the national

---

[10] David M. O'Brien, *Storm Center: The Supreme Court in American Politics* (New York: W. W. Norton & Company, 1993), 380.
[11] Kluger, 752.

government provided moral or authoritative support for the Court's decision. President Eisenhower was strongly criticized for his lack of leadership during this tumultuous time. Many bitter southerners contended that had the president publicly supported the Court's authority in the matter, had he pointed to the supremacy of federal law, or had he merely declared that law (rather than mobs) must rule, much of the frenzy would have died. Moderation would have prevailed, and integration would have progressed much more smoothly. However, Eisenhower never endorsed the *Brown* decision and often expressed sympathy for the upheaval integration was causing in the South. Of course, he did not directly encourage lawlessness. He urged extremists *on both sides* to adopt a more reasonable stance. There was simply no presidential leadership when it was so desperately needed, and the refusal of the Justice Department to act encouraged segregationists in their obstructionist tactics throughout the South.[12]

On numerous occasions rioters attempted to disrupt the implementation of a federal court order. At times the rioters acted with the tacit approval of state and local officials.[13] The Little Rock confrontation was the most infamous. Virgil Blossom, Little Rock superintendent of schools, requested help from the United States Department of Justice after Governor Faubus and local segregationists had harassed him for attempting to comply with federal court orders. It was not until the situation became explosive when Faubus called in the National Guard to bar black students from entering Central High School that President Eisenhower finally responded by calling in the 101st Airborne troops to oversee the peaceful integration of the school.

Following the standoff at Little Rock, the Supreme Court reentered the melee and agreed to review *Cooper v. Aaron* (1958). In *Cooper v. Aaron*, Governor Faubus and the State of Arkansas claimed that they were not bound by the 1954 *Brown* decision. Arkansas had not been a party to the *Brown* suit, but a federal court judge had ordered the Little Rock school board to desegregate. State officials tried to block the school board from complying with that decree. The Supreme Court, in ruling against the state, could have declared simply that state officials had no authority to nullify a federal court order, but the Court went much further. In a decision *signed by all nine members of the Court,* the justices declared in no uncertain terms that the

---

[12] Peltason, 49-50.
[13] Ibid., 51.

Constitution was the supreme law of the land, and, quoting Chief Justice Marshall in *Marbury v. Madison* (1803), "It is emphatically the province and duty of the judicial department to say what the law is." Thus, the Court declared that its interpretation of the Fourteenth Amendment in *Brown v. Board of Education* was the supreme law of the land. The Court noted that Article VI of the Constitution rendered the decision binding on the states, and that every state legislator and executive and judicial officer was solemnly sworn to uphold the U.S. Constitution.

While the Court's pronouncement did not seem remarkable in the 1990s, southern states had questioned the supremacy of the federal government, as well as the Court's authority to interpret the Constitution and declare the law in 1958. The Court's ruling in *Cooper v. Aaron* took at least some wind out of the sails of southern defiance; the Court seemed finally to have taken control again. The pace of desegregation remained painfully slow, however.

In view of the widespread resistance to the Supreme Court's decision in *Brown* and other controversial cases, Gerald Rosenberg argued in *The Hollow Hope* that the Court was incapable of effecting sweeping social change. Proponents of the opposing *Dynamic Court* view contended that the federal courts, through *Brown* and its progeny, played a critical role in bringing about changes in civil rights and activating the civil rights movement. The *Dynamic Court* view held that federal courts served as agenda-setters, legitimizing the protests of blacks, and striking at the consciences of whites.[14]

Rosenberg rejected this notion of the *Dynamic Court*, pointing to the years of resistance to the *Brown* decisions and the Court's almost complete failure to achieve compliance until the legislative and executive branches intervened with the 1964 Civil Rights Act. He noted that shortly after the *Brown* decisions, Thurgood Marshall predicted that complete, nationwide compliance might require up to five years. Marshall further predicted that by 1963, the 100th anniversary of the Emancipation Proclamation, all forms of segregation would have been eliminated throughout the nation.[15] Marshall's sanguine predictions were, of course, not fulfilled. In fact, Rosenberg suggested that far from promoting civil rights, *Brown* may have

---

[14] Gerald Rosenberg, *The Hollow Hope: Can Courts Bring About Social Change?* (Chicago: University of Chicago Press, 1991), 40-41.
[15] Ibid., 43.

hardened resistance to social change. *Brown* released a wave of hysterical racism of gigantic proportions. Thus, reliance on the *Dynamic Court* to promote social change may produce "surprising and unfortunate costs."[16]

Raymond Wolters and other critics of judicial activism characterized the Supreme Court's and lower courts' actions in school desegregation, particularly as the mandate evolved to affirmative action toward *integration*, as social engineering based on judges' earnest desires to address perceived injustices and resultant racial tension.[17] This broadening of the *Brown* mandate, Wolters argued, endorsed a color conscious, rather than colorblind interpretation of the Constitution.[18]

In light of the very limited compliance with *Brown* until the passage of the 1964 Civil Rights Act, one could hardly argue that the Court alone can effect social change. Furthermore, it was not the intent of the framers that the Court should have such a function. None of the branches of government was meant to forge policy on its own. In the case of desegregation in public schools, compliance improved when the judicial branch received the support of the other two branches. However, even the three branches of the national government working in tandem proved incapable of overcoming resentment toward outside interference, deep-rooted prejudices, and middle class indifference to the problems of the poor, all of which worked against the vision of *Brown.*

This is not to say that the Court should not have made the decision it did in *Brown* or that the plaintiffs were misguided in appealing to the judicial branch when the elected branches of government were turning a deaf ear to their pleas. Despite the limitations on the power and influence of the judicial branch, the "conscience" of the Court has at times been "a step ahead" of the conscience of the nation. In the case of school desegregation, the Court's pronouncement that racial segregation in public schools was unconstitutional could well have given members of Congress the courage needed to push through the monumental and highly polemic civil rights legislation of the 1960s. Moreover, any other decision by the Court would have denied the legitimacy of black demands for equal

---

[16] Ibid., 156.
[17] Raymond Wolters, *The Burden of Brown: Thirty Years of School Desegregation* (Knoxville: University of Tennessee Press, 1984), 215, 227.
[18] Ibid., 7.

rights, making a mockery of America's constitutional principles, and perhaps providing just enough support for the opposition that the civil rights legislation might not have passed.

Thus, the Court's decision in *Brown v. Board of Education* established a constitutionally based requirement for ending dual school systems and provided a foundation for national legislation calling for administrative enforcement of the decree. As the following chapter demonstrates, it was the coordinated efforts of the three branches of the national government that paved the way for compliance to begin. The subsequent case studies examine the complexity of attempting to eradicate inequalities in public education through national judicial directives in a society with a relatively high level of tolerance for social and economic inequality and a strong tradition of local control in schooling.

CHAPTER 2

Compliance Begins

When President Kennedy took office in January 1961, the administration's tone on school desegregation and civil rights in general changed markedly. With Robert Kennedy as head of the Justice Department, the Kennedy administration attacked segregation in schools, putting the weight of the Justice Department behind the Supreme and district court orders to desegregate. In June 1963, President Kennedy proposed a civil rights bill aimed at enforcing voting rights and at desegregation in public facilities and public education. Southern resistance was immediate and vocal. Southern Democrats in Congress attacked the bill as an unconstitutional infringement on states' rights. Following President Kennedy's assassination, President Johnson proved to be an adamant, skillful, and tireless crusader for civil rights. In fact, owing largely to his commitment to civil rights, perseverance, and legislative know-how, all of which exceeded those of President Kennedy,[1] a greatly strengthened version of President Kennedy's bill was passed by Congress a year after its introduction.

The battle for passage of the Civil Rights Act of 1964 (P.L. 88-352) was long and acrimonious, including a 57 day filibuster in the Senate. Proponents disregarded Senate norms and bypassed the unreceptive Judiciary Committee, which, like most powerful congressional committees of that era, was chaired by a conservative

---

[1] Charles and Barbara Whalen, *The Longest Debate: A legislative history of the 1964 Civil Rights Act* (Cabin John, MD.: Seven Locks Press, 1985), 87.

southern Democrat. Senators offered over one hundred amendments to the bill and forced them to roll call votes.   Finally, the bill's proponents, who included a core of relatively newly elected liberals from the Northeast and who had the strong backing of the president, prevailed.[2]

Title II of the 1964 Civil Rights Act, Injunctive Relief Against Discrimination in Places of Public Accommodation, engendered by far the most controversy during the congressional battle for its passage. Yet implementation, which many had threatened would incite widespread resistance and violence, took place almost without incident. In fact, President Johnson publicly commended the many civic leaders who supported compliance. He especially applauded the members of Congress who "opposed the Civil Rights Bill with all their strength and eloquence while it was being debated and who, once the bill was enacted, urged their constituents and followers to comply with the 'law of the land.'"[3]

Title IV, Desegregation of Public Education, permitted the U.S. Office of Education (within the Department of Health, Education, and Welfare -- HEW), upon the request of local school boards, to provide technical and financial assistance for the planning or implementation of desegregation programs (sec. 403), but not merely to correct racial imbalance (sec. 401b). Title IV authorized the Justice Department to file suit to desegregate public schools or colleges upon receipt of a written complaint of injured parties, who, in the opinion of the attorney general, were unable to bring suit themselves (sec. 407).

Title VI, Nondiscrimination in Federally Funded Programs, prohibited discrimination on the basis of race, color, or national origin in the carrying out of any federally financed programs (sec. 601).   It authorized federal agencies, upon failure to achieve voluntary compliance from a recipient of federal funds to terminate the funding (sec. 602).

The intervention of the Justice Department in desegregation actions pursuant to Title IV resulted in a dramatic increase in school desegregation. The Civil Rights Act of 1957 had created the Civil Rights Division within the Justice Department, but until the passage of

---

[2] Barbara Sinclair, *The Transformation of the U.S. Senate* (Baltimore: Johns Hopkins University Press, 1989) 43-44.
[3] *Congressional Quarterly Almanac*, 1964, "Civil Rights Act of 1964," 378.

the Civil Rights Act of 1964, the Division had virtually no authority, expertise, or resources to assist in the enforcement of *Brown*.[4] By 1966 HEW had drawn up strict guidelines including much more specific criteria for desegregation than was contained in most court decrees. Freedom of Choice plans were still allowed, but HEW wanted to see specific minimum percentages of blacks in white schools.[5]

Following the passage of the Civil Rights Act of 1964, President Johnson promoted and Congress passed numerous other pieces of civil rights legislation. These included the 1965 Voting Rights Act (P.L. 89-110) and the Elementary and Secondary Education Act (ESEA -- P.L. 89-10, which had civil rights components) of the same year. The latter was the federal government's first attempt to compensate children for their disadvantaged backgrounds through special educational programs. Such compensatory programs would later gain prominence in school districts' plans to offer minority children an equal educational opportunity when integration was either impracticable or insufficient to remedy the effects of past discrimination.[6]

In 1968, finally exasperated with recalcitrant southern school districts, the Court demanded immediate effective integration. In *Green v. County School Board of New Kent County* (1968), the Court struck down "freedom of choice" plans where they failed to achieve unitary, nonracially segregated school systems. Opponents of the "freedom of choice" plans argued successfully that the Court's mandate was not aimed at merely eradicating official (*de jure*) segregation, but at eliminating racially identifiable schools. The Court's new approach looked at effect, rather than purpose or good faith, in assessing the level of compliance with *Brown* (II), and it declared that the time had run out for "all deliberate speed."

That same year, the Departments of Justice and HEW under President Johnson began to initiate school desegregation cases in the North and West,[7] and as a result, school desegregation policy entered a new phase in the 1970s. The courts began to address segregation that

---

[4] David M. O'Brien, *Storm Center: The Supreme Court in American Politics*, 3d ed. (New York: W. W. Norton & Company, 1993), 362-63.
[5] J. Harvie Wilkinson, III, *From Brown to Bakke: The Supreme Court and School Integration: 1954-1978* (New York: Oxford University Press, 1979), 104.
[6] The ESEA and the goals of compensatory education will be discussed more thoroughly in Chapter 3.
[7] O'Brien, 363.

had previously been overlooked because of its more "benign" nature. The cause of segregated schools in the North and West lay in ethnically separate housing patterns, rather than in statute. On closer examination, however, courts found evidence of official action which reinforced racial segregation in schools. Consequently, the courts expanded their definition of *de jure* segregation to include such official action. The courts ordered remedial action which often included busing of students throughout school districts. Suddenly desegregation took on a whole new meaning. A northern public that had previously supported desegregation in the South now vehemently opposed it when it involved the busing of children from their own neighborhoods to distant and unfamiliar schools.

In *Swann v. Charlotte-Mecklenburg Board of Education* (1971), the Court addressed the complex issue of desegregation in metropolitan areas with marked residential segregation. Though Swann was a southern (North Carolina) case, it would have a tremendous impact on desegregation throughout the United States, because it permitted the busing of students, where necessary, for purposes of desegregation.

The Supreme Court, reminding the litigants that judicial authority in school desegregation was only indicated where a constitutional violation had been identified, declared affirmative action, i.e. the pairing or grouping of schools along with busing, an acceptable remedy. The Court held that, in light of past discrimination, broad remedial measures were sometimes necessary to achieve unitary school systems. "Racially neutral" boundary lines were often an inadequate remedy. The Court held that racial balance or quotas could be used as a starting point for a remedial plan to desegregate, but that one-race schools were not in and of themselves proof of discrimination. The burden of proof lay with the school district, however, and the district had to offer students in one-race schools the option to transfer, with the district bearing the cost of transportation. The Court assured the school district that once a unitary district was achieved, the Court would not require that the district make yearly adjustments to its school zones to correct for demographic changes in order to achieve racial balance. Thus, with Swann, the Supreme Court accepted busing as an acceptable method for achieving desegregation, but thus far its desegregation directives were confined to southern states that practiced *de jure* segregation based on state law.

Keyes v. Denver School District No. 1 (1973), the first Supreme Court decision on school desegregation in the North, addressed intra-district busing, as well. The Court called for a broad intra-district remedy based on the trial court's finding of purposeful discrimination in a part of Denver's school district. Justice Brennan, writing for the majority, said that purposeful segregation in a substantial part of the district called for the application of *Brown* (II) and Swann. In approving the district-wide plan for desegregation, Justice Brennan pointed out that segregative acts in one area of the school district could have effected segregation in other areas.

Only Justice Rehnquist dissented in *Keyes*; he rejected the Court's broadening of its definition of *de jure* segregation to include official action that was not based in statute. He also said the Court was going far beyond *Brown* in requiring school districts to take positive steps to mix the races, rather than simply requiring the drawing of neutral boundaries. In other words, Rehnquist rejected the Court's broadening of its mandate from desegregation to integration.

As the Court deliberated *Keyes*, the prelude to the "Battle of Boston," the North's answer to Little Rock, was in progress. Finding extensive purposeful action by school officials to perpetuate the segregation emanating from residential housing patterns, federal district judge Arthur Garrity imposed a district-wide desegregation plan involving two-way busing.

The Boston case[8] exemplified commonplace actions by northern officials that the Supreme Court had come to interpret as evidence of *de jure* segregation. The Boston School Committee had manipulated attendance zones and used optional attendance zones, segregative feeder patterns, and various pupil assignment practices to further racial segregation in its schools.[9] Judge Garrity found the evidence of purposeful segregative action by the school district much more extensive than that in the Denver case.

In his moving portrayal of the upheaval caused by the desegregation order in Boston, J. Anthony Lukas noted the differing undercurrents between northern and southern racial tension. Since colonial days, blacks and whites had lived separately in the North. Lukas suggested that there was some truth in the Negro folk wisdom: "In the South, the white man doesn't care how close you get if you

---

[8] Morgan v. Hennigan 379 F. Supp. (D. Mass.1974); Morgan v. Kerrigan, 401 F. Supp. 216 (D. Mass.1975); 509 F. 2d 580 (CA1 1974); *cert denied* 421 U.S. 963 (1965).

[9] J. Anthony Lukas, *Common Ground: A Turbulent Decade in the Lives of Three American Families* (New York: Alfred Knopf, 1985), 236.

don't get too high; in the North, the white man doesn't care how high you get if you don't get too close."[10]

Judge Garrity's remedial plan, based on the state's Racial Imbalance Law, redrew boundaries throughout Boston. It paired Roxbury, the heart of Boston's black district, with South Boston, the Irish stronghold wherein anti-black sentiment was especially high. The plan set into motion an explosive reaction that, thanks to full media coverage, kept the nation spellbound. Despite the violence that followed Judge Garrity's order, the appellate court upheld Judge Garrity's plan, and the Supreme Court declined to review it.

As desegregation and busing mandates moved north, resistance mounted in Congress, reflecting America's increasing rejection of the judiciary's meddling in local school district affairs, especially when the mandates included busing. President Nixon's administration retreated from President Johnson's active desegregation policy. The Nixon administration reduced the role of HEW to providing technical assistance in achieving court-mandated plans, rather than the more effective, but more controversial, tactic of withholding funding from delinquent school districts.[11]

Nixon's view of federalism called for more local control and discretion in education. He encouraged the passage of anti-busing legislation in Congress. Congressional passage of the Stennis-Ribicoff Amendment to the Elementary and Secondary Education Act in 1970 and 1971 exemplified the tension caused by society's (and the Court's) dichotomous treatment of *de facto* ("northern") and *de jure* ("southern") segregation. In a curious marriage of conflicting motives, the amendment brought together the positions of a staunch states' rightist, Senator John Stennis of Mississippi, and an ultra-liberal integrationist, Connecticut's Senator Abraham Ribicoff. The amendment called for nationwide like treatment of *de jure* and de facto segregation. Senator Stennis pushed for the amendment, feeling confidant that like treatment would cause the North to back off from its hypocritical censure of southern segregation, now that their "innocent" pattern of segregation was deemed equally unconstitutional. Senator Ribicoff, a true liberal, on the other hand, wanted the two types of segregation treated alike

---

[10] Ibid., 234.
[11] James Bolner and Robert Stanley, *Busing: the Political and Judicial Process* (New York: Praeger Publishers, 1974), 142-43.

because he wanted them both uprooted.[12]   Following extensive and acrimonious debate, the amendment passed in both 1970 and 1971, having won the support of conservatives in the South and ultraliberals in the Northeast.

George Wallace's victory in the Florida primary in 1972 demonstrated the salience of the busing issue. Few politicians failed to take note. On March 16, President Nixon asked Congress to sharply limit the courts' desegregation powers.[13] Adopting the carrot approach, the president proposed and Congress passed The Emergency School Aid Act (P.L. 92-318) in 1973.   The Act offered large monetary rewards to school districts that were integrating.[14]

In 1974, the Supreme Court addressed inter-district remedies for segregation in *Milliken v. Bradley*. It ruled that "absent an inter-district violation there is no basis for an inter-district remedy." The Court reversed a lower court order that had called for inter-district remedies based on a finding of *de jure* segregation in the city of Detroit. The lower court had determined that desegregation could not be accomplished by a plan encompassing only the Detroit city district, because the area was overwhelmingly black. It therefore mandated a plan involving 53 surrounding school districts.   The trial judge concluded, "district lines are simply matters of political convenience and may not be used to deny constitutional rights." In rejecting the trial judge's reasoning, Chief Justice Burger pointed to the history of public education in America. He allowed that constitutional violations could call for inter-district remedies, "but, the notion that school district lines may be casually ignored or treated as a mere administrative convenience is contrary to the history of public education in our country."

The Chief Justice declared that the imposition of an integration plan on outlying districts that had never been found guilty of a constitutional violation would be a "wholly impermissible remedy based on a standard not hinted at (in) any holding of this Court." Blacks of Detroit had a constitutional right to attend a unitary school

---

[12] Ibid., 84.

[13] Gary Orfield, *Must We Bus? Segregated Schools and National Policy* (Washington, D.C.: The Brookings Institution, 1978), 335.

[14] Ray C. Rist, *The Invisible Children: School Integration in American Society* (Cambridge: Harvard University Press, 1978), 37-38.

system in that district. The Court remanded the case to the district court for other relief.

The Court was sharply divided in *Milliken*. Chief Justice Burger wrote for the five-member majority. Justices Marshall, Douglas, Brennan, and White dissented, with Marshall calling the decision "a giant step backwards" and an "emasculation" of equal protection. Both Marshall and White in separate dissents pointed to the fact that actions of both city and state officials had resulted in de jure segregation within Detroit. Because an inter-district remedy was necessary to effect meaningful desegregation, and not only city, but also state, official action had caused segregation, then the inter-district remedy was justified, declared Marshall and White. Despite these objections, the Court continued to draw a firm distinction between inter- and intra-district remedies.

In *Milliken v. Bradley (II)* (1977), the Court unanimously held that the district court could order remedial programs as part of a desegregation decree and that the court could order the state to bear a portion of the program costs when state officials had been found responsible for a constitutional violation. In the Detroit case, the district court had found that state officials had directly contributed to the segregated condition of the district's schools. In fact, the Michigan legislature had forbid the implementation of a voluntary district plan to ameliorate the effects of past segregative practices.

The district court imposed a remedial plan including four educational components: remedial reading programs, in-service training for teachers to ease the transition to desegregation, culturally unbiased testing of students, and counseling and career guidance for students. In upholding the district court's requirement that the state share the burden of these educational components, the Supreme Court observed that racial segregation had left its victims educationally disadvantaged and that the "ultimate objective of the remedy is to make whole the victims of unlawful conduct." Special educational programs were needed to restore the victims of segregation to the educational level they would likely have attained in the absence of the violation.

The *Milliken II* decision led to the expenditure of hundreds of millions of dollars[15] in efforts to remedy the effects of past and current

---

[15] Gary Orfield, foreword *to Still Separate, Still Unequal: The Limits of Milliken II's Educational Compensation Remedies*, by Joseph Feldman,

racial segregation on minority children. As increasing numbers of school districts found it impossible to meaningfully desegregate in light of growing residential segregation, administrators turned to "*Milliken II* schools," with compensatory programs, equipment, and facilities, to attempt to enhance the learning environment and elevate the test scores of children disadvantaged by segregation and poverty. Such programs constituted an integral part of the desegregation programs in the case studies discussed in the following chapters.

Despite the Court's rejection of inter-district remedies for intra-district violations, public and congressional opposition to desegregation orders, especially those involving busing, grew in the 1970s. As the Court deliberated *Milliken II,* Congress was debating amendments to the ESEA (P.L. 93-380 -- called the Education Amendments of 1974), and the issues under consideration in *Milliken II* were clearly foremost in members' minds. The amendments, which passed on August 21, 1974, sent a clear message to the Court. They repudiated desegregation efforts to overcome racial imbalance and denied the use of federal funds for busing to achieve racial desegregation. Congress further instructed the Courts that it should not ignore or alter school district lines unless it was established that such lines were drawn or maintained for the purpose of segregation.

President Ford followed in President Nixon's footsteps, taking a cautious approach to the uproar surrounding busing to achieve desegregation. On October 9, 1974, in response to a press inquiry regarding the crisis in Boston, Ford stressed that he had always opposed forced busing to achieve racial balance, and said that he "respectfully disagree(d) with the judge's order."[16] The Ford administration had been looking for an appeal of a federal busing order to support, but the Boston situation proved so explosive that Ford declined to enter the melee with an *amicus curiae* brief.[17] Administration support of the Boston appeal would have sent a strong message of support to defiance of federal court orders.

In September 1975, the Senate passed the Biden Amendment, sponsored by Democrat Senator Joseph Biden of Delaware, which prohibited the withholding of HEW funds from school districts that

---

Edward Kirby, Susan E. Eaton, and Alison Morantz (Cambridge: The Harvard Project on School Desegregation, 1994), 1.

[16] Jon Hillson, *The Battle of Boston* (New York: Pathfinder Press, 1977), 35-36.

[17] Ibid., 261.

had failed or refused to comply with desegregation orders. The U.S. Commission on Civil Rights called the Biden Amendment "unquestionably the most sweeping attack on the civil rights act passed by the Senate in recent years."[18] The Senate passed the Byrd Amendment a week later; sponsored by Majority Whip Robert Byrd of West Virginia, it prohibited the use of HEW funds to require the busing of any student to a school other than that nearest his home for the sole purpose of desegregation. The Civil Rights Commission protested again, calling the amendment an effort to return to "separate but equal."[19] These amendments passed at the height of the turmoil in Boston. They reflected the growing resistance within the public to increasingly extensive mandates from the courts, stiff opposition to busing to achieve integration, and the resultant tension between the elective branches of government and the courts. In the face of unapologetic foot dragging and outright defiance on the part of school systems, the courts heightened their pressure on school systems, oftentimes issuing increasingly explicit and comprehensive orders. However, the resolve of federal judges to fulfill their anti-majoritarian roles could not overcome public resistance, especially when the other two branches of government endorsed that resistance.

In 1977, the newly elected President Carter appointed Joseph Califano as Secretary of HEW, and the department once again adopted the Johnson era policy of actively enforcing civil rights law. Califano promised to "restore the integrity of HEW's civil rights program," declaring that there had been "too much data collection and too little enforcement." HEW threatened to resume its policy of fund cutoffs for non-complying districts. The Office of Civil Rights faced strong opposition in Congress, however, and was restricted by the Byrd and Biden Amendments.[20]

The Justice Department under the Reagan administration again abandoned the enforcement of busing orders and the pursuit of stringent goals and timetables for desegregation. Nationwide, polls showed decisive and increasing resistance among whites to busing to achieve segregation, and support among blacks was only moderate; it generally split down the middle. In addition, President Reagan continued the trend President Nixon began by appointing conservatives to the

---

[18] Ibid., 174.
[19] Ibid.
[20] Orfield, *Must We Bus?*, 316-17.

courts.[21] The Supreme Court's willingness in the 1990s to withdraw from the supervision of school districts reflected this more conservative outlook, which came to characterize the high bench as a result of President Reagan's emphasis on ideology in making judicial appointments.

The inter-branch tension in the years between 1968 and 1990 highlighted the dependency of the judiciary on support from the other branches of government. When the executive and legislative branches did not see eye-to-eye with the court's view on desegregation and busing, the Court's effectiveness suffered. In the years when HEW and the Justice Department acted to reinforce the Court's intent, implementation proceeded more smoothly. Clearly, the courts' credibility and efficacy were highest when the branches of government were working in harmony.

In addressing *de jure* segregation and imposing remedial action, the Court remained ever mindful of the long history of localism in public education, as well as the significance of school district boundaries. The Court steadfastly refused to interfere in local school district affairs in the absence of a constitutional violation. While it did not rule out the possibility of imposing inter-district remedies, the Court indicated that only the most extreme situation would call for such a remedy. The Court thus acknowledged its limited jurisdiction in public school policy making.

Milliken I was the watershed of the desegregation movement in public schools. The Court indicated the point beyond which it would not go to correct a deep-rooted societal problem. It could administer relief in the case of a constitutional violation, but it could not correct injustice resulting from centuries of troubled race relations, residential segregation and disproportionate poverty among minorities.

Milliken I did not diminish school district's responsibility to provide equal educational opportunity, however. In *Milliken II*, the Supreme Court approved court-ordered compensatory education programs where desegregation was impracticable. Such compensatory programs became an integral part of many court-ordered desegregation plans for school districts with residential isolation that rendered

---

[21] Thomas Byrne Edsall and Mary D. Edsall, *Chain Reaction: the Impact of Race, Rights, and Taxes on American Politics* (New York: W. W. Norton & Company, 1992), 218.

impossible the meaningful integration of their schools. The philosophy behind these court directives was essentially the same as the theory behind Title I of the Elementary and Secondary Education Act (ESEA) of 1965. Noting the strong correlation between poverty and low achievement in school, Congress established the Title I program to offer disadvantaged children extra instructional aid to enable them to overcome the obstacles to educational achievement attributed to their disadvantaged backgrounds. Such special educational programs were called compensatory education programs because they were designed to compensate children of poverty for the lack of educational support that children of middle-class families usually received in the home. It is important to understand the theory behind compensatory education programs and the educational benefits they did and did not produce, in order to assess their potential as a remedy for the harm done black children by discriminatory school system practices. As growing numbers of school districts adopted such compensatory programs in the 1970s and 1980s, and as courts began to release school districts from busing orders in the 1990s under the assumption that these programs would help disadvantaged children to overcome their environmental obstacles to achievement, clearly, it was important that the programs produced results.[22] Chapter 3 addresses issues surrounding compensatory education programs. As will be shown, the programs did not fulfill the expectations of those who so enthusiastically endorsed them in the 1960s and 1970s.

---

[22] The Harvard Project on School Desegregation's 1994 study *Still Separate, Still Unequal* (Feldman, et al) addresses the problem of the lack of accountability with such compensatory programs in Prince George's County and other school systems where they were adopted as part of the relief ordered to victims of unconstitutional discrimination. This report is discussed in Chapter 7.

CHAPTER 3

Compensatory Education

Compensatory education, the effort to counteract or compensate for the environmental deficits that impede the educational progress of poor children, first became public policy in America during the Civil Rights Era of the 1960s. The correlation between lower levels of education on the one hand, and high rates of unemployment and lower wages on the other, provided the rationale for extending federal welfare policy to education. The notion of a self-sustaining "cycle of poverty" emerged, where low expectations, minimal encouragement, and limited aspirations for children led to lower academic achievement, which in turn led to poverty in the next generation. Compensatory education was viewed as a means to break the cycle of poverty. A wave of optimism regarding the ability of public education to solve the great societal ill of poverty accompanied the development of compensatory education.

The Elementary and Secondary Education Act (ESEA -- P.L. 89-10) of 1965 constituted the federal government's first significant effort to fund public education. Public education had been a state responsibility historically, and federal aid to public schools had been very controversial since World War II, particularly regarding resistance to funding segregated or church affiliated schools.[1]

---

[1] "First General School Aid Bill Enacted," *Congressional Quarterly Almanac* 1965, 279.

However, in 1965, circumstances combined to provide an atmosphere in Washington highly receptive to the federal government's entry into the funding of public education. The Civil Rights Act of 1964, prohibited the provision of federal funds to segregated schools, eliminating that reservation. The sweeping Democratic victories in the 1964 elections brought to Washington many liberals who generally favored federal aid to education, and public support for President Johnson's Great Society programs provided the incentive to find a compromise regarding aid to private schools. As part of President Johnson's War on Poverty, the federal government would provide assistance to disadvantaged children in an effort to "get at the roots" of poverty. Thus began the federal government's venture into the arena of compensatory education.

In a speech delivered April 1, 1965, President Johnson powerfully conveyed the bill's purpose:

> This bill has a simple purpose: To improve the education of young Americans. . . . With education, instead of being condemned to poverty and idleness, young Americans can learn the skills to find a job and provide for a family. . . . How many young lives have been wasted; how many families now live in misery; how much talent has the Nation lost; because we have failed to give all our people a chance to learn. . . . This bill represents a national determination that this shall no longer be true. Poverty will no longer be a bar to learning, and learning shall offer an escape from poverty. . . . [W]e will liberate each young mind -- in every part of this land -- to reach to the furthest limits of thought and imagination. For this truly is the key which can unlock the door to a great society.[2]

Noting the "strong correlation between educational under achievement and poverty," President Johnson and other supporters of the measure sought to "bring better education to millions of disadvantaged youth who need it most."[3] The Senate Report on the

---

[2] Congress, Senate, Committee on Labor and Public Welfare, *Elementary and Secondary Education Act of 1965*, 89th Congress, 1st sess., 1965, Rept. No. 146, 3-4.

[3] Ibid., 4-5.

ESEA stated that the testimony presented graphically illustrated that poverty produced an environment that hindered children from taking full advantage of educational programs. Environmental conditions and a lack of appropriately adapted educational programs, rather than lower mental aptitude, bore most of the responsibility for the failure of poor children to achieve in school. Title I -- Aid to Educationally Deprived Children, the heart of the measure, thus provided funds for school districts to institute special remedial programs to compensate for the disadvantages endured by children of poverty.[4]

The legislation encouraged local school districts to use imaginative approaches in meeting the educational needs of poor children. Testimony by educators indicated the potential usefulness of such programs and policies as preschool training, reduction of class sizes (lower pupil-teacher ratio -- PTR), remedial programs, especially math and reading, special help in English for non English speakers, after-school study centers, summer school, and breakfasts.[5]

The millions of dollars in aid that the ESEA offered school districts provided a strong incentive to desegregate. The strong correlation between minority status and poverty meant that school districts with many blacks were likely to be eligible for sizable Title I allocations if they desegregated.

Owing to the high level of distrust for state officials and local educational administrators and school boards during the Civil Rights Era, Congress felt it was imperative to retain congressional control over the dissemination of Title I funds. Although localism had been the tradition in educational policy making, the general reaction to suggestions that Title I should allow states or local school boards to decide how best to use the federal dollars was "Do you mean you want to give the money to George Wallace?"[6]

Senator Robert Kennedy was highly skeptical of Title I's ability to establish effective compensatory educational programs for the poor, and he battled fiercely to have strong provisions made for oversight of the program and requirements for evaluation and results. He feared that school administrators, would eagerly accept the generous federal funding, but then do little to ensure that the funds were directed to

---

[4] Ibid., 5.
[5] Ibid., 10-11.
[6] David G. Savage, "Why Chapter 1 Hasn't Made Much Difference," *Phi Delta Kappan*, 68 (April 1987): 582.

programs for the disadvantaged. Kennedy believed that Congress had a special obligation to act on behalf of the poor.[7] Testifying before the Senate subcommittee on Education, he implored:

> [These children] really don't have a lobby speaking for them and do not have parents that can be clamoring down here because they cannot afford to take the bus ride, or cannot afford to fly down here, and they are the ones, I think, who are of concern. They have been ignored in the past. . . . and what I want to make sure of is not just that the money is not wasted, because you can find more money, but the fact that the lives of these children are not wasted.[8]

Kennedy insisted on detailed reporting procedures for recipient schools and especially emphasized that the parents of participant children should be regularly informed of their children's progress. Kennedy viewed the failure of disadvantaged children as a consequence of the disinterest and inefficiency of school administration, and he therefore championed, more than anyone else, the notion of accountability in the implementation of the ESEA.[9]

Through the years, evaluation requirements were developed and refined, and school administrators were expected to justify the use of dollars spent through detailed descriptions of compensatory programs and standardized testing of the participants. Yet, from the start, standardized testing showed disappointing results. Not only did participant children begin remedial reading programs at lower levels than non-participants, they progressed at slower rates.[10]

In the early 1970s, Congress tightened the specifications for Title I funding. The allocations were to go to schools with high concentrations of low-income children, and were to be spent only on students showing great need in basic skill areas (reading, math, and language arts). Finally in the mid 1970s, studies began to show overall

---

[7]Milbrey Wallin McLaughlin, *Evaluation and Reform: The Elementary and Secondary Education Act of 1965, Title I* (Cambridge: Ballinger Publishing Company, 1975), 1.

[8] Congress, Senate, Subcommittee on Education, *Hearings on Elementary and Secondary Education Act of 1965*, 89th Cong., 1st sess., 529.

[9] McLaughlin, 3-4.

[10] Ibid., 61.

positive results for Title I participants.[11] However, the requirement that funds be spent exclusively on disadvantaged children led to the standard pullout programs that garnered increased criticism in the 1980s and 1990s.

Studies indicated that the most effective schools had adopted integrative programs wherein faculty and staff worked together as teams, with each taking responsibility for the whole program. This cooperation violated the sense of the Title I regulations, however, which discouraged such commingling of federal and local services.[12]

With the 1974 decision by the Supreme Court in *Milliken v. Bradley,* compensatory education took on a new meaning. The Court now condoned the use of compensatory education programs to offset the discriminatory effects of segregative actions by school systems, when further or meaningful desegregation was not possible. As increasing segregation affected more and more school districts and public support for busing for purposes of desegregation waned, even blacks, in some cases, came to endorse the provision of compensatory funds as an alternative to further desegregation. With this new impetus for compensatory educational programs in schools, the significance of their effectiveness increased. If such programs were meant to remedy the effects of past discrimination, surely it was critical that they actually worked. Yet, the results, were disappointing.

The first longitudinal study of the effects of Title I, Sustaining Effects, completed in 1984, showed that participants in the program gained at a slightly faster rate than non participants, but those gains were not sustained through junior high school.[13]

Based on the results of the Sustaining Effects study, the Reagan Administration proposed revising Title I into a block grant with other educational programs and reducing the total funding by 25 percent. Supporters of the program defeated the initiative. John Jennings, a Democratic congressional aide from when Title I was first enacted through the 1990s, observed, "The defenders of the program became overly protective and didn't want to make any changes. It caused a hardening of positions rather than reaching for solutions."[14]

---

[11] Benjamin D. Stickney and Virginia R. L. Plunkett. "Has Title I Done Its Job?" *Educational Leadership*, February 1982, 380.
[12] Savage, 582.
[13] David J. Hoff, "Tracking Title I," *Education Week*, 22 October 1997, 16.
[14] Ibid., 17.

Given the persistence of the achievement gap and the very limited success of remedial style compensatory educational programs, educators began considering other approaches to increasing the academic progress of disadvantaged children. Professor Donald Orlich of the Department of Educational Administration and Supervision, Washington State University, suggested that a reassessment of desegregation theory was in order, in light of the results of a "monumental" four-year study on the effects of classroom size on student achievement in grades K-3.[15] The results so strikingly confirmed the benefits of lower classroom size that they clearly called for a reevaluation of compensatory education theory. The study commissioned by the Tennessee state legislature assessed three classroom sizes: 1) self-contained classrooms with one teacher and thirteen to seventeen students (small); 2) self-contained classrooms with one teacher and twenty-two to twenty-five students (regular); and 3) self-contained classrooms with one teacher, one full-time aide, and twenty-two to twenty-five pupils (regular with aide). The sample included 128 small classes, 101 regular classes, and 99 regular classes with teacher aides.[16]   Participant schools were located in rural, suburban, inner city, and predominantly minority areas. Standard Achievement Test scores and Basic Skills First (BSF) scores were used to measure achievement. "In every case, pupils in the small classes made the highest scores on the achievement tests; that is, they outperformed all the pupils in the other two treatment conditions on every measure."[17]

In September 1993, the Clinton Administration proposed revisions to the ESEA, dramatically altering the distribution of Title I funds. His proposal would have directed more Title I funds to high poverty regions at the expense of more affluent areas.[18]   Under the existing program, 95 percent of all school districts qualified for Title I funds.[19]

---

[15]Elizabeth Word et al., *Student/Teacher Achievement Ratio (STAR) Project: Tennessee's K-3 Class Size Study* (Nashville: Tennessee State Department of Education, 1990).

[16]Donald Orlich, "Brown v. Board of Education: Time for a Reassessment," *Phi Delta Kappan*, 72 (April 1991): 631.

[17]Ibid., 632.

[18] Peter Schmidt, "Desegregation Study Spurs Debate Over Equity Remedies," *Education Week*, 12 January 1994, 5.

[19] "Congress Looks to Chapter 1 Rewrite," *Congressional Quarterly Almanac 1993*, 407.

In congressional hearings on the 1993 Reform Proposals for Chapter 1[20] (H.R. 6), David Hornbeck, Chair of the Baltimore Commission on Chapter 1, urged "significant changes" in the program, noting that the gap between minority and poor children on the one hand, and non "disadvantaged" children on the other, had been widening for the previous two years.[21] Longitudinal studies showed that in the past year, Title I participants had progressed no more on standardized tests than non-participating disadvantaged students.[22] Recent data suggested that minority and poor children lagged about a year behind other children at grade four, two to three years behind at grade eight, and three to four years behind at grade twelve.[23]

Hornbeck criticized the employment of pullout programs and extensive use of teacher's aids, which had not been shown to increase the achievement level of children. He said that the Title I funds were spread too thin, so the most needy children were not receiving enough help. Thirty minutes of remedial help per day was insufficient to make a difference in the achievement levels of the most needy children. He urged a complete overhaul of the system.[24]

In 1994, R. W. Connell of the University of California, Santa Cruz, wrote, "there is certainly a need to rethink the underlying logic of compensatory programs, which have not changed in their basic design and political justification . . . since the 1960s."[25] Connell suggested that the pressures of standardized testing and the push for basic skills "fostered a rigid, teacher-centered pedagogy in compensatory and special education programs." Furthermore, pullout programs disrupted the supportive classroom atmosphere that the teacher tried to develop, and the emphasis on expert intervention disempowered classroom teachers.[26] Connell urged the "whole-school change" approach, which would emphasize integrated, rather than pullout programs, and a shift

---

[20]At the request of President Reagan, Congress changed the name "Title I" to "Chapter 1." Upon the request of President Clinton, Congress changed the name back to "Title I" in 1994. For simplicity and to avoid confusion, I have used the term "Title I" throughout, except in quotes or in official titles.

[21]U.S. Congress, House 1993, 2-3.

[22]Ibid., 13.

[23]Ibid., 2-3.

[24]Ibid., 3-4.

[25]R.W. Connell, "Poverty and Education," *Harvard Educational Review* 64 (Summer 1994), 126.

[26]Ibid., 137-39.

toward more participatory and interactive, rather than passive, learning atmospheres.

Lawmakers were unwilling, in the end, to sacrifice federal funds to their own states and districts, and after months of negotiations, Congress left the specifications for distribution of funds largely unchanged, though slightly more funds would go to low income children.[27] In 1995, when Republicans took control of Congress, they tried to cut one billion dollars from Title I's appropriations, but public opposition was so vehement that they abandoned the plan. Despite national research showing the limited benefits of Title I programs, voters did not want federal aid reduced.

A second longitudinal study of the effects of Title I was completed in 1997. Prospects[28] tested forty thousand students in the program from the 1991-1992 through the 1993-1994 school year. Prospects researchers could not "discern a compensatory effect over time" which they could attribute directly to Title I. The report stated, "(Title I) does not reduce the initial gaps in achievement between students."[29] The results did not surprise those who had followed studies of Title I's accomplishments. "There is a long series of studies that suggest . . . we have never lived up to the expectations," observed Maris A. Vinovskis, professor of history at the University of Michigan, who had tracked research on Title I throughout its history. Title I was clearly not helping enough to overcome children's disadvantages.[30]

A companion study of the Prospects study, Special Strategies, led by a group at Johns Hopkins, followed certain specific programs and found encouraging results. The study compared national programs such as the Success for All model and the Comer School Development Program with locally developed Title I programs such as extending the school year and school wide reforms. Special Strategies found significant improvement with some schools adopting school-wide changes, with Success for All,[31] and with the Comer program.[32]

---

[27]"Legislative Summary: Elementary, Secondary Education," *Congressional Quarterly Weekly Report 1994*, 3184.
[28]Abt Associates of Bethesda, Maryland.
[29]Hoff, "Tracking Title I", 18.
[30]Ibid., 17.
[31]*Success for All* was an intensive school wide reform program that focused on reading, writing, and communication skills. It balanced phonics with reading for meaning and sought to have all children reading by the third grade. The program emphasized aggressive early intervention. Robert

Following the 1994 changes to Title I which gave schools more direction in choosing proven programs and steered them away from the pullout programs which had proven unhelpful, demand for the Success for All program skyrocketed. Congress allowed $150 million in the fiscal year 1998 budget for encouraging the implementation of proven, research based programs at Title I schools.

Based on the findings of the Tennessee STAR study, President Clinton proposed in his 1998 State of the Union address allocating federal funds to reduce first, second, and third grade classroom sizes to an average of eighteen students. Some researchers remained skeptical of certain aspects of the STAR study, however. For instance, they wondered why the gains made in the first year of the program did not build from year to year. Furthermore, a Texas experiment in which fifteen schools were given $300,000 each to reduce class sizes to various degrees, resulted in dramatic gains in only two of the schools, and those were schools that had undergone several other reforms simultaneously.[33] Thus, neither traditional remedial programs, nor whole school reforms, nor reducing class sizes significantly were panaceas for achievement gap between middle class and disadvantaged children.

The disappointing results of Title I programs showed that ameliorating the educational disadvantages of minority and poor children would require more than temporary supplementary or remedial assistance. Even the costliest and most well intended programs could not compensate for socioeconomic factors such as low education levels of parents, low expectations, low aspirations, single parent homes, and crime-ridden neighborhoods.

The Supreme Court came to this conclusion in 1995 in the high profile Kansas City desegregation case, *Missouri v. Jenkins*. At the direction of the federal district court, the Kansas City Metropolitan School District (KCMSD) and the State of Missouri had spent hundreds of millions of dollars on an "effective schools" program and

---

Slavin (Johns Hopkins University) and Nancy Madden (husband and wife) developed and oversaw the program.

[32]Dr. James Comer, Director of the School Development Program at Yale, developed an intensive school wide program to improve the academic and social climate in schools. The program relies heavily on parental participation in school decision-making.

[33] Debra Viadero, "Small Classes: popular, But Still Unproven: Clinton Plan Raises Key Research Issues," *Education Week*, 18 February 1998, 16-17.

on magnet schools, following a finding that the vestiges of past discrimination had caused a district wide reduction in student achievement. Yet achievement, as measured by standardized tests, did not improve significantly. Those wishing to continue the costly programs claimed that the achievement gap was a residual effect of past discrimination. The Supreme Court rejected that argument, however, finding that numerous factors beyond the control of the KCMSD and the State of Missouri affected minority student achievement.[34] Following the Court's holding in *Missouri v. Jenkins*, courts released numerous school districts from court supervision, despite increasing segregation and despite the achievement gap between white and minority children.

Thus, following nearly four decades of federally funded compensatory educational programs and more than three decades of court ordered desegregation plans, poor and minority children continued to fare poorly in American schools. Reducing class size and whole school reform programs such as Success for All showed promise, but these were very costly innovations and would require the commitment of states and communities to be successful. Federal funds to reduce classroom size and restructuring Title I to encourage local districts to employ proven methods would not compensate for public ambivalence to the plight of poor children and poor school districts.

The following studies of the desegregation cases in Wilmington, Prince George's County, San Diego, and Cleveland, clearly demonstrate that neither court mandates nor costly compensatory educational programs alone could produce quality educational programs which served poor children well. Residents welcomed the infusion of federal and state dollars into their school systems, but the political pressure to make school systems accountable was lacking. Each of the cases demonstrates the fallacy in expecting the courts to effect equitable or quality public school systems.

---

[34]Missouri v. Jenkins, 115 S. Ct. 2038, is discussed in more detail in Chapters 5 and 12.

CHAPTER 4

The Case of Wilmington, Delaware

Introduction

Because the Wilmington case was one of the original four consolidated in the historic *Brown v. Board of Education* (1954), and because it was the first desegregation case in which the court applied a metropolitan (inter-district) remedy, the results of the court ordered program are of particular interest. The metropolitan plan brought about nearly complete desegregation and was touted as one of the most successful cases of desegregation in the country. In this sense, Wilmington appeared to be a success story. Indeed, in August 1995, the federal district court released the state board and the school district from further court supervision, finding that they had complied in good faith with the remedial order for a sufficient length of time.

Yet, the court order had engendered deep controversy; few people, even within the city of Wilmington, had strongly supported the implementation of the desegregation plan, and opposition had been overwhelming in the suburbs.[1] In 1995, despite the court's recognition of compliance with the desegregation plan, the plaintiffs continued to complain of discrimination, evidenced, among other things, by the lower achievement level of minority students, the higher incidence of disciplinary actions taken against minorities, and the disproportionate number of minorities assigned to lower level courses.[2]

---

[1] Jeffrey A. Raffel, *The Politics of School Desegregation: The Metropolitan Remedy in Delaware* (Philadelphia: Temple University Press, 1980) 36-37.
[2] Peter Schmidt, "Del. Desegregation Case Pivots on Student Statistics," *Education Week*, 1 March 1995, 14.

In his 1980 study of the politics of school desegregation in Delaware, Jeffrey Raffel noted that Delaware had been called a microcosm of the United States. Its southern and northern regions were distinct, and they included city, suburban, and rural areas. Strong party competition existed. The metropolitan areas were plagued by problems characteristic of other American metropolises, including racial segregation and inferior public education. Historically, blacks in Wilmington had virtually no political power in the county government and little in the city government. Their influence was limited to holding a few city council seats and occasionally running for citywide office.[3]

A History of *De Jure* Segregation

As a border state, Delaware had long reflected both southern and northern values and traditions. Though it took the Union side during the Civil War, Delaware refused to ratify the Thirteenth, Fourteenth or Fifteenth Amendments. In response to the Fourteenth Amendment, the legislature declared its "uncompromising opposition" to all "measures intended or calculated to equalize or amalgamate the Negro race with the white race, politically or socially . . . and to making Negroes eligible to public offices, to sit on juries, and to their admission to public schools where white children attend."[4]

The Delaware Constitution, enacted in 1897, required separate school systems for whites and blacks. In 1920 the quality of public education for blacks in Delaware was deplorable. The state began a crash school construction program that produced eighty-seven schools for black children in the 1920s. Pierre S. du Pont, of the wealthy and influential industrial family, donated the majority of the $2.6 million used to build the schools. Yet, extreme inequities remained, and in 1950, when the desegregation cases began to percolate up to the Supreme Court, white schools operated twice as many months per year as did black schools, and there were no four-year high schools for black children south of Wilmington. Delaware remained wedded to the Jim Crow system.[5]

---

[3]Raffel, 17.
[4]Richard Klugar, *Simple Justice* (New York: Random House, Vintage Books, 1975), 426.
[5]Ibid., 427-28.

In 1950, a group of black parents in Claymont, a suburb of Wilmington, brought suit against the State Board of Education, charging that there were gross inequities between Wilmington's Howard High School, to which all black high school children in the area were bused, and the school in Claymont which white children attended. At the same time, the parents of a black elementary school student in Hockessin, a rural village west of Wilmington, brought suit against the state board, complaining that black children were not transported to school by bus, as were white children. The NAACP assisted the plaintiffs in the two cases, *Belton v. Gebhart* and *Beulah v. Gebhart*. The NAACP pursued the Delaware cases as part of its effort to overturn the Court's "separate but equal" doctrine in public schooling, because the inequities between the black and white schools in Delaware were particularly egregious.

Indeed, Delaware's Chancellor Collins Seitz[6] held that because the state had violated the "separate but equal" doctrine by providing clearly inferior school facilities for black children, the black plaintiffs' children were entitled to attend the superior white schools. A monumental victory for the plaintiffs and the NAACP, this was the first time that a court had ordered a segregated white school to admit black children. Chancellor Seitz urged the abandonment of the "separate but equal" doctrine in education, but indicated that he felt that that decision would have to come from the Supreme Court itself. The Supreme Court heard appeals in the Delaware cases, along with appeals in desegregation cases from Virginia, South Carolina, and Kansas. In its monumental 1954 decision *Brown v. Board of Education of Topeka, Kansas*, the Court held that the "separate but equal" doctrine had no place in public education.[7]

Following *Brown v. Board of Education*, the Wilmington school district adopted geographically neutral attendance zones, thereby officially desegregating. The school systems in the two southern, rural counties of the state, which were more "Southern" in their customs and traditions, remained segregated, with a patchwork of black and white districts.

In 1956, Brenda Evans, a black parent in the Clayton School District of southern Delaware, filed a new suit charging that the district

---

[6] Chief Judge on Delaware's Court of Chancery.
[7] See Chapter 18, "Stick With Us," in Kluger's *Simple Justice* for a more detailed description of the development of the Delaware cases.

was not admitting students in a racially nondiscriminatory manner. Evans also charged that the district had not submitted a desegregation plan to the state board of education, whose responsibility it was to develop an effective desegregation plan in accordance with *Brown*.

In 1957, the federal district court found that the state board of education, the superintendent of public instruction and individual districts had taken "no appreciable steps" towards desegregation. The court enjoined the school districts from refusing to enroll black students. It ordered the state board to submit a racially nondiscriminatory plan for the admission, enrollment, and education of all Delaware public school students by the fall of 1957. The Court of Appeals for the Third Circuit affirmed the lower court's decision in 1958.[8] The two-stage plan that resulted called for an initial "freedom of choice" plan followed by the establishment of a wholly integrated school system.

During the 1960s Delaware desegregated the schools in its two southern counties, and by 1967, the last of its officially black school districts were eliminated, which prompted the federal government to declare that Delaware was the first former southern or border state to complete desegregation of its public schools. Yet, inequities remained. During the 1960s, the state board repeatedly introduced legislation to create nondiscriminatory school laws, as the court had required, but none was passed.[9]

Although the city of Wilmington officially desegregated in September 1956, adopting a racially neutral geographic assignment plan, neighborhoods remained quite segregated and most of the schools remained racially identifiable.[10] Furthermore, the local school board created optional attendance areas for certain schools, allowing students to attend schools other than those to which they were assigned, on a space available basis. Additionally, the school district continued to build schools exclusively to serve public housing projects, and as these schools were built, attendance zones were redrawn to foster segregation.[11] Owing to these factors and suburbanization, Wilmington schools remained highly segregated.

---

[8] Evans v. Buchanan, 236 F.2d 688 (3d. Cir 1958).
[9] Plaintiffs' Findings of Fact and Conclusions of Law at 23, Evans v. Buchanan (D.Del. 25 Feb. 1974) (No. 1816-1822).
[10] Ibid., 2.
[11] Ibid., 4-5.

Following the passage of the Civil Rights Act of 1964, HEW pressured Delaware to comply with *Brown*. The state superintendent, the state board, and the Department of Public Instruction (DPI) were aware of various alternatives for desegregating Wilmington, yet the DPI drafted and the legislature passed in 1968 the Educational Advancement Act (EAA), which circumscribed the Wilmington district, while consolidating other districts throughout the state.[12] The EAA stipulated that the Wilmington school district's boundaries would remain coterminous with the city limits, and it limited student enrollment in any newly formed districts to twelve thousand when Wilmington's enrollment was fifteen thousand. Thus, the act precluded the merger of Wilmington with any other school districts, which would have fostered desegregation through intra-district means.

Plaintiffs charged that the legislature left Wilmington out of the reorganization, in response to political opposition to racial integration there.[13] Sponsors of the act said that it was intended to consolidate small, rural districts with too few students to operate a high school. Clarice Heckert, chair of the House Education Committee explained, "We took it for granted that Delaware's schools were integrated, and that we were trying only to improve the quality of education . . . in the poorer, smaller districts, most of them rural"[14] Regardless of intent, the act dramatically impacted the racial composition of Wilmington schools, because it circumscribed the predominantly black school system in a way that eliminated the possibility of integration with adjacent predominantly white areas.

The Desegregation Case Reopens in Wilmington

In 1971 *Evans v. Buchanan* was reopened in federal district court by five black Wilmington parents, with the support of the ACLU and white liberals in Wilmington. The NAACP did not support the suit at the time, because it believed that black children would bear the brunt of any desegregation remedy and that blacks would lose their newly won power in the city school district.[15] Wilmington was by this time predominantly black and the majority of the school board members

---

[12] Ibid., 23.
[13] Ibid., 27.
[14] Raymond Wolters, *The Burden of Brown: Thirty Years of School Desegregation* (Knoxville: The University of Tennessee Press, 1984), 213.
[15] Raffel, 45.

were black, as were the superintendent and many administrators in the district. The Wilmington school board later joined in the suit as a plaintiff, while the state board of education and the state superintendent of public instruction remained aligned as defendants.

As had occurred in many other American cities, the racial composition of Wilmington changed as it went through suburbanization. The percentage of Wilmington public school students who were black grew from 25 in 1950 to 76 in 1970, while the percentage of black children in the suburban districts dropped from 6.4 to 5.3.[16] As Wilmington's school population became increasingly black, achievement levels dropped. A 1973 study revealed that Wilmington public schools experienced the problems of other inner city school systems. Eighty-six percent of Wilmington's third grade students were reading below grade level, and the deficits grew with each school year so that by grade ten, the mean reading level was 6.5, or the expected reading level for second semester of sixth grade.[17]

Public perception of the Wilmington school district was that as the student population had grown increasingly black and poor, academic standards, as well as behavioral standards in the schools had declined.[18] Reports abounded of chaos in hallways, vulgar language, interracial skirmishes, and gang fighting among blacks. In 1973, four state legislators and a Wilmington News Journal Reporter visited several Wilmington schools unannounced and came away with very unfavorable descriptions, including lax standards, general disorder, filth in lavatories, and students sleeping at their desks.[19]

Plaintiffs and their supporters felt that by attaining greater racial balance (the optimal ratio was perceived to be 80 percent white to 20 percent black), poor black students' exposure to middle class values and higher academic standards would improve their academic performance and behavior, without detracting from white students' educational experience. Under the present conditions, blacks were not being served well by low standards in the inner city schools, nor by the indifference some perceived in suburban schools where so few blacks were present that they were often ignored by teachers and seldom encouraged to take positions of leadership.[20]

---

[16]Evans v. Buchanan, *supra* note 9, at 75-76.
[17]Raffel, 22.
[18] Wolters, 208.
[19] Ibid., 195-97.
[20] Ibid., 208.

In reopening the suit, the plaintiffs charged that since *Brown v. Board of Education*, the state board of education had approved or acquiesced in various policies that maintained and fostered a racially segregated public school system. These policies included establishing attendance areas to coordinate with segregated neighborhoods; the use of "freedom of choice" transfer policies, which allowed white students to attend "whiter" schools, rather than the racially mixed schools closer to their homes; reliance upon voluntary faculty transfers which resulted in greater racial identifiability of schools;[21] and mandating, approving, or acquiescing in the choice of school sites and expansion in a discriminatory manner.[22]

The plaintiffs charged that the state of Delaware, through its laws, regulations, and policies, had enforced, approved, or acquiesced in both public and private segregation, including state mandated dual school systems and state mandated or approved segregation in public and private housing. The effects of these policies persisted, charged the plaintiffs. They claimed that the 1968 Educational Advancement Act was designed to perpetuate and did perpetuate a racially discriminatory dual public school system in New Castle County.[23]

The respondents argued that the dual school system had been dismantled when the district adopted its facially neutral attendance plan and pointed out that Wilmington was one of the first districts in the state of Delaware to desegregate. They argued that current segregation resulted from private choices, rather than official policies on the part of the state or county.[24]

On July 12, 1974, the federal district court found that the Wilmington schools had never been desegregated and that the dual school system still operated. The court held that the state board of education, despite its repeated protests to the contrary, was indeed responsible for the desegregation of Delaware schools and that it was guilty of noncompliance with *Brown*. The court declined to rule on the question of whether the Educational Advancement Act was unconstitutional, saying the question was premature. It ordered the defendants and invited the plaintiff Wilmington school board to submit

---

[21]Evans v. Buchanan, *supra* note 9, at 71.

[22] Ibid., 65.

[23] Ibid., 60-61.

[24] Raffel, 45.

alternate intra- and inter-district desegregation plans to the court by September 15.[25]

Later that month, in the landmark *Milliken v. Bradley* (1974), the Supreme Court rejected an inter-district remedy for the segregation found within the Detroit school district. The Court remanded the Delaware case to the district court to review in light of the ruling in *Milliken*. Following the Supreme Court's rejection of an inter-district remedy for an intra-district violation in *Milliken*, the district court in the Wilmington case could consider relief involving more than the Wilmington district, only upon finding that the school districts in New Castle County were not significantly autonomous, or upon finding that the state or the suburban school districts had committed racially discriminatory acts which contributed to inter-district segregation.[26] The district court invited the ten suburban school districts of New Castle County to intervene as defendants and present evidence regarding the amended complaint.

All the suburban school districts adopted the position of the state board. The suburban school districts argued that *Milliken* governed the Wilmington case in virtually every respect. They said that Wilmington schools were predominantly black because the whole district had become predominantly black. Furthermore, they noted, though there might have been state action that had furthered segregation within the schools in Wilmington, the court had found similar federal, state, and local action in the Michigan case, yet the Supreme Court had ruled out an inter-district remedy. The school districts, like the state, argued that the Educational Advancement Act was not unconstitutional, because it had not drawn or redrawn the Wilmington school district boundaries, but had retained the boundaries established in 1905. Though the state admittedly had had the power to alter the boundaries of the Wilmington district, it was under no constitutional obligation to do so, just as the state of Michigan also had had the power to alter school district lines, but had not been required to do so to bring about desegregation.[27]

The court was not moved by the defendants' arguments, however. It cited Federal Housing Administration policies, as well as county and

---

[25] Evans v. Buchanan, 379 F. Supp. 1218, 1221-1224 (D. Del 1974).

[26] Evans v. Buchanan, 393 F. Supp. 428, 432 (D.Del. 1975) (Layton dissenting).

[27] Brief of Intervening Defendants, Evans v. Buchanan (D.Del. 27 Nov. 1974) (No. 18116-1822).

city public housing policies, as factors contributing to the concentration of minorities in parts of Wilmington and their virtual absence from its suburbs. Through the early 1970s, housing authorities had built low-income housing projects, whose tenants were overwhelmingly minorities, almost exclusively within Wilmington, rather than dispersing them throughout the suburbs. Upon reviewing the evidence, the court found, "By the variety of federal, state and local conduct . . . ,[28] governmental authorities have elected to place their 'power, property, and prestige' behind the white exodus from Wilmington and the widespread housing discrimination patterns in New Castle County." Governmental authorities were therefore "responsible to a significant degree for the increasing disparity in residential and school populations between Wilmington and its suburbs in the past two decades."[29] The court held that this federal, state, and local conduct constituted segregative action with inter-district effects under *Milliken*. The court noted further that the case produced extensive evidence that racial balance in housing and racial balance in public schools were closely related. As in many other metropolitan areas, discriminatory housing policies which resulted in segregated residential areas allowed school systems to implement attendance policies that ostensibly were based on neighborhood school plans, but which resulted, with minimal extra effort on the school system's part, in strikingly segregated schools.

The court concluded that whereas in the Detroit case, the suburban school districts had never been implicated in *de jure* segregation, in the Wilmington case, previous to *Brown*, the city and suburbs had cooperatively participated in *de jure* segregation. The Wilmington district and the suburban districts therefore were not meaningfully separate and autonomous. Since the 1950s, the districts had operated independently of each other, and the suburbs had operated unitary districts. However, "[because] since *Brown* governmental authorities

---

[28]In addition to the discriminatory housing policies, the court described various official actions, including inter-district transportation of black and white students in the suburbs to Wilmington schools that were predominantly black or white, respectively; liberal transfer policies by the Wilmington school board which promoted segregation; and state subsidization of inter-district transportation to private and parochial schools (Evans v. Buchanan, *supra* note 22, 432-36 *passim*).
[29]Ibid., 437-38.

have contributed to the racial isolation of city from suburbs, the racial characteristics of city and suburban schools are still interrelated."[30]

On the question of the constitutionality of the Educational Advancement Act of 1968, the court said that it could not conclude that the part of the act that precluded the consolidation of Wilmington with other school districts was purposely racially discriminatory. However, the court observed, "Because the Educational Advancement Act, racially neutral on its face, had a significant racial impact on the policies of the State Board of Education, it constitutes a suspect classification."[31] Furthermore, the general assembly, in passing the act, contributed to racial segregation by effectively redrawing school district lines.   Thus, the court held unconstitutional the general assembly's exclusion of Wilmington from consideration by the state board of education for consolidation.[32]

The remand opinion holding the defendants guilty of unconstitutional segregation heightened public anxiety about the prospect of desegregation, in particular, busing. In 1975, the Positive Action Committee (PAC) formed to oppose busing for the purpose of desegregation actively. The group generated a great deal of publicity with its slogan "It's time to wake up, folks," and its strong ideological appeals. It held heavily attended meetings and actively lobbied the state legislature to take anti-busing stands. PAC flyers carried a school bus labeled "The Kidnap Express;" its leaders implied that their opponents used brainwashing and Nazi propaganda, and charged that they were trying to control school children.[33]

The group's leader, James Venema, railed against the tyrannical court's abuse of power and noted the irony in the court's use of the Fourteenth Amendment to discriminate among citizens based on race.[34] On the other hand, by providing a venue for the public to express their frustration, and by its commitment to non-violence, PAC arguably helped diffuse unrest when desegregation actually began.   The group held no anti-busing rallies at that point.[35]

---

[30]Ibid., 437-38.

[31]Ibid., 442-43.

[32] Ibid., 446-47.

[33] Raffel, 155.

[34] Wolters, 231.

[35] Ibid., 231-32.

Virtually all state legislators opposed busing and sympathized with the public's resistance to the court's authority. Several New Castle County legislators strongly denounced busing before citizens' groups, such as PAC. Responding to PAC demands and general public sentiment, the legislature formed a joint committee in 1975 to study the impact of the district court's proposed remedies, to attempt to obtain a stay, and to obtain legal advice. University of Chicago Law School Professor Philip Kurland, legal consultant to the defendants, advised the legislature that any explicit legislative act intended to thwart desegregation would corroborate the plaintiffs' contention that state action was furthering school segregation. Realizing that anti-busing action could damage the state's appeal, the legislature dissolved the joint committee in September 1975. The committee's final report advised the legislature not to enter the case at that time and advised the legislature to adhere to the law. Thus, fear of jeopardizing future appeals by the state appeared to be the primary restraining force on the legislature.[36]

A group calling itself The Delaware Equal Educational Process Committee (DEEP) had formed early in the litigation process and declared that it would support desegregation, even if it entailed busing. The leaders of DEEP tended to be tied to religious and city groups and interests. Though DEEP was generally viewed as far out of touch with the mainstream, and it had only four hundred members, while its counterpart, PAC, claimed ten thousand, its very extremism arguably helped to pull the majority back from the brink of outright defiance.[37]

On November 27, 1975, the United States Supreme Court summarily affirmed the lower court's call for an inter-district remedy. The lower court subsequently invited both parties to the suit and anyone else interested to submit proposed Wilmington-only or inter-district desegregation plans. In May 1976, the court rejected nineteen submitted plans, observing that according to *Milliken*, the remedy "must be commensurate with the scope of the violation," and that it must place the victims of unconstitutional discrimination in "substantially the position which they would have occupied had the violation not occurred." The court found that "where the violation found resulted in the operation of a dual school system, the Court must

---

[36]Raffel, 89-91.

[37] Ibid., 121.

order the 'greatest possible actual degree of desegregation,' consistent with the practicalities of the situation."[38]

Notwithstanding its determination to fashion an effective remedy, the court went to great lengths to minimize federal court intrusion. Judge Murray Schwartz, who had replaced the three-judge panel for the remedy phase of the proceedings, rejected demands that he prescribe or define a good educational plan:

> We were urged throughout the hearings in the case to be concerned with the quality of education offered by the area schools. That is much more properly the concern of local officials and the parents of children in the schools. Our duty here is not to impose quality education even if we could define that term. . . . We do not find there is a mandate for district courts to concern themselves with how well the educative function is being performed.[39]

Judge Schwartz specified that each school within the system should have between 10 and 35 percent minority students, and he asked the state legislature to devise an inter-district plan, but provided, in the case of legislative default, that a single county-wide system, governed by a five-member interim board be appointed by the state board. In June 1977, the Court of Appeals for the Third Circuit upheld the lower court's decision, except for the 10 to 35 percent minority requirement.[40]

Thus, by mid 1977, the lower court had established: 1) that the defendants were guilty of unconstitutional discrimination resulting in racial segregation in public schools, and 2) that an inter-district desegregation remedy was applicable. The Supreme Court affirmed these rulings. Despite the unequivocal stance of the courts, however, the public seemed to be in denial of the increasingly obvious outcome of the litigation. Desegregation, especially with busing, was so sensitive an issue that few elected or appointed community or state leaders dared suggest planning for it, lest they be accused of supporting the policy.

---

[38]Evans v. Buchanan, 447 F. Supp. 982, 986-87. (Citations from Milliken v. Bradley, 416 F. Supp. at 339 and 341).

[39]Evans v. Buchanan, 416 F. Supp. 328, 364-65 (D.Del. 1976).

[40] Evans v. Buchanan, 555 F.2d 373 (3d Cir. 1977).

Public Reaction

As the case progressed through the courts, public anxiety grew. A 1993 article in Wilmington's *The News Journal*, which recounted the turbulent years before the final court order of 1978, noted the disruption caused by people who exploited the public's fears regarding the safety and well-being of their children. "[T]here were demagogues willing to fan the fires of understandable anger. They played on people's worst fears. They challenged the validity of the court's decisions. They never preached violence, but speeches at their meetings were emotionally charged. The climate was ripe for trouble."[41]

The interim board of education, which the court had charged with devising a workable desegregation plan, was unable to complete its task. Parochialism inevitably hampered the board's decision-making process, as members were instructed by the general assembly to represent various districts' interests. Furthermore, some members' vehement ideological opposition to busing for desegregation made it virtually impossible to devise a viable plan.[42]

Divisiveness within the interim board mirrored the turmoil that plagued metropolitan Wilmington as the litigants battled within the court system and the prospect of an inter-district desegregation plan, including busing, grew increasingly imminent. Many community leaders and government officials joined forces to promote rational discussion and disseminate information responsibly, hoping to avoid the strife that wracked other communities, such as Boston and Richmond.[43] Business executives, elected officials and other community leaders met regularly over breakfast in secret to discuss desegregation planning and implementation. Initially, the group's efforts were very tentative, because any talk of planning for desegregation appeared to imply support of desegregation and busing. However, as the inevitability of a final desegregation order became increasingly certain, the breakfast group became an effective force in

---

[41]John H. Taylor, Jr., "Looking Back on the Long Ride," *Wilmington News Journal*, 5 December 1993, 1(F).

[42]Raffel, 67.

[43] Taylor, 1(F).

planning for a smooth implementation of the eventual desegregation plan.[44]

The Wilmington school district found itself in a delicate position as a plaintiff in the case. By the mid 1970s, the population of Wilmington was predominantly black and the school population had become overwhelmingly black. Thus, blacks had gained control of the Wilmington school board and hired a black superintendent of schools, along with many other black administrators. A majority of the school principals in the Wilmington district were black by this time, as well. Ironically, in seeking to improve the educational opportunities for black children through desegregation, the black leadership risked losing its only base of power in the city. Because the student population of the Wilmington district was overwhelmingly minority, the two most feasible desegregation plans were a single metropolitan district or the formation of pie-shaped wedges uniting parts of Wilmington with sections of its overwhelmingly white suburbs. Both remedies effectively would dissolve the Wilmington district. It was impossible to design a desegregation plan that would not result in the loss of political control of the district by blacks.[45]

Although the legislature tamed its rhetoric to avoid damaging its image with the court, it passed several symbolic resolutions, including 1977 resolutions disavowing the new board of education and urging President Jimmy Carter to remove Judge Schwartz from the bench.[46] Though the general assembly was unable to avert the final decision by the court, its antagonistic stance contributed to the emotional upheaval engendered by the prospect of forced desegregation. Reason took a back seat to rhetoric, and the general assembly appeared impervious to the inevitable outcome of the court's order. "The legislators were cheered on by a public that wrongly believed that nothing would happen if the legislature didn't act. They ignored the fact that even an appeal to the U.S. Supreme Court had failed to reverse the desegregation ruling."[47]

Executive action within the state contrasted sharply with legislative action and rhetoric. Although he was ideologically opposed

---

[44] William Trombley, "Strike Perils Busing Plan in Delaware," *Los Angeles Times,* 30 October, 1978, 22.

[45] Raffel, 66.

[46] Ibid., 98-99.

[47] Taylor, 1(F).

to busing, and although he had no official responsibility with regard to public education, New Castle County Executive Melvin Slawik appointed a Committee of Twelve, later known as the Delaware Committee on the School Decision (DCSD), to advise the county government on how to prepare for the pending court decision. Wilmington Mayor William McLaughlin, who took office in January 1977, openly favored planning for desegregation. He spoke out for peaceful implementation and worked cooperatively with other officials towards those ends. Sherman W. Tribitt, governor of Delaware from 1972 to 1976, also supported the DCSC, though he personally was opposed to busing.[48]

Tribitt's successor, Pierre S. du Pont IV, whose term began in January 1977, immediately took an active role in preparation for desegregation. Though he personally opposed busing and had supported anti-busing measures as a Delaware congressman, as governor he eschewed any notion of resistance and urged responsible compliance.[49] Governor du Pont's was a voice of reason amidst the emotional clamor of others.

The state board did little to prepare for the desegregation, viewing that task as a responsibility of local authorities. Bowing to public pressure, local school administrators prepared only minimally for desegregation, because even discussing the subject heightened white anxiety. Superintendents avoided doing anything that could be perceived as acquiescing in desegregation or busing.[50]

Thus, until the final order was issued in January 1978, little constructive communication transpired between the boards and administrators on the one side, and the public on the other. Legislative representatives forfeited the opportunity to participate in the formation of the desegregation plan, instead fueling public anxiety through inflammatory rhetoric. State and local education officials shirked their responsibility to inform the public and to involve citizens in rational planning for desegregation. Though some business and community leaders worked effectively to smooth the process, even they felt the need to meet in secret, so sensitive was the topic of desegregation and busing. With few exceptions, of those who held elective positions or

---

[48] Raffel, 101-04.

[49] Ibid., 105.

[50] Ibid., 78.

who were responsible for public school policy, only executive leaders had the courage to urge compliance with the court's eventual directive.

Given this political climate, it would be virtually impossible for the court to provide a system that would treat minority children equitably. The court would impose a desegregation order, and on the surface it would appear that Wilmington's was a model desegregation plan in terms of its comprehensiveness and compliance with the busing plan, but serious equity issues would remain. Had political officials stepped in earlier to encourage public participation in the plan, had they offered constructive suggestions as to how to meet the court's mandate, rather than encouraging constituents to defy the courts, they might have been able to forge a desegregation plan that the public would have more readily accepted. Furthermore, they would not have offended their minority constituency, leaving them feeling alienated. As in other communities torn by desegregation and busing, if political leaders had shown leadership, the desegregation era likely would have been much less traumatic, and both whites and minorities would have felt less abused. In Wilmington, the resentment of the black community festered throughout the desegregation era and into the post desegregation era, because blacks continued to feel that the school system was insensitive to the educational needs of black children and that it failed to offer them an equal educational opportunity.

The Final Desegregation Order

The interim board of education's having failed to submit a pupil assignment proposal to the court, the court eventually ordered the state board to appoint a new five-member board of education (called the New Castle County Planning Board of Education -- "NCCPBE") to replace the interim board. The court charged the new board with developing a complete desegregation plan by September 30, 1977, and preparing for the assumption of authority over the new school system.[51]

The new board (NCCPBE) was politically moderate; it consisted of four whites and one black, four men and one woman. It submitted two plans, neither of which satisfied the court, so the court directed the NCCPBE to offer additional proposals, in response to which the NCCPBE established a six-member Pupil Assignment Committee. The Pupil Assignment Committee submitted three alternative

---

[51] Evans v. Buchanan, *supra* note 32, at 988.

proposals, including a "9-3" assignment plan which would reassign all students from the predominantly black districts (Wilmington and Delaware) to predominantly white districts for nine school years, and all students from the predominantly white districts to predominantly black districts for three consecutive years. The court ordered implementation of the 9-3 desegregation plan.

As was the custom in desegregation cases, the federal court deferred to the policy-making authority of the local school board as much as possible in fashioning an acceptable desegregation plan. The court allowed the NCCPBE the flexibility to design the assignment plan, establishing and altering attendance area boundaries as needed, breaking feeder patterns if desired, allowing transfers, and utilizing whatever other reasonable desegregation tools the board deemed necessary to achieve an optimal 9-3 configuration.[52]

The desegregation order included ancillary components, and the court stressed their necessity "to cure the constitutional infirmity and restore the victims of discrimination as nearly as possible to the position they would have assumed in the absence of a violation."[53] The order included eight types of ancillary relief:

1. In-service training for administrators, faculty, and staff to ease the desegregation process;
2. The implementation of an affirmative reading and communication skills program which would not resegregate students; ·
3. The provision of curriculum materials that reflected cultural pluralism;
4. The implementation of an effective and nondiscriminatory counseling and guidance program;
5. Establishment by the new board of nondiscriminatory guidelines for new construction and school closings;
6. The provision of an "appropriate" human relations program "to protect the individual dignity of students and teachers and to prevent racial myths and stereotypes from prevailing in schools undergoing desegregation;"
7. The development of a code of student rights and responsibilities regarding student conduct, suspension, and expulsion, among other things;

---

[52] Ibid., 1008.
[53] Ibid., 1017.

8. Reassignment of administrators, faculty, and staff in a nondiscriminatory manner.[54]

The court provided for the transfer of governing authority from the eleven boards to the New Castle County Planning Board of Education, who's appointed members would hold their positions for two years, after which the board would become elective. The plaintiffs requested that the court continually monitor the transition to a fully desegregated system, but the court repeatedly emphasized its desire to remain unobtrusive and leave policy-making decisions to locally elected officials. The court maintained that its provision for the representation of the Wilmington district on the school board would protect the plaintiffs' interests, while facilitating "the Court's desire to studiously avoid undue interference with school board functions."[55]

Finally, the court addressed the financial aspects of the final order. It directed the state to maintain its financial support for the affected districts at the fiscal year 1976-1977 or 1977-1978 level, whichever was higher. In addition, the court directed the state to pay the bulk of the transition costs, with the school district taking on an increasing portion of the financial responsibilities until the 1985 fiscal year when the state's fiscal obligations toward the desegregation effort would end.[56]

The order resulted in the reassignment of about 21,500 of the district's 63,540 students when the busing plan was implemented on September 11, 1978.[57] Kindergarten children and special education students were exempted from the desegregation plan. Kindergartners remained in neighborhood schools, and special education students retained their previous school assignments.[58]

---

[54] Evans v. Buchanan, No. 1816-1822 (D.Del. 9 Jan. 1978) (order at 11-13).

[55] Evans v. Buchanan, *supra* note 32, at 1018-20.

[56] Ibid., 1037-1039.

[57] Trombley, "Desegregation in Wilmington a 30-Year Fight," *Los Angeles Times*, 30 October 1978, 16.

[58] Delaware Department of Public Instruction, "Regulations for the Reorganization of the New Castle County School District – 1980" (Dover: Delaware Department of Public Instruction, 1980), 41.

Desegregation Takes Place

Despite the fact that surveys showed that 90 percent suburban parents opposed busing,[59] the mood in Wilmington following the announcement of the court's final order was rather calm. Governor du Pont, in his state of the state address, referred to the decision and said, "I, and most of us in Delaware, disagree with that dictate, but we nevertheless have a constitutional duty to obey it."[60]

Dr. Carroll W. Biggs, the superintendent of the new school district, conceded that the level of frustration among whites was very high, partly because they felt that they had not taken part in causing the discrimination. Biggs planned to reassure parents that there would be discipline in the schools and that their children would be safe. PAC vowed to appeal the decision and called the governor and other officials "defeatists" for advising compliance with the order despite their opposition to busing.[61]

Public opinion regarding the final order was divided among blacks. Wendell Howell, the president of the Wilmington school board strongly supported desegregation, having attended an integrated Roman Catholic high school himself. "I know the values I picked up just by going to school with those white kids. It did make me seek higher goals in life." Howell stressed that the key problem in the black community was low self-esteem and self-doubt. "Blacks, more than whites, question the ability of blacks to do a job. We doubt ourselves." Many blacks were unhappy with the desegregation plan, which placed a much heavier burden on black students, busing them outside their neighborhoods for nine years, whereas white children would be bused only three years. "The blacks won the case," said Charles Grandison, an aide to Mayor William McLaughlin, "but they still think they're getting shafted." Grandison expressed confidence, however, that the Wilmington area had a leadership committed to compliance with the order, and that the disruption and violence that had plagued other cities undergoing desegregation would not afflict Wilmington.[62]

---

[59] Raffel, 74.

[60] Steven V. Roberts, "Leaders of Wilmington, Del., Seek Smooth Start of Busing," *New York Times*, 2 February 1978, 16(A).

[61] Ibid.

[62] Ibid.

Seven of the suburban school districts and the state appealed the final order, claiming that the remedy was excessive and that it inappropriately dissolved democratically elected school boards (and districts) by "judicial fiat."[63]   However, on July 24, the Court of Appeals for the Third Circuit upheld the lower court order.

Though the state planned to appeal the appellate court's decision, Attorney General Richard R. Wier, Jr. held out little hope that the Supreme Court would reverse the appeal court's ruling. Wier called on parents and school officials to accept the decision. "The time has come for all of us, black and white, young and old, to put our differences behind us and to work together to insure that desegregation, as ordered by the courts, is not only implemented, but implemented peacefully and in good faith."[64] Thus, apparently convinced of the finality of the court's order, given the failure of all appeals, school officials moved quickly following the announcement of the decision to inform the public and to ask for its assistance in shaping and implementing the plan. A system of citizens' advisory councils (CACs) was planned, and student leaders took part in training workshops.   This activity caused protests in March, when three thousand students from nearly all the county's schools boycotted classes (one thousand were suspended), but the new board made it clear that it was moving ahead with implementation.[65]

By virtually any measure, New Castle County was fully desegregated in September 1978.   Eighty-five of the ninety-three regular schools in the district were within 10 percent of the district average of 24 percent black.[66]   During the first week of school, enrollment was about 90 percent of that expected.   School officials were delighted with the remarkably peaceful implementation of the busing plan and the smooth transition.[67]   However, a major disruption lay ahead.

An acrimonious five-week teachers strike shook the district beginning in October, the dispute centering on a demand by suburban

---

[63] Trombley, "Desegregation in Wilmington," 16.

[64] "Delaware Districts Lose Busing Appeal," *New York Times*, 25 July 1978, 10(A).

[65] Raffel, 84.

[66] Ibid., 187.

[67] "Supplementary AP material on busing," *New York Times*, 12 September 1978, 88.

teachers that their salaries be raised to equal the higher wages paid the Wilmington teachers. Finally, the two sides agreed to freeze the former Wilmington teachers' salaries at the current level for eighteen months, while gradually raising the salaries of the former suburban teachers.[68] Most of those who did not participate in the strike were Wilmington teachers, and their crossing the picket lines generated a great deal of bitterness between the two groups. Resentment lingered long after the strike ended.[69]

As the first year of desegregation progressed, tensions surfaced as white parents charged that there was a double standard with regard to discipline; they felt that black students were held to lower standards of behavior. Minority parents charged that minority students were being suspended in greater numbers than white students. Parents of high achievers felt that the curriculum was being diluted. Some parents complained of the amount of time that was lost to discipline. There were reports of intra-class segregation. Thus, while the newly integrated schools opened smoothly in 1978, after the settlement of the teachers' strike, various issues and problems still remained. However, Superintendent Carroll Biggs noted at a meeting of the Breakfast Group in February 1979, that these were the same problems other communities faced with the implementation of desegregation.[70]

Some black parents withdrew their children from public schools in order to spare them the long bus rides to the suburbs and sent them to private Catholic schools. However, most could not afford private school. The fact that the suburban children were bused into city schools for only three years rendered it easier for their parents to avoid the city schools altogether by placing their children in private schools for those years.

Jim Reilly, a lifelong resident of Wilmington, who remained in the public school system for one year following desegregation, recalled in 1995 that from a white child's perspective, the greatest anxiety regarding the order to desegregate was the disruption it would cause.

---

[68] Gregory Jaynes, "Wilmington Teachers End Strike With Approval of Three-year Pact," *New York Times*, 22 November 1978, 14(A).

[69] Ebrima Ellzy-Sey, founding member of the Coalition to Save Our Children, chairman of the Education Committee of the Wilmington NAACP, and retired Red Clay District school teacher, interview by author, Wilmington, 4 June 1995.

[70] Raffel, 194-95.

Classes were split, and children worried about where they would be assigned and which of their friends would accompany them. Reilly's elementary school, which had been about 90 percent white, was closed, and he was sent to a school that was about 75 percent white. He recalled no racially motivated incidents at his new school.[71]

Reilly's parents had been very supportive of the public education. Two older daughters attended Wilmington area public schools and went on to Yale. As the first year of desegregation progressed, however, his parents perceived a decline in the public schools, and they feared that Jim would not receive the same education his sisters had received. Consequently, they placed Jim in Wilmington Friends Quaker School for the 1979-'80 school year, and he remained there through the twelfth grade. Four of Reilly's classmates transferred with him to Friends Quaker School, and he estimated that as much as 20 percent of his class may have transferred to private schools in the first years following the desegregation order. He knew of several teachers who left the public schools to teach in private schools, as well.

Raffel argued that in New Castle County, relatively little white flight that could be attributed to the busing order occurred. He attributed much (31 percent) of the decline in white enrollment between 1974 and 1977 to declining birth rates in the county. Raffel claimed that about 24 percent of the decline was attributable to white students leaving the public school system for private schools. He noted that the extent to which this shift was due to busing was unclear.[72] This rate of white flight was relatively low and corresponded with the lower rate of white flight where metropolitan desegregation plans, as opposed to inner-city district plans, were implemented, claimed Raffel.[73]

Wolters, on the other hand, stressed that the decline in white enrollment, and especially the 23 or 24 percent increase in white enrollment in private schools was "striking testimony to the fact that resourceful parents can evade the best-laid plans of sociological jurisprudence." Furthermore, he suggested that a decrease in the white population of New Castle County, at a time when the white population in other Delaware counties was increasing, reflected white reluctance to moving into a community with forced busing.[74] Whether the court's

---

[71]James Reilly, interview by author, 4 June 1995, Wilmington..

[72]Raffel, 179-80.

[73]Ibid., 187.

[74] Wolters, 247.

jurisprudence was sound or not, clearly there were effective ways for people to avoid the court's authority.

Between 1978 and 1981, much dissatisfaction arose regarding the restructured metropolitan school district. The administration of four attendance zones within the one mega-district was cumbersome, and school officials and the public were generally dissatisfied with the large size of the district. Thus, the Department of Public Instruction developed and the state board approved a plan for reorganization of the New Castle County School District into four districts. The district court granted the state's request for approval of the plan in 1981, and on July 1 of that year, the four-district plan became official. The four newly formed districts, Red Clay, Colonial, Brandywine, and Christina, followed the attendance zones of the single metropolitan district. Each consisted of somewhat natural groupings of the ten former suburban districts, along with a portion of the former Wilmington District. The court's plan was made into state regulation, as were parts of the revised tax system that funded the desegregation plan.[75]

State law established nominating districts within each of the four school districts for the election of representatives to the respective school boards. The law allowed that nominating petitions be signed by anyone within the respective school districts, however, and it required at-large elections. The provision for nominating districts was meant to ensure minority representation on the boards, but the at-large elections resulted in suburban domination of the school boards and therefore generated resentment among minorities.[76] This issue, which remained contentious in the 1990s, is discussed further in the following chapter.

Thus, following decades of litigation, the last few years of which were characterized by rising public anxiety and turmoil regarding the prospect of school desegregation and busing, the transition to a restructured school system, including desegregation and busing, went relatively smoothly. Several factors likely contributed to the peaceful implementation of the busing order, including the determination of community and business leaders that Wilmington would not be the

---

[75] Jack Nichols, assistant state superintendent for administrative services, Delaware Department of Public Instruction, interview by author, 6 June 1995, Dover.

[76] Ellzy-Sey, *supra* note 62.

scene of the type of chaos and violence that wracked such cities as Boston and Richmond, the steady leadership shown by Governor du Pont and other executive officials, and perhaps the time that transpired between the 1974 finding of unconstitutional discrimination and the 1978 implementation of the remedy, which allowed residents to adjust to the inevitability of the final decision and accept the court's authority. Public frustration was high immediately following the announcement of the final order in January 1978, but by September, when school started, the public seemed to have been generally resigned to the decree, if not supportive of it. Some students left the public school system during the years leading up to and immediately following the final order, and some perceived a decline in the public school system in the six to eight years following desegregation, but the system rebounded, and by the mid 1980s, faith in the public school system appeared to have been restored.[77]

As the 1990s approached, the system had been desegregated for over ten years, and there were no outward signs of differences between Wilmington and suburban schools. Following a relatively smooth implementation and more than a dozen years of compliance with the court order, the time seemed ripe for returning to court to ask for release from supervision. Yet, efforts to reach a settlement and the trial that resulted in a declaration of unitary status brought out long simmering frustrations among blacks, revealing problems in the school district that appeared to be a model of successful desegregation. A significant achievement gap between whites and minorities, as well as disproportionate placement of black students in low level classes, led advocates for minority students to charge that the integration within the system was superficial and that students remained segregated and inequitably treated within schools. These frustrations highlighted the limitations of the courts in providing equity and quality within schools in the face of a resistant or indifferent community and in the face of vastly different socioeconomic conditions within the student population.

---

[77] Reilly, *supra* note 64.

CHAPTER 5

Wilmington in the 1990s

Introduction

Few school districts were as desegregated as those in the Wilmington area following the 1978 district court decision. In 1994 Gary Orfield, director of the Harvard Project on School Desegregation, noted the success of the metropolitan desegregation plan in Wilmington, in terms of levels of integration and the low incidence of white flight.[1] In 1995, the four Wilmington school districts had a combined enrollment of about fifty thousand students, 31 percent of whom were black.[2] Though busing had become routine for both city and suburban parents and children by the mid 1990s, frustration was growing amongst blacks and whites, and most seemed eager to have the court's supervision and busing ended. Both black and white parents seemed eager to have their children attend school closer to their homes.[3]

There was no longer any significant inequality among the schools, because the Wilmington schools were operated as parts of the four restructured school districts, rather than as a separate and distinct district. In contrast with many other prominent school desegregation

---

[1] Feldman, Joseph, Edward Kirby, Susan E. Eaton, and Alison Morantz, *Still Separate, Still Unequal: The Limits of Milliken II's Educational Compensation Remedies* (Cambridge: The Harvard Project on School Desegregation 1994), 2.
[2] Peter Schmidt, "Del. Desegregation Case Pivots on Student Statistics," *Education Week*, 1 March 1995, 14.
[3] Eric Ruth, "Schools: equality is understood," *Wilmington News Journal*, 28 December 1994, 1(A).

cases, school funding, or the lack thereof, was not a significant issue in the Wilmington case. As the Court of Appeals for the Third Circuit had noted in 1958, the state of Delaware assumed a particularly high level of responsibility for public education, and state funding of education was quite generous. In the mid 1990s, Delaware ranked fifth in the nation in per capita expenditures on public education.[4] State funding of education rose steadily since 1975-1976, when the state spent $1,511 per pupil through 1993-94, when it spent $6,420 per pupil.[5] Districts received 70 percent of their funding from the state and about 22 percent was locally secured, with about 99 percent of the local revenues derived from property taxes.[6]

Thus, Wilmington seemed to be a success story in terms of the evolved *Brown* mandate and federal courts' capacity to guide a public school system through the transition from a discriminatory dual school system to a unitary, integrated school system that truly offered an equal educational opportunity for all. However, minority students continued to achieve at significantly lower levels than white children. The central questions in the mid 1990s were whether the state and school districts had complied in good faith with the court's desegregation order and who or what was responsible for the persistent achievement gap between whites and minorities.

Request for Release

In 1993 the state and the four Wilmington area school districts returned to district court to request release from court supervision based on their continual good faith compliance with the 1978 court order. Attorney General Oberly assured the public that the state would not be "gerrymandering" attendance zones to resegregate black and white students. He noted that the Constitution forbade such action. However, release from the court decree would end the requirement that the school districts reassign students each time population shifts resulted in racial imbalance. Instead, the districts would be able to employ such programs as school "choice" or magnet schools to retain a level of racial balance in schools. The parties to the desegregation suit

---

[4] Jack Nichols, assistant state superintendent for Administrative Services, Delaware Department of Public Instruction, telephone interview by author, 18 October 1995.
[5] Delaware DPI, "Delaware School Finances," May 1994, 14.
[6] Nichols, *supra* note 4.

had been negotiating in an attempt to reach a settlement, but the state felt that negotiations were not progressing quickly enough. Negotiations continued while the state pursued its goal through the court system.[7]

Throughout the era of judicial oversight, the state and the school districts had complied with the two main components of the desegregation order, the 9-3 plan[8] and the requirement that a full set of grades be maintained in Wilmington, to minimize disruption if the court order were to be overturned. The court had been quite unobtrusive with regard to educational policy making, except for setting these two basic requirements, and the state and school districts never had been charged with noncompliance with these two requirements.[9] From the state's and the school districts' point of view, the time was ripe for release.

However, the Coalition To Save Our Children, the group which since May 1990 represented the plaintiff class, objected to the state's request for release, claiming that the school districts had not eliminated certain vestiges of past discrimination. They cited the achievement gap between whites and minorities, the disproportionate placement of minorities in lower-level classes, disproportionate rates of disciplinary action, including suspensions and expulsions, and higher dropout rates for minorities as evidence of continuing discrimination.[10] The state argued that the gap was related to socioeconomic level, and not race. It stressed its compliance with the court order since 1978.[11]

With regard to the defendants' claims that they had always complied in good faith with the court's order, Ebrima Ellzy-Sey noted with frustration Red Clay Consolidated's poor record of compliance. "They blatantly avoid court orders," he charged. Observing that the residents of Red Clay included the "movers and shakers" in Wilmington and the state, Ellzy-Sey contended, "Red Clay is the richest, but they seem to think the federal court doesn't apply to them."[12] Indeed, the court had found in 1991 that the Red Clay

---

[7] Sandy Dennison, "Panel hopes to end '78 busing order," Wilmington News Journal, 31 October 1991, 1(B), 5(B).
[8] The 9 - 3 plan is described in the previous chapter.
[9] Nichols, *supra* note 4.
[10] Schmidt, "Del. Desegregation Case," 14.
[11] Nichols, *supra* note 4.
[12] Ebrima Ellzy-Sey, founding member of the Coalition to Save Our Children, chairman of the Education Committee of the Wilmington NAACP,

Consolidated School District still had "substantial problems" which were "vestiges of past discrimination" and which had to be eliminated before achieving unitary status.   Yet, the court did not address the plaintiffs' substantive complaints with regard to Red Clay's infractions; it merely required additional reporting.[13]

Another Coalition complaint was that the districts did not hire enough minority faculty.   The state contended that there simply were not enough minorities in the faculty hiring pool.   The Coalition claimed, however, that state policies were to blame for the low number of blacks in the hiring pool.   It charged that Delaware's use of the highest minimum standards on the teacher performance exam, a national test which only a few states used to screen teaching applicants, eliminated many minority applicants and intimidated others.   Ellzy-Sey noted that the faculty never had been fully integrated, but that since 1991, when a large number of teachers took early option retirement, the districts had hired few minority teachers, so faculty integration was particularly poor in the mid 1990s.   The Coalition remained unconvinced that the state and the districts had made sufficient efforts to hire minority teachers.

Ellzy-Sey claimed that the four-district plan was flawed from the start and never served the interests of minority children well.   Prior to desegregation, Wilmington was the richest of the county's school districts, owing to various endowments that supplemented the district's revenues from the state and local property taxes.   Splitting up the Wilmington district had been particularly burdensome to these children.   Minority families moved frequently within the city of Wilmington, observed Ellzy-Sey.   Prior to the desegregation order, such moves had been minimally disruptive with regard to the children's education, because they had remained in the same district. However, following implementation of the desegregation plan, a move of a few blocks within the city of Wilmington could mean transfer to a different school district and the likelihood of greater adjustments for the student.   Other evidence of the school systems' declining ability to meet the needs of minority students was the sharply declining college matriculation rate.   Prior to 1978 three city high schools served

---

and retired Red Clay District school teacher, interview by author, 5 June 1995, Wilmington.

[13] Coalition To Save Our Children (formerly Brenda Evans, et al.) v. State Board of Education (formerly Madeline Buchanan, et al.) No. 1816-1822-SLR, slip op. at 8 (D.Del., 2 March 1994).

African-American children, and about 65 percent went to college. In 1995, virtually no African-American children in the city of Wilmington attended college, according to Ellzy-Sey.[14]

Unemployment figures for black youth had risen sharply since desegregation, and Ellzy-Sey attributed this decline to the deterioration of the cooperative relationship between schools and the business community in Wilmington since the Wilmington school district had been restructured. Prior to desegregation, businesses offered students internships and work-study opportunities, which Ellzy-Sey estimated resulted in employment offers perhaps 90 percent of the time. The district had had an effective liaison office that coordinated internships and the hiring of high school students. However, since desegregation, the four school districts had not had a cooperative relationship with the business community, and unemployment among black youth had risen.

Other evidence of the decline in the school system's responsiveness to minority children's needs was the lack of participation by minorities in school music programs. Prior to desegregation, there had been bands in each of the inner city schools. In the 1990s almost no minority children participated in the school bands. Another sign of alienation was the fact that minority children rarely sought out school counselors. Ellzy-Sey observed that African-American children did not trust counselors. Even minority teachers and counselors were not as supportive of minority children as they could be. "They've succumbed to the pressure of their colleagues (to be more responsive to majority children's needs). By the fourth grade (African-American) children are alienated from school."[15]

Many minority parents who attended Wilmington schools had negative experiences that remained with them in their adult years. Ellzy-Sey suggested that such parental experiences and attitudes affected children's ability levels when they started school, and they affected their attitudes and achievement levels as they progressed through the system. Thus, the Coalition remained dissatisfied with several aspects of the state's and the school districts' compliance with the court order. Furthermore, its members feared that without continued judicial oversight, the school districts would revert to a neighborhood school system, which would result in marked resegregation. They sought to retain the court's protection to preclude

---

[14]Ellzy-Sey, *supra* note 12.
[15]Ibid.

such changes and to ensure that the school districts would not resume the discriminatory practices they had engaged in prior to the 1978 order.

The Failed Consent Decree

The parties to the suit continued negotiating a settlement, even after the state and the school districts returned to court to request release. The state board president and the Coalition reached tentative agreement in November 1993 for release from the court order. However, negotiations broke down later that month, and Judge Schwartz, who had become deeply involved in the negotiation process, recused himself from the case. Judge Sue Robinson was appointed to replace him.[16]

Negotiations resumed shortly thereafter, and on December 16, 1993, the state board of education approved the tentative settlement. The plan included extensive reporting requirements and provided for continued judicial oversight, despite the fact that the parties stipulated to the declaration that the school districts would be deemed legally unitary. Furthermore, the agreement aimed to use the court's authority to effectuate substantive educational remedies that were not a part of the original remedial order.[17]

Governor Carper called for support of the consent agreement in an article he wrote in the *Wilmington News Journal*. The governor noted that the consent decree declared that Brandywine, Christina, Colonial, and Red Clay Consolidated school districts had attained unitary status and ended the court's jurisdiction, except for enforcing the settlement. With the court's approval, the school districts would be released from the obligation to adjust attendance zones whenever schools fell more than 10 percent outside the district-wide ratio of white to black students. After four years, the districts would attain full flexibility in student assignment. Governor Carper explained that the agreement called for numerous educational programs based on New Directions goals and Delaware 2000 that would benefit all Delaware children.[18] Such substantive requirements aimed at educational quality, though

---

[16] John H. Taylor, Jr., "Looking Back on the Long Ride," *Wilmington News Journal*, 4 December 1993, 1(F).

[17] Dennison, "Del. Board oks school deseg plan," *Wilmington News Journal*, 17 December 1993, 1(A).

[18] Thomas R. Carper. "Desegregation settlement will benefit Delaware children," *Wilmington News Journal*, 5 December 1993, 3(F).

well intended, would evoke strong misgivings on the part of the court, which adamantly held the position that its role was to ensure equity, not quality, in the school system.

The agreement also promoted Delaware's goal of "ensur[ing] the recruitment, retention and development of highly qualified and accomplished educators" by elevating the quality of its teaching corps and helping to ensure that minority children had positive minority role models in the classroom. The plan allowed for the recruitment of qualified non-education majors and strengthened the state's ability to recruit qualified minority teachers from other states to increase the number of minority teachers in the classroom. It also funded scholarships for graduating high school students who committed to teaching in Delaware.[19]

In addition, the settlement called for the elimination of at-large voting and the substitution of in-district voting. This proposed change addressed the minority complaint of under representation on the school boards resulting from the fact that their votes were diluted by majority votes throughout the districts. Minorities claimed that the board members were "hand-picked" by the mayor and/or other elites.[20] All four district school boards approved the settlement at simultaneous meetings on January 24, 1994. Their votes of approval were all contingent upon the state's funding the educational programs outlined in the agreement.[21]

However, Senate approval of the settlement failed by one vote on the day following the release of a letter from Judge Robinson raising several questions about the tentative settlement.[22] The state subsequently asked Judge Robinson to rule on the questions she had raised concerning the consent agreement, arguing that the matter of whether the court "intended to approve the agreement" was "a decisive one in the resolution of the case."[23] The court therefore expressed its "tentative, but substantial concern regarding the enforceability of the settlement agreement as proposed" in a memorandum opinion dated March 2, 1994.

---

[19] Ibid.

[20] Ellzy-Sey, *supra* note 12.

[21] Dennison, "Crafting a Settlement," 1(A).

[22] Ibid.

[23] The Coalition To Save Our Children v. State Board of Education, *supra* note 13, at 11.

Judge Robinson noted that while the parties stipulated that a unitary school system had been achieved, the plaintiffs agreed to that point (in their own words) "solely for the purposes of settlement." The agreement specified that the court would retain jurisdiction only "as may be required to enforce this Consent order." Yet, the agreement failed to specify the extent or the duration of such limited jurisdiction.[24]

The consent agreement required extensive reporting obligations for the state board and the districts until the end of the 1997-1998 academic year. These included, among other things, annual, bi-annual, or quarterly reports on suspensions, expulsions and arrests by race, grade and infraction, district and school; racial composition of students by district, school, and classroom; special education; and drop-outs by race, school, and district. The agreement specified that the district reports be filed with the state board, the Coalition and the Hispanic interveners and that the Coalition would have the right to file a complaint with the court within sixty days of the filing of any report, if it was unsatisfied that the district(s) had complied with the consent agreement.[25]

The court clearly was troubled by the extent of the proposed judicial oversight in a closed desegregation case in which unitary status had been declared. The court observed that the most significant provision of the consent agreement "should be the declaration of 'unitary status,'" because this had been the stated goal of the litigation since 1956. The court added that the significance of the declaration of unitary status in the consent decree was virtually nullified by the lengthy list of continued oversight requirements. Referring to the list, the court declared:

> The preamble to the settlement agreement demonstrates that the parties' declaration of unitary status is not consistent with the terms that follow. Thus, the settlement agreement replaces the goal of achieving unitary status with compliance to the terms of the agreement as written. The agreement, as illustrated above, is written so as to provide multiple goals to

---

[24] Ibid.
[25] Ibid., 22-23.

implement an assortment of new educational initiatives to address broad-based problems.[26]

The court noted that any complaints regarding the substance or the implementation of the requirements could result in the imposition of further remedial relief by either the state board or the court, and such relief could be required indefinitely. Thus, in removing the only "cognizable goal in school desegregation cases," that of achieving unitary status, the parties eliminated the only standard by which to judge the appropriateness of further remedies or compliance with them. Under such circumstances, the litigation had no foreseeable end.

The court reiterated its previous stance that matters of educational quality remained the province of local educators and not the court. "The fourteenth amendment (sic) requires an equal education. There is no constitutional guarantee of a quality education. The constitution (sic) is satisfied if all . . . students . . . receive an equally bad education, regardless of race."[27] The court opined that the settlement agreement "takes the Court where it has declined over the decades to venture -- into the educational process itself." It concluded that the settlement agreement was designed to use the authority of the court to effect broad remedies that the court had never before imposed. Thus, the court declared that it found the agreement "ill-conceived," and said that it was "reluctant to venture down the path chosen by the parties.[28]

Thus, Judge Robinson stressed the limited jurisdiction of the court in desegregation cases. She observed that it was not within the court's purview to compel school systems to provide a quality educational program. She refused to be pulled in that direction by a settlement agreement when the court had steadfastly resisted imposing such demands throughout the course of the litigation.

Following the court's negative assessment of the consent agreement, the parties abandoned further attempts to negotiate and focused on the trial that would address the defendants' request for release from court supervision.

---

[26]Ibid., 26.
[27]Evans v. Buchanan, 447 F. Supp. 982 at 1000, quoted in Coalition to Save Our Children v. State Board of Education, *supra* note 13, at 27.
[28]Ibid., 29.

The Trial

The trial took place from December 19, 1994 through January 6, 1995. The court heard testimony from top national experts in desegregation, along with that of school district officials. In opening arguments before the court, Thomas Barr, counsel for the plaintiffs, claimed that black students had lost ground and accused the defendants of assuming that "there is no way to teach black children better."[29]

Dr. Christine Rossell, a desegregation expert who testified for the defendants, studied the racial compositions of the four districts and found that while Red Clay had experienced racial imbalance at a rate higher than what was recommended by the state, the four districts together were almost perfectly racially balanced. All of the districts, including Red Clay, were "significantly less racially imbalanced than the national court ordered sample."[30] Dr. David Armor, another well-known desegregation expert, also testified that the schools had a long record of compliance with the court's guidelines.

In response to this expert testimony, the plaintiffs charged that while figures showed that the districts were well integrated, tracking or ability grouping within schools resulted in classroom segregation, and this segregation was evidence of continued discrimination on the part of the school districts.

An editorial appearing in the *Wilmington News Journal* while the trial was ongoing blasted both parties in the suit for the narrowness of their arguments which attempted to place blame for the lower achievement level of disadvantaged black children, rather than offering solutions:

> Based on the narrowness of the arguments, nothing much is going to get solved in court. Whether or not the schools are ruled to be properly desegregated, the problem of low achievement among a substantial portion of students needs to be met. Solving that problem should be the first order of business whichever way the court case goes.

---

[29] Schmidt, "Delaware Desegregation Case," *Education Week*, 1 March 1995, 14.

[30]*Coalition to Save Our Children v. State Board of Education*, 901 F. Supp. 784, 797 (D.Del. 1995).

It is simply not acceptable to say that poor children should not be expected to perform as well as their more affluent peers. That flies in the face of the experience of millions of children in America who came from backwoods gulches, back alleys, tobacco roads, from slums, and from tenements in urban jungles and managed -- in the American public school system--to join the ranks of the best and the brightest. The country is built on their achievements. Write off those people and you write off the nation's future.[31]

The editorial suggested that policy makers consider consolidating the four districts to eliminate socioeconomic disparities among the districts and more efficiently distribute resources. Such a move could have eliminated redundant administrative layers in favor of one smaller central administrative office, with a higher level of site-based management (more authority delegated to school building administrators). The editorial concluded, "In such a system, perhaps, arguments about the abilities of poverty-stricken students could become what they should be, useful debates about how to use resources to solve the problem rather than useless sophistries to justify inequities."[32]

Before Judge Robinson had written her opinion, the Supreme Court released its opinion in the highly significant Kansas City case, *Missouri v. Jenkins* (1995). Judge Robinson relied on this ruling, along with two other recent Supreme Court rulings, *Oklahoma v. Dowell* (1991) and *Freeman v. Pitts* (1992), in which the Supreme Court supplied guidelines for release of school districts from court supervision following good faith compliance with desegregation orders.

In the Missouri case, the district court had found that segregation in the Kansas City school district had caused a system-wide reduction in student achievement, and the court consequently ordered a wide range of "quality education programs" for Kansas City public school students, to achieve its goal of "eliminat(ing) all vestiges of state imposed segregation." The remedial order included reducing classroom size and doing whatever was necessary to restore the Kansas City,

---

[31]Editorial, "New Castle County Schools: Outcome of deseg case will not solve achievement problems," *Wilmington News Journal*, 30 December 1994, 14(A).
[32]Ibid.

Missouri School District (KCMSD) to AAA status, the highest classification awarded by the state board of education. The district court implemented an "effective schools" program, under which it required the state to fund special programs at the school district's twenty-five racially identifiable schools, as well as its other forty-three schools. By the time of the Supreme Court appeal, the cost for these quality education programs had exceeded $220 million.[33]

Because the district court had found no inter-district violation, it could not order an inter-district remedy, and it declined to order additional reassignment of students to alter the minority ratio in district schools, because of the concern that such a requirement would "increase the instability of the KCMSD and reduce the potential for desegregation." Instead, the court ordered the quality education programs, the establishment of magnet schools, and the restoration of AAA status to maintain and perhaps increase non-minority enrollment. The court ordered the district to convert every high school and middle school and half of the elementary schools in the district to magnet schools. The cost for the magnet school program, including transportation, from its inception had totaled $448 million. The court had also ordered a total of $540 million in capital improvements and $200 million in salary assistance.[34]

In 1994, the state of Missouri had requested release from court supervision, claiming that unitary status had been attained through good faith compliance, but the defendants maintained and the district and appeals courts agreed that unitary status had not been attained because student achievement remained below the national average. Because the court earlier had determined that lower achievement levels were a vestige of past discrimination, and achievement levels remained below average, the defendants argued and the court agreed that continuation of the remedial quality educational programs was warranted. The school district was still far from reaching its potential with regard to student achievement.[35]

The Supreme Court rejected this argument, however. It held that the district court's attempt to create a magnet school district of the KCMSD to serve the inter-district goal of attracting non-minority students from the surrounding school districts was not within the

---

[33] Missouri v. Jenkins, 115 S.Ct.2038, 2042-43 (1995).
[34] Ibid., 3043.
[35] Ibid., 2046.

court's broad remedial powers. The Court observed that it was possible that increased expenditures could have increased the number of non-minority students attracted to the district, but "this rationale is not susceptible to any objective limitation." Spending in the KCMSD far exceeded that in the neighboring school districts.[36]

The Court observed that the district court had never determined the incremental effect of segregation on student achievement and had never provided the school district with specific goals regarding the quality of education programs. "The basic task of the District Court is to decide whether the reduction in achievement by minority students attributable to prior *de jure* segregation has been remedied to the extent practicable. Under our precedents, the State and the KCMSD are 'entitled to a rather precise statement of [their] obligations under a desegregation decree.'"[37] The Court held that many factors beyond the control of the KCMSD and the state affected minority student achievement and that "[i]nsistence upon academic goals unrelated to the effects of legal segregation unwarrantably postpones the day when the KCMSD will be able to operate on its own."[38]

In the early 1990s, the high Court had signaled its readiness to release school districts that had demonstrated good faith compliance with desegregation orders. Hence the Wilmington defendants had good cause to believe that the district court would look favorably upon their request for release. The announcement of the *Missouri v. Jenkins* opinion, which directly addressed and disposed of a central question in the Wilmington case, responsibility for the achievement gap, bolstered the Wilmington defendants' position further.

---

[36] Ibid., 2052-54.

[37] Ibid., 2055 (inner quote from Oklahoma v. Dowell, 111 S.Ct.636).

[38] Ibid., 2056.

In a forceful concurring opinion beginning, "It never ceases to amaze me that the courts are so willing to assume that anything that is predominantly black must be inferior," Justice Clarence Thomas urged judicial restraint in desegregation cases and warned against judicial use of social science. Using such terms as "judicial overreaching" and "extravagant us(age) of judicial power," Justice Thomas charged that the equity powers of the federal courts had been used expansively and wrongly. "In this case, not only did the district court exercise the legislative power to tax, it also engaged in budgeting, staffing, and educational decisions, in judgments about the location and aesthetic quality of the schools, and in administrative oversight and monitoring" (Missouri v. Jenkins, 115 S.Ct. 2038, 2071(1995)).

In August 1995, Judge Sue Robinson granted the defendants' request, acknowledging their good faith compliance and observing that the achievement gap between minorities and whites was a national trend, and not the result of discrimination unique to the four districts.[39] The impact of the Supreme Court's ruling in the Missouri case was unmistakable. Judge Robinson repeatedly stressed the limited role of the courts in desegregation cases, reflecting the high Court's more conservative posture in the 1990s.

The 1995 Opinion

On August 14, 1995, Judge Sue L. Robinson declared that the school districts of New Castle County had attained unitary status. In the opinion, Judge Robinson stressed the oft-expressed goal of the Supreme Court of returning court-supervised school districts to local control. She also noted that when the district court had called for an inter-district remedy in 1974, it had observed:

> We do not find in [*Brown I* and *II*] a mandate for District Courts to concern themselves with how well the educative function is performed. The decision in *Brown* was rather that the operation of a dual school system, based on race, is an impermissible classification under the Fourteenth Amendment. There has been much discussion, and there undoubtedly will continue to be much writing upon the topic of whether black children learn better in desegregated classrooms. Our holding does not rest upon these considerations, not least because judges are unqualified and inexpert in answering such questions.[40]

Judge Robinson thus declined to address the pedagogical merits of desegregation and focused on remedying the violation of the Fourteenth Amendment's equal protection clause.

---

[39] Coalition To Save Our Children v. State Board of Education, *supra* note 30.
[40] Ibid., 790. (Citing Evans v. Buchanan 416 F.Supp. 328 , 364-65 (D.Del. 1976)).

<u>The Green Factors</u>
In assessing the level of compliance of the four school districts and looking for vestiges of racial discrimination, Judge Robinson followed the Supreme Court's guidelines as set forth in *Green v. County School Board of New Kent County* (1968).[42] Citing the testimony of desegregation experts Drs. Christine Rossell and David Armor, Judge Robinson declared in the Findings of Fact "the 4 districts are among the most racially balanced schools in the United States."

Regarding the plaintiff's charge that the practice of tracking, or ability grouping, rendered classrooms segregated, Judge Robinson found that excluding special education and bilingual classes in the 1993-94 school year, an average of 85 percent of the students in the four districts attended classes that were within $\pm$ 20 percent of their school's minority ratio. This rate was one half to one third of the imbalance found in a national sample of schools collected by the Office of Civil Rights, United States Department of Education. The judge noted that school systems had long used tracking, or ability grouping. The question for the court was whether such tracking or ability grouping was done on the basis of race or to promote racial segregation.[43] Thus, the court reiterated that substantive questions regarding the quality of educational programs or practices were not within the purview of the courts.

Regarding the second *Green* factor, faculty and staff assignment, the court found that for certified staff (teachers, psychologists, speech and hearing therapists, etc.), approximately 80 percent of the schools in the four districts had fallen within a $\pm$ 10 percent variance of their minority ratios each year since the desegregation plan began. In every year except 1981, over 90 percent of the schools had fallen within a $\pm$ 15 percent variance.[44]

---

[42]The facets, commonly referred to as the *Green* factors, were student assignment, faculty and staff assignment, transportation, extra- curricular activities, and facilities. Judge Robinson noted that the plaintiffs agreed that federal supervision should end regarding transportation and facilities.
[43] Coalition To Save Our Children v. State Board of Education, *supra* note 30, at 800.
[44]Ibid., 804.

The court found that while classified staff (bus drivers, secretaries and clerical workers, custodians, food service workers, etc.) were not integrated, they had relatively limited contact with students. They often worked at schools within walking distance of their homes, and given the fact that their wages were very low, the negative impact of transferring them to schools more distant from their homes would far outweigh any benefit to students from having racially unidentifiable classified staffs.[45]

Regarding extracurricular activities, the court was satisfied that while participation in such activities was not "racially balanced," participation was open to all students provided they met academic requirements established by the Delaware Secondary School Athletic Association (DSSAA), such as taking a full academic load and passing a specified number of major subjects.[46]   Having thus addressed the Green factors, the judge proceeded to address compliance with the ancillary relief required in the 1978 order.

Compliance with Ancillary Relief Requirements
The ancillary relief requirements in the 1978 order contained eight components: 1) in-service training; 2) reading and communication skills; 3) curriculum; 4) counseling and guidance; 5) school building construction, site selection and use of existing schools; 6) recognition of human values; 7) standards of conduct; and 8) staff.[47]   Regarding in-service training, the court found that all four districts offered a "rich array" of in-service programs for the faculty. Early in the desegregation era, the focus of these programs had been desegregation.   Later, the focus broadened to include race equity and multiculturalism issues, as well.[48]

The New Castle County School District (NCCSD) initiated a reading program in 1978 and the program continued after the four school districts were formed.   Students in grades two through nine were provided reading assistance if they read at one year or more below grade level as measured by standardized tests.   Students in grades ten through twelve were given assistance if they tested at two or more years

---

[45]Ibid., 803.

[46] Ibid., 804-806.

[47]The parties stipulated prior to trial that the requirements regarding school construction and site selection were satisfied. The requirements regarding staff were addressed under the *Green* factors.

[48]Ibid., 809.

below grade level. Most special instruction was given in small groups within the classroom.[49]

With regard to curriculum, the court observed that both the state DPI and the districts had adopted policies stressing multiculturalism, diversity, and global education. The four districts developed their own curricula following these guidelines, oftentimes involving members of the community.

The court observed that the school districts had developed and implemented counseling and "recognition of human values" programs, both of which were intended to ease the students' transition to a desegregated school setting, promote fair and equitable treatment, and ensure the physical and emotional well-being of the students.[50]

Judge Robinson also found that the school districts had satisfactorily complied with the court's 1978 requirement to establish standards of conduct. She conceded that the standards were often vague, allowing for subjective interpretation, a reference to the plaintiffs' charge that discipline procedures were applied in a discriminatory manner.[51] Judge Robinson concluded that the conduct codes were not applied in a discriminatory manner, accepting defense expert testimony that the rates of disciplinary action against black students were equal across the four districts, were lower than the national rate as reported by the Office of Civil Rights, and were lower than the percentage of black youths arrested in Delaware.[52]

Regarding the "achievement gap" between white and minority students, Judge Robinson cited the data provided the court by the defense demonstrating the inferior socioeconomic condition of black students, concluding that these socioeconomic disadvantages, rather than discrimination on the part of the school district explained the lower achievement levels of minority students. The opinion noted: 1) black households were 2.54 times as likely as white households to have a reporting householder without a high school diploma, 2) black households were 6.47 times as likely as white households to have children categorized as being in poverty, 3) blacks were 2.86 times as likely as whites to be unemployed, 4) black households with children were 3.21 times as likely as white households with children to be

---

[49]Ibid., 810-12.
[50] Ibid., 812-14.
[51]Ibid., 816.
[52]Ibid., 817.

headed by a single parent, 5) black children were 5.25 times as likely as white children to have received inadequate prenatal care. The judge cited the following figures on student achievement: 1) in 1992, on standardized tests, the average reading score for white sixth graders in the four districts was 55.6, and the average score for black sixth graders was 39, with a national norm of 50; 2) the average math score on standardized tests in 1992 was 52 for white students and 36 for black students, with 50 being the national norm.[53]

Judge Robinson cited Dr. David Armor's use of regression analysis comparing educational outcomes as measured by standardized test scores to socioeconomic status measured by four indicators: 1) free lunch status of the students; 2) AFDC status of the students; 3) percentage of adults with college education, separated by race; and 4) percentage of renters, separated by race and gender. Dr. Armor found that this comparison of socioeconomic factors with achievement levels explained 80 to 96 percent of the achievement gap. Judge Robinson noted that the black/white achievement gap was a nationwide phenomenon, reported as early as the 1960s in the "Coleman Report," one of the first studies on equality in educational opportunity. Judge Robinson concluded, "Because the environment outside school is so strong, cumulative, and varied, schools cannot overcome such environmental/differences (sic) among children."[54]

The court also acknowledged the disproportionate placement of minority students in special education classes, (minority enrollment in the four districts was 31.1 percent, whereas minority enrollment in special education classes was 45.4 percent) and observed that this was a national phenomenon and a national concern. The court found no evidence that minority children were treated differently than whites with regard to special education placement. Nor did the court find evidence that the districts used placement in special education classes to separate children by race.[55]

With regard to the defendant's charge that the higher dropout rate for black students evidenced continued racial discrimination within the school districts, Judge Robinson observed, "Dropping out of school is a process, symptomatic of poor performance, discipline problems, and lack of participation in extracurricular activities and guidance

---

[53]Ibid., 818.
[54]Ibid., 818-19.
[55]Ibid., 820-21.

programs." The judge acknowledged the overall higher dropout rates for blacks; however, in Colonial, the most socioeconomically homogenous of the four districts, she noted the white dropout rate was significantly higher than the black rate.[56]

In conclusion, Judge Robinson stressed the temporary nature of judicial oversight of school systems undergoing desegregation. She reiterated that the Court of Appeals for the Third Circuit had rejected any specific racial percentage requirements for the school districts. She noted that current racial percentages had been achieved through the elimination of the neighborhood school concept and that the only way these percentages could be sustained was by remaining under desegregation plan indefinitely. Judge Robinson held that the school districts had complied in good faith with the two fundamental requirements of the 1978 order, the 9-3 plan and achievement of "unitariness," as well as fulfilling their obligations under the ancillary relief portion of the order. She concluded that there was no credible evidence that the differences between black and white children's performance in school resulted from the former *de jure* segregated school system.

Judge Robinson declared:

> The continued existence of racial discrimination in our society as a whole, and the effect of that discrimination on the ability of a black child to enter school on an equal footing with more privileged white school mates, are not matters in dispute in this litigation. And, indeed, as the years have passed since *Brown I* and *II*, it has become apparent that the school desegregation process has been unable to eliminate or overcome racial discrimination in the "myriad factors of human existence" outside the school environment, as predicted by the Supreme Court in *Swann,* 402 U.S. at 22.[57]

Holding that the four districts had complied in good faith with the 1978 order, Judge Robinson observed:

> The doors of the public school system have been opened to all children, regardless of their color. All children, regardless of

---

[56]Ibid., 821-22.
[57]Ibid., 823.

their color, are presented with the opportunity to learn and to succeed, building upon their education. It is time for the federal court to end its supervision of the public school system of Northern New Castle County.[58]

Thus, relying heavily on the precedent set in *Missouri v. Jenkins*, as well as the court's history in this case of resistance to interference with substantive educational or pedagogical issues, Judge Robinson declined the plaintiff's request to continue jurisdiction in an effort to eradicate or reduce the racial imbalance, the achievement gap, and the other disparities between black and white students in the district. Taking a restraintist position, Judge Robinson refused to broaden the judicial mandate to include educational quality issues, instead stressing the imperative to return the school district as soon as possible to local and state educational policy makers. Thus, while Wilmington had been a showcase example of successful integration, with its metropolitan scope, the desegregation plan had fallen short of the hopes of those who had envisioned its eliminating the disparities in achievement, drop-out rates, placement within schools, or discipline problems between whites and non-whites. Judicial oversight resulted in elimination of the dual school system, but once the constitutional violations had been eliminated, the court's authority to impose the desegregation plan ended, and a return to neighborhood schools, which would clearly be racially isolated, would likely eventually occur.

The Aftermath

The Coalition To Save Our Children petitioned both Judge Robinson and the Court of Appeals for the Third Circuit for a stay of the opinion, but both declined. For several reasons, the opinion would not result in significant policy changes in the 1995-96 school year, and it was unlikely to result in fundamental changes in the near future. Because Judge Robinson handed down the decision in mid August, so close to the beginning of the school year, student assignments and busing contracts were already in place. Any changes would take place gradually, because policy- making was bound by facilities and geography. The school systems lacked the buildings to support a wholesale change to neighborhood schools. Describing the court as a

---

[58]Ibid., 824.

"benevolent despot," DPI Assistant for Administrative Services Jack Nichols stressed that the court's oversight had been quite unobtrusive. Except for the imposition of the 9-3 plan, the school districts and state board of education had maintained their policy-making powers during the seventeen years of judicial oversight. Hence, release from the court order would result in little immediate change, especially given the fact that lack of facilities prohibited a return to neighborhood schools.[59]

Though many parents, both black and white, had grown weary of busing, some minority parents expressed apprehension that resegregation would occur, given the fact that the districts were no longer under any obligation to comply with the 1978 decree. School boards could reassign students, as long as they did not do so with the intent to resegregate blacks and whites. "It's disappointing," commented Lem Joyner, a member of the Coalition To Save Our Children. "The feeling in the minority community is that this will lead to a re-segregated school system, because whites haven't wanted to go to school with us anyway. I'm sorry, but that's the way it's always been."[60] Though some reassignments were likely to take place, major changes were impracticable for the near future; after seventeen years of busing and population growth and shifts, many children did not live near any school.

Coalition member Ebrima Ellzy-Sey expressed frustration with the state's position that the problem with under-achievement among minority children was rooted in socioeconomics, which meant that the state took no responsibility for the achievement gap. "They've given up on black and minority kids, to say they just can't learn because of their socioeconomic conditions. If that's their position, then we may have to look at taking black children out of public schools."[61]

In 1995 an educational reform movement called New Directions for Education, whose motto was "Excellence and Equity for All Children," was attempting to raise educational standards throughout the state. At the state level, the program focused on setting rigorous standards. The local districts bore the responsibility for curriculum design,

---

[59]Jack Nichols, assistant state superintendent for Administrative Services, Delaware Department of Public Instruction, telephone interview by author, 18 October 1995.

[60]Ruth, ""Deseg trial draws to early close," *Wilmington News Journal*, 7 January 1995, 4(A).

[61]Ellzy-Sey, *supra* note 12, telephone interview by author, 27 October 1995.

development, and implementation to meet the standards established by the state. The state was in turn responsible for comprehensive assessment.[62] This program was not directed at minority student achievement, *per se*, but it was hoped that the revised curriculum, along with rigorous assessment, would help educators determine how they could meet the special needs of minority and disadvantaged children more effectively.

Educators were considering developing more objective criteria for academic placement, or considering other choices than academic tracking, in order to raise the achievement levels of minority students. Professor Jeannie L. Oakes of the University of California at Los Angeles testified in the 1994-95 trial that ability grouping or tracking often placed blacks in lower-level classes, even when the same test scores did not place white students in lower-level classes. She noted that criteria for judging abilities were often subjective and vague. "The whites are advantaged in every case."[63] Grouping students by their supposed abilities often locked blacks into classes where they were not challenged and which therefore offered little hope of a bright future. Oakes testified that remedial programs actually damaged achievement, and just one year in a segregated, low-level track could have a detrimental effect.[64]

Following the August 1995 decision, the general assembly passed a measure approving "school choice" and charter schools. By supporting the school choice policy, the legislature indicated its preference for abandoning the 9-3 student assignment plan. According to the law, each school district was required to publish the number of seats available in each school, but the school districts likely would attempt to maintain the approximately 75 to 25 percent mix in the schools, at least until the appeal process was complete.[65]

The assembly approved five charter schools in the Wilmington area districts for the 1996-97 school year and an additional five for the 1997-98 year. The charter schools would be state funded, and their curriculum required state approval, but it would be specially designed to meet specific needs or goals. That is, the charter schools could be alternative schools for students who did not function well in traditional

---

[62] Nichols, *supra* note 58.
[63] Ruth, "Deseg trial" 4(A).
[64] Ibid.
[65] Ellzy-Sey, *supra* note 60.

schools, or they could have a special focus, such as math-science or fine arts. For the 1996-97 academic year, the assembly approved the transformation of Wilmington High School in the Red Clay district to a math-science center that would be run by private industry.[66]

On July 24, 1996, the full Court of Appeals for the Third Circuit denied the application of the Coalition To Save Our Children to overturn their ruling that upheld Judge Robinson's August 1995 declaration of unitary status for the Wilmington school system. Pleased with the court's decision, Governor Carper issued an official statement:

> For all of us striving to improve education in New Castle County and throughout the state, this decision is good news. A crucial part of Delaware's education reform plan involves increasing local school autonomy and placing decisions in the hands of those who know our schools best. This decision puts us one step closer toward fulfilling that important objective -- restoring local control of our schools.[67]

In November 1996, the Coalition announced that it would not appeal the release to the United States Supreme Court, thereby officially ending the litigation. Instead, it issued a "call to arms" to the community to keep school equity issues at the top of the public agenda. The Coalition joined the Delaware NAACP in urging citizens to exert "unprecedented pressure" on the governor, the state and local school boards, and educators to ensure that poor and minority children were not "disenfranchised" in any redistricting that might take place. The Coalition and the NAACP both sought the reunification of the Wilmington school district and its separation from the suburban districts that had been unified during court supervision.[68]

The community was divided on the question of whether the districts should return to a neighborhood school system with the traditional kindergarten through fifth grade or kindergarten through sixth grade configuration, or whether they should maintain the desegregation plan under which students attended one school for

---

[66] Ibid.

[67] State of Delaware, Office of the Governor, press release 22 August 1996.

[68] Beth Miller, "Deseg case officially laid to rest," *Wilmington News Journal,* 20 November 1996, 1(A).

kindergarten through third grade and another for fourth through sixth grades. The Brandywine district held four public hearings in late 1996 to discuss how to respond to the release from court oversight. A return to neighborhood schools would clearly render the schools racially identifiable. Furthermore, a change in assignments would have resulted in inequities or required an expensive school construction program. Thus, the board of education for the Brandywine district decided to retain the court ordered attendance plan with minor modifications in the feeder patterns to accommodate demographic changes.[69]

The Red Clay Consolidated School District saw significant changes following the release from oversight, not because it changed its assignment plan, but because of the large number of students who chose to return to schools nearer their homes through the school choice plan. Both city and suburban parents and students were taking advantage of the school choice program, although city children were more readily accommodated because there was more space available in the city schools. Red Clay planned to open two magnet or theme schools in city schools with declining enrollments during the 1998-99 school year. Both schools would have full day kindergarten, which was popular with parents of all ethnicities.[70]

The Christina School District returned its fourth grade suburban students to their neighborhood schools immediately following the declaration of unitary status, and they changed their city schools to theme or magnet schools. Fourth graders who chose to remain in city schools were allowed to do so. Residents of the district were divided as to whether the district should return completely to a neighborhood school system. While many supported that course of action, others argued that the district should work to make the city schools more attractive so that students and parents would select them. Deputy Superintendent Frank Rishel said that the district expected to revert eventually to a neighborhood school plan for the whole district, while maintaining theme schools in the city.[71]

The Colonial School District was attempting to remain within the guidelines of the desegregation plan and maintain racial balance within

---

[69]Diane Emerson, administrative secretary, Superintendent's Office, Brandywine School District, telephone interview by author, 30 April 1998.

[70]Dr. Gail Ames, School Choice, Red Clay Consolidated School District, telephone interview by author, 5 May 1998.

[71]Dr. Frank Rishel, Deputy Superintendent of Schools, Christina School District, telephone interview by author, 5 May 1998.

their schools as much as possible. They had received many applications for returning to neighborhood schools under the choice law, but most of these requests were based on childcare needs. The district had no plans for changing to a neighborhood school policy that would render the schools racially identifiable.[72]

Thus, following the declaration of unitary status, the districts made no comprehensive change to a neighborhood school system. However, with the changes in Christina, the significant number of students who were applying to enroll in schools closer to their homes under the school choice law, and the public pressure to provide more classroom space in the suburbs, the trend appeared to be in the direction of returning to neighborhood schools. All four districts appeared to be committed to maintaining theme or magnet schools in the city to encourage suburban students to enroll there. The NAACP and Coalition members were concerned that inequities between city and suburban schools would increase as greater numbers of suburban students left the city schools.

In 1998, Coalition member Ebrima Ellzy-Sey said that he expected the Coalition would be taking the school districts back to court, because inequities persisted, and he felt they had worsened since the school districts' release from court supervision. He felt that intra-school segregation had increased, owing to tracking, although he had no statistics, because the districts were no longer required to provide such information.[73]

Ellzy-Sey said the Coalition had not appealed the Third Circuit's upholding of the release, because of the conservative complexion of the Supreme Court. "With the present Supreme Court, we didn't want to be the ones that would throw everything that had been gained out. With the present Supreme Court, I don't think we could have gotten a favorable ruling. So sometimes you have to (wait) till the time's right." The Coalition served as a watchdog in the school systems, advocating for minority students. Ellzy-Sey said the Coalition had a good working relationship with all four districts and were able to communicate effectively their concerns to the school boards.[74]

---

[72]Denise Murphy, Administrative Secretary in the Office of Information and Support, Colonial School District, telephone interview by author, 6 May 1998.
[73]Ellzy-Sey, *supra* note 12, telephone interview by author, 30 April 1998.
[74]Ibid.

Regarding the Coalition's and the NAACP's earlier support for the reestablishment of an independent Wilmington school district, Ellzy-Sey said that he no longer supported that suggestion. However, he approved of the idea of merging Brandywine with Wilmington, and Red Clay with Christina. He noted that Brandywine had long been more cooperative with the plaintiffs in the case, and the parties had made some trade-offs that had satisfied both sides, so he felt that the Brandywine School District was more receptive to minority concerns. Brandywine parents had voiced strong objections to resegregating the system.

Jack Nichols of the State Department of Education observed that while there had been no immediate comprehensive changes following the declaration of unitary status, the Wilmington area school systems were attempting to respond to "the clamor for neighborhood schools while at the same time not abandoning the city schools." He expected that the busing plan would eventually be phased out, owing to popular and legislative support for neighborhood schools. Nichols noted that the fear in many areas that funding would decline as schools became resegregated was not an issue in Delaware, because the state provided 66 percent of the funding for schools and districts paid only 24 percent.[75] Furthermore, the state subsidized less wealthy districts with a forty-seven million dollar equalization fund. Thus, in Delaware there was relatively little disparity in funding among school districts.[76]

However, the concerns of the Coalition and the NAACP were not directly funding related. Advocates for minority students felt that minority children were the victims of discriminatory attitudes and class placement and that these factors contributed to the achievement gap between black and white students in the district. If the city and suburban school systems became increasingly racially distinct, these perceived inequities would likely grow, they predicted.

Conclusion

At the close of the twentieth century, the school system that had been a model of successful metropolitan desegregation had earned unitary status and appeared to be inching back toward a neighborhood school

---

[75]The federal government provided about 8 percent of education funds in Delaware.

[76] Nichols, *supra* note 4, telephone interview by author, 4 May 1998.

system that would clearly leave the schools racially identifiable. The community appeared to support the concept of magnet or theme schools in the city to draw suburban students, but the Christina experience suggested that the draw of the neighborhood schools was stronger than that of the magnet or theme schools. San Diego's experience with a voluntary integration program, which is the subject of Chapters 8 and 9, suggested the same thing. While magnet schools and a voluntary integration program drew a significant number of enthusiastic participants, the school district remained highly segregated.

Wilmington's desegregation plan had provided an almost perfectly integrated school system, yet the goals of those who pressed for integration had proven elusive. Many argued that the court ordered plan did not provide meaningful integration, nor did it provide equity in the education service delivered to black and white students, because blacks were disproportionately placed in lower level classes. Despite the fact that the court's authority had proven insufficient to provide equitable education, in the view of the Coalition and the NAACP, these groups sought continued surveillance by the court, because they feared that conditions would worsen without the court's guidance. Yet unless they anticipated retaining court supervision indefinitely, political pressure on the school system to reduce disparities in the delivery of educational programs and pressure on community and state policy makers to reduce the socioeconomic disparities between black and white families likely would have been more productive in improving the educational opportunities and outcomes of black children.

Epilogue

The "theme" program launched to try to entice suburban students into voluntarily attending city schools following the court's 1995 release of Wilmington from judicial oversight was largely unsuccessful. Six Wilmington schools serving fourth through sixth graders adopted programs focusing on science, math, business, the arts, foreign language, and ecology. However, only 171 suburban students chose to attend the theme schools, whereas 1,214 chose to attend suburban schools, which led to severe overcrowding in the suburban schools. The following year even fewer suburban students chose to enroll in the city theme schools. Some observers said the programs at the theme schools were not well-developed, while others felt that the draw of neighborhood schools was simply stronger.[77]

Delaware's Neighborhood Schools Act of 2000 mandated an end to long-distance busing and a return to neighborhood schools. The impetus for passage of the bill apparently came from Christina School District parents who had formed a group called the Christina Coalition for Neighborhood Schools and had lobbied state legislators actively.[78] While some parents and students looked forward to the reassignment of students in their familiar neighborhoods, others expressed regret at what would be lost – fairly high racial balance in the schools and social interaction with students outside their neighborhoods. Furthermore, building space in suburban neighborhoods was insufficient to house all the suburban students, and building programs would be very costly.[79]

Forty years after desegregation began in Wilmington, tens of millions of dollars had been spent in integration and compensatory programs that did not produce the programs' ultimate objectives, meaningful integration and higher achievement levels for minority students. Leaving the court's protective mantle behind left some Wilmington residents uneasy. However, only continual pressure on the school systems and the active engagement of parents and other community members could possibly achieve the quality and accountability these activists sought.

---

[77]Thompson, "In Christina, long rides bring a cry for change: After a failed attempt to attract kids to the city, the parents put on pressure," *Wilmington News Journal* (www.delawareonline.com), 17 December 2000.

[78]Dennis Thompson, Jr., "Change didn't come without persistent parents and a lot of pressure," *Wilmington News Journal*, (www.delawareonline.com) 17 December 2000.

[79]Thompson "Shorter bus rides coming – with a cost: Christina led the charge, but soon many districts will face the challenge" *Wilmington News Journal* (www.delawareonline.com), 17 December 2000.

CHAPTER 6

The Case of Prince George's County, Maryland

Introduction

Prince George's County, which borders the nation's capital to the east, grew tremendously in the latter half of the twentieth century, with families migrating from the District of Columbia. Population growth transformed the economy and way of life, as the formerly rural landscape of tobacco farms gave way to residential areas and shopping malls. As urbanization took place, the adult population became younger, and the children of these younger parents flooded the county's schools.[1]

Historically, Prince George's County, like its southern counterparts, operated a dual school system, pursuant to state law. Pupils, faculty, and staff were assigned and school sites were chosen on the basis of race. Entrenched residential segregation facilitated the segregation of the county's schools.[2] Moreover, following World War

---

[1]*A Long Day's Journey into Light: School Desegregation in Prince George's County* (Washington, D.C.: U.S. Commission on Civil Rights, 1976), 2-3.

[2]The Federal Housing Authority guaranteed loans, and the Resettlement Administration built housing for middle-income white families from the 1930s to the 1960s, establishing distinctly segregated residential areas in the outskirts of Washington (U.S. Commission on Civil Rights 1976, 57). Subsequently, discriminatory practices among realtors contributed to residential segregation.. Agents would "steer" black buyers to "black" areas, or as blacks moved into a "white" area, agents would induce whites to

II, the black school population in the county increased more rapidly than the white school population as blacks acquiring middle-class incomes sought middle-class neighborhoods in which to raise their families.

All Deliberate Delay

Following the Supreme Court's May 1955 ruling in *Brown II*, the Prince George's County board of education appointed a twenty-one member biracial fact-finding committee to study the district's segregation problem. The board formulated and unanimously adopted a policy based on the recommendations submitted by the committee, under which students were assigned to the schools they had previously attended; however, parents could apply to have their children attend a school closer to their homes. The resolution stated: "No child will be denied the privilege of attending any school he wants to attend unless it is administratively not practical to admit the child because of overcrowded conditions, or other valid reasons." The resolution further specified that the board "reserves the right during the period of transition to delay or deny the admission of a pupil to any school . . .".[3] During the 1955-56 school year, ninety-seven black students sought admission to previously all-white schools; the board of education granted sixty-seven and denied thirty of those requests.[4]

On April 10, 1956, the board of education adopted a "freedom of choice policy." The provisions of that policy included: 1) individual choice in enrollment, subject to availability of space and transportation services, with the school board reserving the right of final placement approval; 2) enrollment in the school nearest the student's home, in his or her present school, or in another school upon request, if administratively feasible; 3) reservation of the school board's right to delay or deny the admission of any student to any school "if it deem[ed] such action wise, necessary, and in the best interest of the public safety and community welfare."[5] At this time 13 percent of the

---

sell their homes at reduced prices, by telling them the area was "going" (*A Long Day's Journey*, 60).

[3]Mike Monroney, "Prince George's Schools Take Integration Step," *Washington Post*, 10 August 1955, 27(A).

[4] Laurence Stern, "Voluntary Integration Approved By County," *Washington Post*, 11 April 1956, 1(A).

[5]*A Long Day's Journey*, 18.

district's school population of approximately fifty-thousand was black. The school district operated under this freedom of choice plan, so popular in the southern states, with minor revisions, through the mid-1960s.

Under the freedom of choice plan, the school district continued to reinforce the residential segregation in the county through its program of site selection and school construction.   Consequently, whether students stayed at their originally assigned schools or requested transfers to schools nearer their homes, they remained in segregated schools.   Transfer policies accentuated the problem by allowing students to enroll in schools where they would be in the majority. Thus, despite the school district's official policy of desegregation, the schools remained racially identifiable as a result of official attendance requirements.[6]   During the decade that the school district operated under its freedom of choice policy, only about 20 percent of its black students attended racially mixed schools.   Some black students were bused thirty-two miles round trip to the all-black Fairmont Heights High School near Washington during this period.[7]

During the 1960s, black parents and community leaders increased their pressure on the school board to comply with the *Brown* mandate. In May 1964, the school district took its first tentative steps toward compliance with the Court's mandate in *Brown II*, adopting the superintendent's "Suggested Next Steps in Desegregation Program." The proposals included eliminating some instances of cross-county busing of black students to all-black schools and assigning the affected students to area schools.[8]   Additionally, the board of education rescinded its policy requiring formal application by black students to attend integrated schools closer to their homes.   The new board policy allowed students to notify the principals of the integrated schools that they would like to enroll there.[9]   Yet there was no substantive reversal in policy.   The school district continued to build schools that were racially identifiable.[10]   Nine years after the *Brown II* decision, Prince George's County schools remained effectively segregated.

---

[6] Complaint at 4, Vaughns v. Board of Education of Prince George's County (D. Md. 1972) (No. K-72-325).
[7] "Events Leading to School Order," *Washington Post*, 30 December 1972, 12(A).
[8] *A Long Day's Journey*, 22-23.
[9] Ibid., 143.
[10] Ibid., 22-23.

A Modest Start

With the passage of the Civil Rights Act of 1964, the Department of Health, Education, and Welfare (HEW) began to pressure the board of education to escalate its desegregation or risk losing federal funds. Thus, on June 22, 1965, ten years after the Court's decision in *Brown II*, the board of education of Prince George's County adopted and submitted to HEW a desegregation plan described as a unitary educational system which would be operated without regard to race, color, religion, or national origin. Of the eighteen all-black schools in the county, six received some white students under the plan, one was closed, one each was "desegregated" in 1966 and 1967, one continued to operate until a replacement facility was built, and eight schools were "organized on a unitary area basis," though all but one of these eight retained all-black enrollments.[11] These all-black schools were located in the Fairmont Heights area, which was populated almost entirely by blacks. The plan also called for desegregated staffing and desegregated busing operations.[12]

An article in *The Washington Post* described the desegregation plan as "far-ranging" and said it marked a breakthrough in integration in the county. The plan was hailed for abandoning the freedom of choice policy, which had drawn criticism from civil rights groups because it perpetuated segregation. The school board projected that the plan would increase the percentage of black children attending desegregated schools from the current 20 percent to about 55 percent that fall and 60 percent by 1967.[13]

As the nation's largest suburban school system, the Prince George's County school district captured the attention of the HEW. HEW regularly reviewed Prince George's County's compliance status and required more comprehensive desegregation plans when it discovered inadequacies. In July 1968, HEW informed Superintendent William S. Schmidt that current HEW policy (adopted in March 1968) required that school systems be completely desegregated by the beginning of the 1969-70 school year.[14] Yet, the Office of Education (HEW) withdrew its proposal for desegregation after residents voiced

---

[11] Ibid., 23-25.
[12] Maurine Hoffman, "Prince Georges Desegregated Most Schools," *Washington Post*, 23 June 1965, 1(A).
[13] Ibid.
[14] *A Long Day's Journey*, 206-7.

strong objections at public hearings. With the Supreme Court's ruling in *Green v. New Kent County* (1968) rejecting freedom of choice plans and calling for desegregation *now*, HEW stepped up pressure on recalcitrant school districts, threatening federal fund cutoffs if immediate results were not forthcoming.[15]

The school district and the OCR worked through the summer of 1969 to develop a proposal acceptable to the OCR. On November eleven, following an ultimatum issued by the HEW that the school system must immediately desegregate two all-black schools or lose $12 million in federal aid, the school board approved a desegregation plan that radically redrew attendance zones in an attempt to eliminate the last vestiges of the dual school system. The plan redrew the attendance areas of eighteen schools, but the main focus was to integrate the all-black Fairmont Heights Senior High and Mary Bethune Junior High School. HEW held that these schools were vestiges of the dual school system, because unlike other one-race schools serving single neighborhoods, they served several communities.[16] The plan called for the busing of an additional four hundred students and the transfer of forty-five hundred of the county's secondary school pupils to accomplish the desegregation.[17]

The board approved the plan in a five to three vote after an emotional discussion in which Board President Carroll Beatty, who voted against the plan, declared that the majority of both the black and white communities opposed the plan and that he "would rather have a court tell me to do this than justify this to the people of our community." Board member Ruth Wolf, who supported the plan broke into tears following the vote, saying, "I know it's not a popular decision in my community, but I think it's morally right." Wolf noted that she was the only board member directly affected by the vote; her daughter would be transferred to Mary Bethune Junior High.[18]

Intense public opposition to the board's action ensued. Board members who voted for the plan reported receiving threatening

---

[15] Ibid., 26.
[16] "Parents Wary of Area Desegregation Plan," *Washington Post*, 30 November 1969, 1(D).
[17] Lawrence Meyer, "Pr. George's Meets HEW School Order," *Washington Post*, 11 November 1969, 16(A).
[18] Ibid.

telephone calls and requested police protection of their homes.[19]   Prince George's County Commissioner and former president of the county council of PTAs Gladys Spellman declared that the plan was "abhorrent to all facets of the community, black and white,"[20] and she predicted that the schools would soon become resegregated because whites would leave the area.[21] U.S. Representative Lawrence J. Hogan (R.Md) called the plan "idiotic" and said it would "disrupt the education of a considerable number of students in Prince George's." Commissioner Spellman suggested that the County Commissioners ask Hogan to request an extension from HEW, but Hogan responded that it would be inappropriate for him to ask HEW to override a plan adopted by the board of education.   He revealed that he had asked HEW Secretary Robert Finch to reconsider the Department's ultimatum that the school district must desegregate the two all-black schools.[22]

Following the November 17 meeting of the board of education, members met with county commissioners and legislators to explain their action. Delegate Arthur King, one of fourteen state delegates and three senators to attend the meeting, and the only black member of the legislative delegation, noted the irony in the concern of some board members and elected officials that the board's plan called for busing of students. "When I went to school in Prince George's, you bused me (for purposes of segregation) but you called it transportation. Now you're transporting people across the street, but you're calling it busing."[23]

Parents of children attending the majority white Bladensburg High School were most vocal in their opposition to the plan. Bladensburg High School would lose 536 white and 99 black students to the formerly all-black Fairmont Heights High School.[24] Among those slated to leave Bladensburg High were all of the high school aged children from nearby Cheverly, a neighborhood of mainly white-collar government and professional people.

---

[19] Meyer, "Top Level Talks Slated on Schools" *Washington Post*, 15 November 1969, 1(B).

[20] Meyer, "Plan 'Abhorrent' In Pr. George's," *Washington Post*, 14 November 1969, 1(C).

[21] Meyer, "Top Level Talks," 3(B).

[22] Meyer, Plan 'Abhorrent,'" 9(C).

[23] Meyer, "Pr. George's Reaffirms School Plan," *Washington Post*, 18 November 1969, 2(C).

[24] Meyer, "Pr. George's Meets HEW," 16(A).

Dissatisfaction among Cheverly residents was overwhelming. The Cheverly Citizens Association, whose meetings usually drew about thirty people, called a special meeting on November 25. It drew two hundred residents, the vast majority of whom opposed the board's plan. A few Cheverly residents expressed support for the plan, however, including Ann Cushman, president of the Bladensburg PTA, whose son was transferred to Fairmont High.[25]

A group of white parents from Bladensburg, calling themselves "Citizens for Action, Inc." (CFA) called the board's plan "a tragic subversion of the rights and will of the people" and called for the replacement of the appointed board by an elected one. The group had only one hundred members, but claimed that it represented the views of the majority of the county's residents. The group charged that the board's action gave "erroneous dignity and acceptance" to the Department of HEW's "accusation of a dual school system." It supported School Board President Beatty's recommendation of a court test of the HEW directive.[26]

Black parents in the increasingly middle-class Fairmont Heights area expressed apprehension about the proposed revisions, as well. Responses to the impending changes ranged from "stark disbelief through deep apprehension to cautious optimism. Enthusiasm [was] notably absent."[27] At the same time, they believed that the only way to better the quality of their children's education was through integration, and they deeply resented the resistance of Cheverly residents to the move, especially the threats of a white exodus from Prince George's County in response to the desegregation plan.[28]

Public indignation grew, and pressure on the board of education and administration mounted. On December 1, 1969, Superintendent Schmidt requested technical assistance and aid under Title IV of the Civil Rights Act of 1964 to contend with the "tremendous amount of public . . . [resentment] which is building up in our county regarding

---

[25]Meyer, "In All-White Cheverly: Apprehension, Protest," *Washington Post*," 30 November 1969, 8(D).

[26]Douglas Watson, "Parents Hit Pr. George's School Plan," *Washington Post*, 16 November 1969, 1(D).

[27]David W. Hardy, "Black Fairmont Heights: Fears, Cautious Optimism," *Washington Post*, 30 November 1969, 9(D).

[28] Ibid.

the Board's plan for the integration of Fairmont Heights Senior High School and Mary Bethune Junior High School."[29]

Though the plan was implemented, its effectiveness was questioned. On November 5, 1970, the regional director of the Office of Civil Rights expressed "extreme concern" to the new Superintendent of Schools, Carl W. Hassel, regarding the high number of transfers of white students from the Fairmont Heights Senior High School. The director of OCR advised the superintendent to review all previously granted transfers and rescind those that did not meet the new criteria or that were found to be falsified. The school board declined on a five to four vote to review the transfers that had already been granted for that year.[30]

In May 1971, following the Supreme Court's decision in *Swann v. Charlotte-Mecklenburg*, OCR Director J. Stanley Pottinger required that the school district, by the 1971-72 school year, 1) develop a new desegregation plan for student assignment on a nonracial basis and 2) reassign faculty on a nonracial basis. The school board remained intransigent. Three days after receiving Pottinger's notice, it rejected a proposal to develop a definite plan to integrate students and schools by September 1971. On July 28, 1971, Director Pottinger informed Superintendent Hassel that the school district was in noncompliance with Title VI of the Civil Rights Act of 1964. He gave the board one more chance to comply before he commenced enforcement action.[31]

An overflow crowd of seven hundred attended an emotionally charged board of education meeting the following evening, during which fifteen of nineteen speakers urged the board to oppose any additional desegregation that would require further transfers and busing. Representative Hogan urged the board to reject the proposed staff plan for further desegregation and fight the HEW's directive in the courts.[32] Hogan declared that the HEW order involved "idiocy" and the "misguided zeal of social experimenters." The school board's attorney, Paul M. Nussbaum, informed the board that based on the recent *Swann* decision, the courts would likely consider nine schools, eight of which were 80 percent or more black, segregated, owing to vestiges of the former dual school system, rather than housing segregation. Yet, the

---

[29]*A Long Day's Journey*, 29-30.
[30]Ibid., 30.
[31] Ibid.
[32]Watson, "Integrate or Face Fund Loss, U.S. Orders Prince George's," *Washington Post*, 30 July 1971, 1(A).

sharply divided board, which had directed its staff to design a plan for desegregation of the nine predominantly black schools, refused to act on the plan that evening, despite their attorney's advice and the OCR's threat of legal action and a fund cutoff.[33] On September 5, 1972, the OCR found the school district in noncompliance with Title VI.

Vaughns I

In the meantime, on March 29, 1972, the parents of eight Prince George's County School district students filed suit against the school system in *Vaughns v. Prince George's County Board of Education* (1972). Many of the charges in the suit had been raised by the HEW in its battles with the school district. The central complaint was that the school district had never fully dismantled the dual school system that had operated under state law until *Brown v. Board of Education.* Furthermore, the school district had perpetuated the dual school system through its site selection and construction of new schools after 1954. The plaintiffs were joined in their suit by school board members Jesse J. Warr, the only black member of the board, and Ruth S. Wolf, both of whom had urged further desegregation of the county's schools through redrawing of attendance areas and site selection for new schools.[34]

At the time the lawsuit was filed, 20 percent of the school district's student population was black, yet 73 percent of the black students attended schools that were more than 30 percent black, 61 percent attended schools that were more than 50 percent black, and 40 percent attended schools that were more than 80 percent black. Conversely, 47 percent of the white students attended schools that were 95 percent white, and 66 percent attended schools that were more than 90 percent white. Just 18 percent of the black students and 24 percent of the white students attended schools that were between 10 and 30 percent black, the approximate district-wide ratio. Only 49 of the district's 232 schools fell within the 10 to 30 percent black ratio.[35]

The complaint charged that most of the racial imbalance within the system's schools could be attributed to 1) racially gerrymandered

---

[33] Ibid., 16(A).

[34] Herbert H. Denton, "NAACP Sues County, Asks More Integration," *Washington Post*, 30 March 1972, 9(A).

[35] Complaint, *supra* note 6, at 5-6.

attendance zones, 2) school site selection and construction resulting in the schools' opening as racially identifiable schools, 3) racially based faculty and staff assignments, 4) transportation routing to effect segregation, 5) a liberal transfer system whereby white students in majority black schools could transfer to majority white schools, and 6) the school district's failure to take affirmative steps to dismantle the dual school system and eliminate the racial identifiability of its schools. During the eighteen-year period between the *Brown* decision and the filing of the complaint, the district had more than tripled in student population and had built 128 schools, affording the school administration ample opportunity to promote integration of the system. Despite the November 1969 pledge by the board of education (at the insistence of HEW) to begin desegregating the district's faculty, the schools' faculties remained racially identifiable.[36]

The plaintiffs charged that the school district's persistence in operating a segregated system resulted in an inferior education program afforded black students, as measured by standardized tests. Further, the school facilities, educational materials, and resources allotted for educational programming and planning were inferior in the predominantly black schools.[37]

On June 25, 1972, Judge Frank Kaufman issued a summary judgment, holding that Prince George's County had not fully eliminated the vestiges of its former dual school system and that it was not in compliance with *Brown, Green,* and *Swann.* He ordered the school board to develop a constitutional plan for desegregation by August 22, 1972. The board filed a plan with the court on August 22 for desegregating its senior high schools, but pleaded with the judge to delay implementation of any plan, because "chaos" would result if it were put into effect on September 5, the start of the new school year.[38] Consequently, the judge postponed the desegregation order, but required the board of education to present alternative plans by December 4, 1972 for desegregation of its elementary and secondary schools. Desegregation would take place January 29, 1973.

On December 29, 1972, Judge Kaufman announced his opinion in *Vaughns.* He observed that the school district's own records indisputably showed that the former dual school system had never been

---

[36] Ibid., 7-9.

[37] Ibid., 12.

[38] "Events," 12(A).

dismantled. Judge Kaufman made particular note of the district's record of school construction. Since the *Green* decision in May 1968, which called for an end to *all deliberate speed* and demanded desegregation *now*, the district had constructed thirty-five new schools, of which twenty-four were racially identifiable upon opening. The district had continued its practice of constructing racially identifiable schools even after the 1971 *Swann* decision, in which the Court emphasized the importance of new school construction in achieving and maintaining a desegregated system. Judge Kaufman declared that "factual and legal background . . . compel the conclusion that regardless of the reason why, the Prince George's County School Board has disregarded the mandates of the highest Court of our land."[39]

The judge noted in his opinion that following his August 31 requirement that the school board draw up alternative plans for desegregation, the school district staff, in consultation with the attorneys for both parties to the suit, had eventually submitted a plan that the court deemed constitutional. However, the board of education rejected the plan by a five to four vote at a December 22 meeting because, among other things, there had been insufficient time to consider the plan. His patience with the board exhausted, Judge Kaufman declared that the board had had more than sufficient time to draw up and consider a constitutional proposal, and the court therefore rejected outright any board objection based on insufficiency of time.[40]

The plan accepted by the court called for a "relatively small number of schools" to remain more than 90 percent white, but for no schools, except two which would be "paired," to remain more than 50 percent black. The plan divided the school district into eleven "neighborhood sectors," with no children to be bused outside his or her own sector. Approximately one-sixth of the school district's students would be transferred. The plan would increase the percentage of students eligible for busing from 48 to 56 percent. It provided for an average busing time of fourteen minutes one way and a maximum of thirty-five minutes one way. The court noted that the school district did not dispute the fact that further desegregation could not be accomplished without busing. The district argued instead (in essence)

---

[39]Vaughns v. Board of Education of Prince George's County, 355 F. Supp. 1051, 1052-53 (D. Md. 1972).
[40] Ibid., 1054 (footnote 12).

that busing to achieve desegregation "is wrong." [41] Yet, Judge Kaufman noted, the district had relied on extensive busing to maintain its highly segregated system.

Judge Kaufman ordered implementation of the plan on January 29, 1973, the start of the second semester of the current academic year. Graduating high school seniors were exempted from the midyear transfer. Chastising the school board for its irresponsibility in refusing to bring forth a satisfactory desegregation plan in a timely manner, the judge noted that it had been informed that "at no time (since July 1972) has there been more than four out of eight or nine members who were ready to recommend to the Court any plan which in the opinion of this Court even approaches compliance with constitutional standards."[42] The opinion stipulated that the court would retain jurisdiction of the case so that it could oversee implementation of the decree.

Following the announcement of the court's opinion, School Board President Chester E. Whiting, one of the five board members who had voted against the staff plan, immediately announced that the board intended to appeal Judge Kaufman's order. Board member Ruth Wolf, who had supported the plan, (and who was a plaintiff in the lawsuit) expressed regret that the board had not acted voluntarily and instead "had to be told by a federal court to obey the Constitution."[43]

On January 29, 1973, nearly two decades after *Brown* and following years of resistance, Prince George's County implemented Judge Kaufman's desegregation plan. The transition went remarkably smoothly, despite a rash of demonstrations and acrimonious meetings in the weeks just prior to the change. To their credit, politicians who had vehemently opposed the desegregation plan urged compliance with the law and discouraged disruptions at the schools or along bus routes. The administration was credited for its thorough planning and coordination of the first day under the new desegregation plan. Numerous parents said that they were apprehensive about busing their children to unfamiliar schools, but it was time to comply with the law, and further defiance would be futile.[44] "If adult overseers in Prince

---

[41] Ibid., 1057 (footnote 19).
[42] Ibid., 1062 (footnote 31).
[43] Herbert H. Denton, "Desegregation Deadline Set," *Washington Post*, 30 December 1972, 12(A).
[44] Philip A. McCombs, "Prince George's Desegregation of Schools Peaceful, Smooth," *Washington Post*, 30 January 1973, 10(A).

George's County schools were exceedingly organized and somewhat nervous, (the) students themselves seemed almost defiantly indifferent to desegregation."[45] One student remarked, and others agreed, "It's the parents who are causing all the problems. The kids are really nice about busing, but the parents couldn't accept it."[46]

Sylvester Vaughns, Sr., who had volunteered his son's name for the lawsuit was satisfied with the decision, remarking that he had filed suit because "I have a moral and religious conviction that the separation of the races is wrong." His son, Sylvester Jr., expressed some ambivalence about the action that resulted in his transfer to a new high school. "I'd rather be going to school with black people. . . . You know, we've got more in common." Despite his regret at leaving friends at his old high school, the younger Vaughns said that he felt desegregation was necessary to insure blacks a better education.[47]

On January 29, the Maryland State Senate saluted Prince George's County for desegregating its schools "peaceably and *on schedule*" (emphasis mine). On the Senate floor, numerous members congratulated the county. One senator noted that the county had acted only in response to a court order.[48]

Though the transition was smooth, enrollment in private schools jumped following implementation of the court order. A week after it had gone into effect, the First Baptist Church of Riverdale acquired a new building that could house an additional eight hundred for the church's school. The Baptist school had an enrollment of five hundred, but had recently received applications for an additional 370 students. The school was integrated, though predominantly white. Other private schools in the area reported a "flood" of inquiries, but most were already at capacity. Owing to apparent white withdrawals, several formerly "black" schools were several percentage points more black than had been projected. For the most part, black students enrolled as directed in white neighborhoods.[49]

---

[45]Tom Huth, "Kids Were Ready Before Today," *Washington Post*, 30 January 1973, 1(C).

[46]Ibid., 3(C).

[47]Charles A. Krause, "'I'd Rather Be With Blacks,'" *Washington Post*, 30 January 1973, 3(C).

[48]"Pr. George's Saluted on Desegregation," *Washington Post*, 30 January 1973, 10(A).

[49] Philip McCombs., "Mixing Goal Not Reached, *Washington Post*, 3 February 1973, 1(B), 3(B).

Though the administration had optimistically predicted that enrollment would return to normal within a few days after desegregation began, the expected white enrollment at the county's schools never recovered. School officials estimated that about three thousand students likely left the system owing to dissatisfaction with desegregation.[50]

For two years following implementation of the desegregation order, the school district filed status reports with the court. On February 20, 1974, the school board and the plaintiffs entered into a consent decree concerning faculty hiring, promotion, site location, and opening enrollment of new schools. The decree stipulated that all schools remain desegregated. On March 13, 1975, after two years of court-supervised compliance, the court issued a memorandum and order relinquishing jurisdiction. However, the decree stated that either party had the right to reopen the case and resume the court's jurisdiction.[51]

Vaughns II

During the 1970s, the population of Prince George's County shifted dramatically. Between 1967 and 1986, Prince George's County experienced the largest percentage increase in black student enrollment with the largest decrease in white enrollment in the United States. Many attributed the white exodus to busing and the elimination of "neighborhood schools." Many black families migrated to the county during the same period, causing the percentage of blacks in the county to rise from 13 percent in 1971 to 40 percent in 1981. The public school population shifted even more dramatically. In nine years black enrollment shot from 24 to nearly 50 percent.[52] Segregation patterns in the schools became much more pronounced. On January 29, 1973, the day the desegregation order went into effect, only thirteen of the district's 228 schools were outside the court's guideline for racial identifiability (less than 10 percent or more than 50 percent black). By

---

[50] *A Long Day's Journey*, 426.
[51] "Vaughns Highlights," (Upper Marlboro: Prince George's County Public Schools), 1 unpublished.
[52] Margaret Shapiro and Leon Wynter, "Pr. George's Faces Busing Case Renewal," *Washington Post*, 2 September 1981, 9(A).

May 1973, only four months later, ten more schools had fallen outside the guideline.[53]

Racial identifiability of the district's schools grew steadily, and by 1980, ninety-seven schools (44.9 percent) were racially identifiable. This percentage fell within three points of the percentage of racially identifiable schools in Prince George's County as of September 1972, before the implementation of the desegregation order. More than two-thirds of the schools that were racially identifiable in 1980 were at least 75 percent black. Yet in several areas at the outskirts of the county, some schools had enrollments more than 90 percent white.[54]

In September 1981, the NAACP, which was not one of the original litigants in the *Vaughns I* case, along with some of the original plaintiffs and additional plaintiffs, petitioned the court to reopen the case and resume jurisdiction, in light of the resegregation that had taken place in the districts' schools. Sylvester Vaughns, Jr. was not a litigant in the case initiated by the NAACP, having lost interest in the desegregation cause. The court reopened the case and resumed jurisdiction on September 28, 1981. On October 8, at Judge Kaufman's request, the NAACP and the other plaintiffs filed a new complaint against the board of education and administration and asked that the two cases be consolidated. The request for the new complaint arose in response to the school board's charge that the NAACP had raised new issues, such as the discriminatory assignment of blacks to special education classes, which were not a part of the original suit.[55]

The 1981 complaint charged that the school district had "failed to achieve stable desegregated status" in the school system. It declared that the board of education had "impeded desegregation" by closing schools, adjusting boundaries, and unilaterally imposing modifications to the 1973 desegregation plan. Further, the plaintiffs charged the school board with racially discriminatory policies within the county's schools with respect to special education, classroom assignment, student discipline, and faculty assignment. The complaint noted the steady and rapid increase in segregation within the district since the implementation of the desegregation plan through their action and inaction, including opening and closing schools, altering attendance

---

[53] Complaint at 3, NAACP v. Board of Education of Prince George's County (D. Md. 1981) (No. K-81-2597).
[54] Shapiro and Wynter, 9(A).
[55] Margaret Shapiro, "Rehearing Set in '72 School Case," *Washington Post*, 29 September 1981, 11(A).

areas, transferring students, and altering transportation routes.[56] The plaintiffs asked the court to reassign students and alter attendance zones to ensure that the school system would achieve and maintain desegregated status, reassign faculty and hire additional minority faculty to reflect the racial composition of the district and the labor market, and require that the district eliminate its discriminatory policies with regard to classroom assignment, special education assignment, and disciplinary measures.[57]

The board of education responded that it had achieved unitary status with the desegregation of the school system in 1973, and that this was confirmed by the court's relinquishment of jurisdiction in 1975. The defendants argued that previously segregated school systems did not bear the perpetual responsibility of redrawing attendance zones to ensure that they maintained a standard of racial balance. Citing *Pasadena City Board of Education v. Spangler* (1976) and *Swann* (1971), the defendants declared, "Indeed, the Supreme Court has held that unless there has been intentional resegregation, the federal courts lack the power--jurisdiction--to direct the school boards' actions."[58]

Judge Kaufman dismissed the board of education's argument that the court had no authority in the case after having relinquished its jurisdiction in 1975. The *Vaughns II* trial took place in March, April, and May 1982, and in June 1983, the court held that a unitary school system had not been achieved with regard to student assignment, but it found in favor of the defendants with regard to faculty hiring, faculty reassignment, special education assignment, talented and gifted enrollment, and discipline. In September the court established "flexible" 10 to 80 percent guidelines for pupil assignment, requiring the board take into consideration in making all its decisions the "need to achieve unitary status as quickly and as reasonably as possible."[59]

Following numerous meetings between the attorneys for the NAACP and the board of education, the parties submitted a memorandum of understanding which was approved by the court in June 1985. The agreement stipulated that by the 1987-88 school year,

---

[56] Complaint, *supra* note 53, at 3-4.

[57] Ibid., 9.

[58] Memorandum in Support of Motion to Dismiss for Lack of Jurisdiction and in Opposition to Plaintiffs' Motion for Consolidation at 4-5, NAACP v. Board of Education of Prince George's County, (D. Md. 1981) (No. K-81-2597).

[59] "Vaughns Highlights," 2.

at least 80 percent of the district's pupils were to attend schools that were between 10 and 80 percent black, and by the 1988-89 school year 85 percent of the district's students should be in schools 10 to 80 percent black.[60] Under the agreement, the district began a magnet school program to attract blacks to predominantly white schools and whites to predominantly black schools.

Further, the parties agreed that certain of the system's schools were too difficult to desegregate, so the district would allot extra compensatory funds to these schools, in accordance with the *Milliken II* decision. In 1985, 10 of the system's 174 schools were designated *Milliken II* schools.[61] The following year eleven more *Milliken II* schools were designated.[62] These schools would offer numerous special programs, including all day kindergarten, a pupil-teacher ratio (PTR) in regular classrooms of twenty to one, full time math and reading resource teachers, and summer school remedial instruction for children who otherwise would not be promoted the following year.[63]

As a result of the dramatic shifts in population in the thirteen years since the 1972 court order, the busing plan was no longer effective, and in some cases it was counterproductive. Therefore, the memorandum of understanding called for reassessment by the school board to reduce the number of black students who were being "unnecessarily bused" and to reduce the time and distance that some black students were being bused as a result of the 1972 court order. Finally, the defendants recommitted to hiring and promoting qualified blacks in all positions in the school system.[64] Thus, the parties were once again in agreement over measures to be taken to achieve the highest level of desegregation reasonably feasible in Prince George's County.

Conclusion

Following over a decade of denial, resistance, and delay, the Prince George's Public Schools had adopted a desegregation plan aimed at reducing racial isolation and improving achievement levels of minority

---

[60] Memorandum, *supra* note 58, at 3.

[61] Memorandum of Understanding, NAACP v. Board of Education of Prince George's County at 3 (D. Md. 1981) (No. K-81-2597).

[62] Feldman, et al., 39.

[63] William A. Bradford, Jr., Letter to Paul Nussbaum re: Milliken II Relief, 21 June 1985. (filed with Memorandum of Understanding, *supra* note 61).

[64] Memorandum of Understanding, *supra* note 61, at 4-5.

children.   However, demographic changes soon necessitated adjustments in the student assignment plans, and by the mid 1980s, the student population had become so black that busing for purposes of desegregation was no longer practicable in many areas.   The court thus reduced the busing requirements in some areas and ordered the district to implement compensatory educational programs to reduce the deleterious effects of racial isolation.   However, the causes of the achievement gap between white and minority children would prove much too complex for court-ordered remedial programs alone to surmount them.   Furthermore, the *Milliken II* schools and programs posed a new set of dilemmas, including equity between magnet and non magnet schools and the question of discriminatory admissions criteria.

By several standards, opportunities were improving for minorities in Prince George's County by the 1980s.   The standard of living among minorities was rising.   The dual school system had been eliminated, and improved academic programs were in place. Furthermore, blacks had made political gains, achieving positions of leadership within the school system and in the county administration. Yet, minority achievement lagged, and feelings of distrust and resentment between blacks and whites lingered, a legacy of the bitter legal battle to desegregate the schools and resistance to the court's authority.

The following chapter addresses the problems faced by Prince George's County school system in the 1990s.   After more than twenty years of court supervision, during which time the schools became increasingly segregated, the board of education of Prince George's County proposed a plan for returning to a neighborhood school system with compensatory educational and other programs to enhance the learning environment in the schools.   Skeptics of the board's proposal pointed to the general failure of compensatory programs, since they were first widely administered under the ESEA of 1965, to achieve significant measurable improvement in the test scores of disadvantaged school children.   Recognizing the limits of any one type of compensatory program, the school board proposed a multifaceted plan which was aimed at resurrecting the neighborhood school concept, employing a variety of remedial programs, expanding the magnet school program, and encouraging greater parental and community involvement in the schools.

CHAPTER 7

Prince George's County in the 1990s

Introduction

By the mid 1990s, the student population of Prince George's County Public Schools was approximately 70 percent black, and many residents viewed the court order (memorandum of understanding) under which the school system had been operating since 1985 as outdated and ineffective. Prince George's County was the only district in the Washington, D.C. area that was still under a court order to desegregate. Many of those who originally supported the court's intervention by this time conceded that the emotional and financial costs of the desegregation plan had been high, while the plan's impact on academic achievement had been limited. The lack of improvement in performance was especially notable in light of the fact that the county became wealthier as it became predominantly black during the 1980s. Neither the court's supervision, nor the improved living standard within the county had improved standardized test scores significantly.[1]

The 1985 memorandum of understanding required that magnet and *Milliken II* schools be established to remedy the effects of past discrimination where desegregation was not feasible, but the court order did not require any standard for success. Feldman, Kirby, Eaton, and Morantz, authors of the Harvard Project on School Desegregation's 1994 study entitled *Still Separate, Still Unequal*, suggested that without addressing achievement or including educational goals, the

---

[1] Lisa Leff, "For Schools, Coot Order Provided No Shortcut to Excellence," *Washington Post*, 13 September 1993, 10(A).

1985 plan could hardly have been expected to meet the Supreme Court's demand to "restore victims of discriminatory conduct to the position they would have occupied in the absence of such conduct," as expressed in *Milliken II.*[2] The Court's idealistic goal remained elusive for Prince George's County, where desegregation was increasingly impractical and compensatory programs had not fulfilled the promise their architects envisioned.

In 1993, 86 percent of the approximately eleven thousand students (10 percent of the school population) who were bused for purposes of desegregation were black, and half attended schools that would have been majority black with or without the busing plan. John Rosser, a former vice-president of the NAACP conceded that, given present conditions, the critics of busing for purposes of desegregation in Prince George's County may have had a point. "Nobody says, 'I want my child in a school that has a certain number of whites.' They say, 'I want my child in a good school.' There's a difference."[3]

In the 1994 election for county executive, successful candidate Wayne Curry, an attorney who was among the blacks who first desegregated Bladensburg High School, supported replacing the busing plan with a system of high quality black schools.[4] His electoral success indicated the degree to which attitudes among blacks regarding busing in Prince George's County had evolved in the previous two decades.

The low achievement levels of Prince George's County students presented stark evidence of the limits of the court's ability to improve the educational opportunity offered by the school system. In 1994, the standardized test scores of the district's elementary schools were below the state average,[5] just as they had been since before the court order was implemented in 1972. The school system had set a goal of having 75

---

[2]Joseph Feldman, Edward Kirby, Susan Eaton, and Alison Morantz, *Still Separate, Still Unequal: The Limits of Milliken II's Educational Compensation Remedies* (Cambridge: The Harvard Project on School Desegregation, 1994), 40.

[3]Leff, "Demographics Foil P.G. Schools' Efforts to Achieve Racial Balance," *Washington Post*, 12 September 1993, 24-25(A).

[4] Leff, "Mistrust, High Costs Conspire Against Alternatives," *Washington Post*, 14 September 1993, 6(A).

[5] *1994 Maryland School Performance Program Report: State, School System and Schools, Prince George's County Public Schools*, (MSPP) (Upper Marlboro, Md.: Prince George's County Public Schools, 1994), 16 and 24.

percent of its students performing within or above the satisfactory range in language arts, mathematics, science, and social studies by the year 2000.[6] Student performance was far below that goal in 1994, but the superintendent's statement within the 1994 Maryland School Performance Program report (MSPP) said that the district would use the MSPP data, along with other locally developed criteria, to help guide improvement in student performance in the district.[7]

Despite increasing disenchantment with the desegregation plan among blacks, the NAACP was reticent to relinquish the court's protection while many black children continued to perform poorly in school.[8] In 1993 board member Kenneth R. Johnson suggested that a barrier of mistrust between the black and white communities in Prince George's County impeded the formation of a consensus that would lead to the court's withdrawing its order. The decades of resistance to desegregation by the county's white-dominated school board and the board's decision to fight the NAACP all the way to the Supreme Court following Judge Kaufman's 1972 order to desegregate had long been sources of animosity. Johnson reflected, "what the busing brought was nobody trusting anybody. We need to let go of some of the fears that have grown up with us over the years."[9] Part of the lingering mistrust and unwillingness to relinquish the court's protection may have stemmed from the fact that while 70 percent of the student population was black, the superintendent and five of the nine school board members were white, and the faculty remained disproportionately white. In the 1994-95 school year, 63.1 percent of the faculty was white, 35.5 percent was black, .72 percent was Hispanic, .48 percent was Asian, and .13 percent was American Indian.[10]

Despite these statistics, the reversal of the racial composition in Prince George's County had dramatically altered the political landscape, giving blacks political power and the potential to guarantee equitable funding to schools in black neighborhoods. School board member Dr. Alvin Thorton, noted that while blacks had no political power in 1972, in the mid 1990s, they were administrators and county

---

[6] Ann Gourley, test development specialist, Prince George's County Public Schools, telephone interview by author, 26 April 1995.

[7] MSPP, *supra* note 5 at 23.

[8] Leff, "Demographics," 24(A).

[9] Leff, "Mistrust, 6(A).

[10] Bonnie Jenkins-Bundy, director of public affairs, Prince George's County Public Schools, telephone interview by author, 6 April 1995.

executives.   There was no real *wealth* among blacks, but there was income and significantly higher education levels among black parents. Dr. Thorton, a political scientist at Howard University, suggested that as black families had moved into the middle class, the need to expose black children to white children in school had decreased.[11]

Yet, despite increasing black efficacy, the higher socioeconomic level of Prince George's County residents, the efforts to desegregate, and the implementation of special educational programs in schools where desegregation had not been feasible, student performance remained disappointingly low.   Franklin Jackson, a black lawyer who ran a mentoring program at one county high school, felt that parental and teacher expectations of students had declined since 1972 when the court order was implemented.   Jackson reflected, "Back then, while you had more racial conflict than you do now, there was also much more of a commitment to excellence.   It's almost like we expect [children] to do worse as the system becomes darker."[12]

School officials explained the lack of progress by pointing to drug-related violence, the skyrocketing divorce rate, and too much television viewing.   They claimed the overriding problem was poverty, however. More than one-third of the county's students qualified for free or reduced school lunches.   Some school advocates suggested lack of public commitment, rather than actual poverty, was the real problem. While poverty rates in the county were declining, per pupil expenditures were also declining.[13]

The fact that 75 percent of Prince George's County households did not have children in school may have at least partially explained the lower level of financial support for public education.   The county's population was aging and the percentage of children attending private schools had increased since the 1970s.[14]   These trends resulted in a lower percentage of the population's directly benefiting from expenditures on public education.   Hence, these residents may have felt ambivalent about financially supporting the public school system.

Despite these overwhelming challenges to the school district, there were several reasons for optimism in the mid 1990s.   In 1995, the

---

[11]Dr. Alvin Thorton, member, board of education of Prince George's County, telephone interview by author, 17 March 1995.

[12] Leff, "For Schools, Court Order Provided No Shortcut to Excellence," *Washington Post*, 13 September 1993, 10(A).

[13] Ibid.

[14] Jenkins-Bundy, *supra* note 10, 14 September 1994.

school board hired Jerome Clark as superintendent. The first African-American superintendent in Prince George's County, Clark assumed the position with promises of improving student performance, restructuring the management teams that supervised schools, and increasing community involvement to produce school reform.[15] He threatened to remove top administrators if the substance and quality of the schools did not improve, and he later threatened to "reconstruct" schools, removing principals and forcing teachers to reapply for their jobs, if student scores dropped. "The whole thing is accountability, Clark declared in August of 1995.[16] Yet, despite Clark's attractive and energetic vision for the school district, student performance declined.

In January 1998, the Maryland Department of Education announced that nine Prince George's County schools were among the lowest performing in the state and they were put on "official notice" that they must show improvement or face "reconstitution." The Maryland School Performance Assessment Program measured school performance in terms of student achievement as measured on standardized tests. During the previous year, Prince George's County schools declined slightly while all but five other Maryland school systems improved. Only Baltimore ranked lower than Prince George's County. A report released in March showed that the nine schools experienced high staff turnover, too few classroom teachers and aides, and a lack of parental involvement. These schools were required to submit improvement plans by the end of March and long-term improvement plans in June. Officials in the State Department of Education expected that it would take the schools as long as five years to show significant improvement. If after five years there were no real gains, then the state was considering turning the operation of the schools over to a university or private education company.[17] A quarter century of judicial oversight had clearly not produced the educational opportunity envisioned in *Brown*.

---

[15] DeNeen L. Brown, "Schools Chief Tried Moving a Mountain," *Washington Post*, 22 June 1998, 1(A).
[16] Eric Lipton, "The Struggle of a County's Schools," *Washington Post*, 21 June 1998, 1(A).
[17] Brown, "Defining the Problem in Pr. George's," *Washington Post*, 26 March 1998, 5(D).

The Continuing Struggle to Meet the Court's Mandate

On the surface, Prince George's County Public Schools appeared to have much to offer its students. The district seemed to be aggressively addressing the achievement problem by establishing goals, raising academic standards, and restructuring management. An early 1990s district development that showed promise was *Equity 2000*, an intervention program initiated in the 1992-93 school year by the College Board of Princeton University, in cooperation with the Prince George's County Public Schools. Placing special emphasis on mathematics, the program aimed to close the gap between the college-attendance and success rates of both minority and non-minority students in the district. In its first three years of implementation, the program had moved steadily toward realization of its goal of successful completion by all students of Algebra I by the end of the ninth grade and geometry by the end of the tenth grade. Furthermore, significant progress had been made toward the elimination of low level tracking, with high-level opportunity for all.[18] This goal addressed the problem of segregation *within* schools, the disproportionate placement of minorities in less challenging non-college preparatory classes, a condition found in many areas throughout the United States, even where school *systems* were relatively integrated.

The *Milliken II* and magnet schools established under the 1985 memorandum of understanding offered enhanced and specialized programs for children who wanted to be challenged. Elementary *Milliken II* schools had PTRs of twenty to one. They each had full day kindergarten, a full-time counselor, a full-time media specialist, tutorial support, summer programs, and computer upgrades.[19]

These *Milliken II* schools also used the Comer Process to involve parents in substantive school policy making. In the mid 1990s, approximately fifty of the county's schools were using the Comer School Development Program, designed by Dr. James Comer, Director of the School Development Program at Yale, to engage the talents, strengths and interests of parents, students, and staff to develop in collaboration policies, and practices that improved the academic and

---

[18] *Annual Report to the Community* . (Upper Marlboro, Md: Prince George's County Public Schools, 1994), 21.
[19] Ibid.

social climate of schools.[20] The Comer Program reflected the growing consensus among educators that parental support and direct involvement in the education of their children was essential to academic success.

In addition to the eleven thousand students who were bused for purposes of desegregation, nine thousand students voluntarily traveled by bus to attend magnet schools. The school system spent approximately $564 extra per student per year (10 percent more) in *Milliken II* schools, and $347 extra per student per year (6 percent more) in its magnet programs. Most of the funds paid for extra teachers, equipment, and supplies. The magnet and *Milliken II* schools remained extremely popular with parents and students.[21]

The magnet school program offered a variety of eighteen focused academic themes. For instance, the Academic Center stressed strong achievement in basic academics within a highly structured atmosphere, where disciplined behavior, regular attendance, and punctuality were emphasized. The Biotechnology Program offered a four-year college preparatory program in molecular biology, biochemistry, and technical career training. The Biotechnology Program offered a complementary set of course offerings including Advanced Placement classes in English, the social sciences, and mathematics. Other magnet programs emphasized the creative and performing arts, language immersion, humanities and international studies, and communication studies.[22] Numerous schools offered Talented and Gifted (TAG) programs for identified talented and gifted students. Some schools were "devoted magnets," which meant that all enrolled students participated in the enriched programs. In other magnet schools, students participated in the enriched programs upon request. During the 1993-'94 school year, 70.4 percent of the participating students were black.[23]

Noting the popularity of the magnet schools and alluding to rhetoric that surrounded the busing issue, school board member Alvin Thorton observed, "The most successful children are those who are bused. Children come down to the school district and beg to be bused."[24] This was part of the strategy behind the magnet school

---

[20] Ibid.

[21] Leff, "Demographics," 24(A).

[22] *School System of Choices* (Upper Marlboro, MD: Prince George's County Public Schools, 1994).

[23] *Annual Report to the Community*, 35.

[24] Thorton, *supra* note 11.

programs, which recognized that parents and students resented forced busing, especially if it did not achieve significant racial balance or if it were viewed as detrimental to the quality of education. The magnet programs were designed to entice students and parents to integrate schools in order to take advantage of special educational opportunities.

However, the school board's Community Advisory Council (commonly known as the "Committee of 100"), which monitored the implementation of the 1985 memorandum of understanding, observed in its 1991 *Interim Report* that an unintended consequence of the *Milliken II* and magnet schools was that the standard comprehensive schools had come to be seen as "poor neighborhood schools." Most creative principals and teachers were pulled from these schools to operate the magnet and *Milliken II* schools, which received extra funds for special educational programs and equipment. Furthermore, many of the more active parents moved with their children to these schools. One of every five county students was enrolled in a magnet program. These developments drained the comprehensive schools of leadership and funds. The Committee of 100 recommended that the district equalize the funding of its comprehensive schools and magnet and *Milliken II* schools.[25]

Despite the popularity of the *Milliken II* schools and the envy they engendered, in 1994, the Harvard Project on School Desegregation's report *Still Separate, Still Unequal* expressed concern over the lack of evidence that the extra funds expended in the magnet and *Milliken II* schools had increased achievement levels. The Harvard Project reported that the district had conducted only one study that indicated that students in these schools progressed at a higher rate than those in comprehensive schools. A study conducted by the school district in 1989 showed that third grade black students in *Milliken II* schools moved from the 57th to the 63rd percentile on the California Achievement Test between third and fifth grades, whereas their contemporaries in comprehensive schools remained in the 58th percentile during the same time period.[26]

These findings were encouraging, but as the Harvard report noted, they might simply have mirrored other evaluations that indicated that compensatory programs registered the greatest effect in the elementary schools years, and these gains leveled out in subsequent school years.

---

[25] *Annual Report, supra* note 18, 2-5.
[26] Feldman, et al., 41.

The report concluded, "it seems that *Milliken II* programs, while developed to provide equity, have, in the view of many, created a new kind of inequity." Attempts to rectify these perceived inequities would "force increased spending on unproven programs" as patterns of increasing and likely irreversible racial isolation emerged.[27]

Gary Orfield, Director of the Harvard Project, was highly critical of the implementation of compensatory educational programs under *Milliken II* and charged that, owing to the absence of accountability, the promises of the Supreme Court's decision had not been fulfilled. In the foreword to the project's report, Orfield wrote, "In fact, there is usually no serious independent monitoring of what the schools so (sic) with the money during the years they get it and no policy that guarantees help to new segregated schools that develop by (sic) while the remedy is still in place."[28] Orfield charged that in the four school systems, Detroit, Little Rock, Prince George's County, and Austin, studied by the Harvard Project, the plaintiffs usually were not "consulted seriously" with regard to the remedy. Furthermore, "[W]hat was presented as a remedy for the harms of segregation typically did not identify those harms and did not measure whether they were cured."[29]

Orfield called for a reassessment of the Court's decision ruling out inter-district remedies for intra-district segregation problems in *Milliken I*, in light of the poor management of court-ordered compensatory programs and the lack of substantive results.[30] The Harvard Project report concluded, "until there is a guaranteed cure for the myriad problems that stem from racial and economic isolation and the continuing effects of intentional segregation, *Milliken II* remedies, as they are currently implemented, simply give 'separate but equal' another chance."[31] Ironically, Orfield noted that the two states with the highest levels of racial integration in schools, Delaware and Kentucky, operated successful city-suburban desegregation plans in their largest metropolitan areas. He suggested that greater efforts to integrate should have been made in other metropolitan school systems, rather than using compensatory educational programs as an alternative.[32]

---

[27] Ibid., 42-44.

[28] Ibid., 2.

[29] Ibid.

[30] Ibid.

[31] Ibid., 63.

[32] Ibid., 2.

Yet, as noted in Chapter 5, in Wilmington, black students continued to lag in achievement, and they were disproportionately represented in basic and remedial classes. The plaintiffs in the case fought release of the district from court supervision, based in part on the achievement gap, but the court, shortly after the Supreme Court's ruling in *Jenkins v. Missouri* (1995), released the school district following years of compliance with the court order.

The fact that the achievement level of black students continued to lag, despite the racial balance achieved suggested that the causes of the achievement gap were very deep-rooted, and integration alone was no panacea. Yet, compensatory programs had not produced satisfactory results, either. Orfield suggested that if compensatory programs were to be a remedy for past discrimination, "it is extremely important that the plans produce some real gains." He advised strict supervision of school districts to ensure that compensatory programs indeed benefited the victims of past discrimination. "Ironically," he observed, "although educational remedies may seem far less obtrusive and far less likely to general (sic) community resistance than desegregation, the court must be prepared to be much more intrusive educationally if any beneficial change is likely to occur."[33] The Harvard Project's report suggested that a combination of "effective educational remedies and racial integration [was] the most promising way for meeting the Supreme Court's mandate." However, in suggesting a more intrusive role for the courts, Orfield posited a legitimate and *effective* judicial role in educational policy making.

The Supreme Court rejected this argument in *Missouri v. Jenkins*, which paved the way for numerous school districts to be released from court supervision following years of compliance, despite an achievement gap between whites and minorities. Furthermore, Orfield's recommendations ignored the history of desegregation in American schools, replete with examples of the inability of the courts to render school systems equitable in the face of public opposition or ambivalence. Equitable and effective schools could only be achieved through a grassroots political movement, with states and communities insisting that their school systems offer an equitable and quality education to all.

---

[33] Ibid.

Thus, Orfield's contention that closer monitoring of compensatory educational funds was necessary to ensure accountability was apt, but his suggestion that the courts continue to be the agent of change ignored the evidence that courts, despite their most vigilante efforts, had been unable to render school systems accountable or achieve integration. Courts could not ensure that funds were spent wisely or appropriately, that teachers were prepared or fit, that curricula were challenging and appropriate. *Milliken II's* mandate which allowed for compensatory educational programs to restore victims of segregation to the level of achievement they would have achieved without segregation clearly implied accountability. Common sense and fiscal responsibility demanded accountability. However, communities would have to provide the vigilance necessary to render school systems equitable and excellent.

Revival of the Neighborhood School System

In January 1995, the school board officially adopted a plan aimed at enhancing the educational programs in all its schools, while gradually (over six years) returning to neighborhood school assignments. Entitled *Proposed Phased Implementation of Neighborhood School Assignments: A Six Year Plan*, the proposal embodied four elements: 1) the phased elimination of desegregation-based student assignments as school space became available; 2) the continuation of the magnet school program; 3) the gradual improvement of the system's comprehensive schools, bringing them to the level of "model comprehensive schools," along with the creation of additional *Milliken II* schools; and 4) a continued commitment on the part of the school system to eradicating the vestiges of desegregation through educational improvements directed toward equity and excellence.[34]

The proposal recognized two enrollment trends: 1) increasing student population from 113,570 in 1993-94 to an expected 121,858 in 1999-2000; and 2) continuing changes in the racial demographics by 1999-2000 from 68.9 percent black and 31.1 percent other in 1993-94 to 76.7 percent black and 23.3 percent other. New schools would be

---

[34] *Proposed Phased Implementation of Neighborhood School Assignments: A Six Year Plan* (Upper Marlboro, Md.: Prince George's County Public Schools, 1994), 1-2. (hereinafter *Proposed Phased Implementation*).

needed to accommodate these students, and the school board suggested that the construction of these schools should reflect a neighborhood assignment pattern, rather than the mid 1990s assignment patterns which were aimed at promoting racial integration, but which had been rendered ineffective by changing demographics."[35]

The board's proposal called for converting five high schools, two middle schools, and twenty-seven elementary schools to *Milliken II* status. In the mid 1990s, these schools were within the court's desegregation guidelines as presently understood, but would fall outside those guidelines once the neighborhood school plan was phased in.[36] The goal was to convert the comprehensive schools to "model comprehensive" schools by allocating additional resources to these schools, enhancing the quality of the teaching, and lowering the pupil-teacher ratio (PTR) to twenty-five to one.[37] This projected PTR was considerably higher than the thirteen to seventeen student classroom found most beneficial in the Tennessee STAR study, but such a low PTR appeared to be an unrealistic goal for Prince George's County at that time.

As proposed, the plan would cost $347 million over six years.[38] A major portion of money would go to new school construction and additions to existing schools to accommodate increased population and to bring schools back into neighborhoods.[39] Many neighborhood schools had been abandoned when desegregation took place in the 1970s. No one knew how these funds would be secured, however. Governor Glendening committed $20 million in his budget proposal for the following fiscal year, but the legislature would have to approve the expenditure.[40]

Because the cost of the proposed plan was so high, its implementation almost certainly would necessitate tax increases. Hence, the school administration faced the formidable task of convincing white residents, who comprised about half of the electorate, but only 24 percent of the school population, to finance the proposed plan.[41] The lack of evidence of increased achievement since the

---

[35] Ibid., 2.
[36] Ibid., 8.
[37] Jenkins-Bundy, *supra* note 10.
[38] Thorton, *supra* note 11.
[39] *Proposed Phased Implementation*, 6-7.
[40] Thorton, *supra* note 11.
[41] Leff, "Mistrust," 5(A).

establishment of the existing magnet and *Milliken II* schools would make the school board's effort to convince the taxpayers to support the increase difficult.

In response to concerns about accountability, the school board allotted funds in early 1995 for assessment of the relative progress of students in comprehensive, magnet, and *Milliken II* schools. The Effective Schools Research Study, directed by Dr. Eugene Adcock, would measure progress of third, fifth, and eighth graders.[42] The study would begin immediately and did not depend upon the implementation of the board's neighborhood schools proposal, which needed to secure funding and court approval.

The proposal stressed the school system's commitment to academic excellence for all students and to accountability. The proposal included special programs and efforts aimed at raising the achievement levels of black male students, who, as a cohort, were furthest from the district's achievement goals of meeting or exceeding state and national standards in mathematics, science, reading, writing, and social studies.[43]

The NAACP responded to the board's proposal with a list of thirty-three concerns, and in early 1995 the board and the NAACP were attempting to resolve these issues before asking Judge Kaufman for permission to implement the plan. The NAACP's thirty-three concerns regarding the board's proposals were complex, but generally fell within four categories: 1) whether the proposal was actually an attempt to resegregate; 2) whether the necessary funding for the proposal would actually be available; 3) whether *Milliken II* schools were really appropriate; and 4) whether they moved in a "fundamentally different constitutional direction which [was] at odds with the philosophical approach of the NAACP."[44]

Professor Thorton noted that the proposal attempted to introduce into the legal and political communities a new concept of *outcomes*, rather than ratios, to demonstrate that the children were being offered an equal educational opportunity. This new emphasis would increase the school system's responsibility to the court. Dr. Thorton reported that the Committee of 100 "endorsed (the school board's proposal) with some reservations," and suggested that the proposal seemed to have the

---

[42] Jenkins-Bundy, *supra* note 10.

[43] *Proposed Phased Implementation, supra* note 39 attachment IX, sec.A.

[44] Thorton, *supra* note 11.

support of the community. The question was whether the NAACP and the board of education could move away from their traditional stances, said Thorton. "The NAACP stresses ratios of integration, and the board says 'we've done all we can.'"[45]

As the Prince George's County Public Schools moved toward requesting release from judicial oversight, accountability and financing appeared to be the primary issues of concern, and these two factors were clearly interdependent. The board of education's *Proposed Phased Implementation of Neighborhood School Assignments* attempted to meet the evolving demands of a school community that had grown weary of an obsolete busing order by enhancing the quality of the educational program in all its schools. Unfortunately, the proposal's merit could not be known before its implementation, and without guarantees of effectiveness, the public understandably would be reticent to finance such an expensive undertaking.

If the Effective Schools Research Study uncovered evidence of significant gains among magnet and *Milliken II* school students relative to the progress of comprehensive school students, the court and the NAACP would possibly be more willing to accept the board's proposal, and the public might be more willing to finance it. The enthusiastic support of the participants in the magnet and *Milliken II* schools and their parents appeared to be insufficient to overcome the skepticism of these three critical entities.

Request for Release

In July 1996, the board of education announced that it would ask Judge Peter J. Messitte, who had taken over the case in 1994 from Judge Kaufman, to release the district from the busing order under its *Proposed Phased Implementation of Neighborhood School Assignments.* The school system was nearly 72 percent black by then, and the busing plan no longer served its purpose of integrating students. Nor were the enrollment guidelines for the magnet school program workable. For the 1996-97 school year there were five hundred spaces for white children that went unused, while forty-one hundred black students were wait-listed. The board sought to return to a neighborhood school system, while continuing the popular magnet school program. Though the board and community were eager for

---

[45] Ibid.

release from the court order, they did not want to lose state funds for the desegregation programs they operated.[46] The plan under which the school district hoped to be released called for $172 million from the state and county for the construction of new neighborhood schools and the renovation of old ones. It called for an additional $174 million in the system's operating budget for reducing class sizes, purchasing equipment, improving the curriculum, etc. The plan suffered a major setback when Prince George's County voters rejected a plan to lift the county property tax cap and allow county officials to raise extra revenues for school construction.[47]

In December 1996, Judge Messitte appointed four researchers to an advisory panel to investigate whether race-based busing was still useful for the district. The panel announced its findings the following summer, that the district had done what it could to integrate its schools and end discriminatory practices.[48]

In October 1997, the board of education approved a settlement with the NAACP that was based on the *Proposed Phased Implementation of Neighborhood Schools Plan* with certain modifications. The agreement called for $250 million contributions each from the state and the county.[49] Part of the $500 million included in the settlement was directed toward adding twenty-nine *Milliken II* schools in the district, bringing the total to fifty. A Washington Post analysis of the academic progress made by students in *Milliken II* schools showed disappointed results, however.

The *Milliken II* schools had reduced class sizes, extra guidance counselors, computer labs, and cultural programs, along with field trips. Nevertheless, in standardized test scores, the *Milliken II* schools fell at the low end of the district's schools, and the district ranked second lowest in the state, with only poverty-plagued Baltimore falling lower.[50] Such poor results were not unique to Prince George's County.

---

[46] "New Dynamics in Prince George's" *Washington Post*, 2 August 1996, 20(A).

[47] Lisa Frazier, "Prince George's School Plan Hurt By Tax Revolt," *Washington Post*, 1 December 1996, 1(B).

[48] "Prince George's Busing Realities," *Washington Post*, 4 July 1997, 20(A).

[49] Frazier, "Prince George's School Board Votes to End Busing," *Washington Post*, 25 October 1997, 7(H).

[50] Dr. Louise Waynant, Deputy Superintendent of Schools for Prince George's County, confirmed in April 1998 that two studies, which were adjusted for poverty, showed mixed results. However, the *Milliken II*

Most such enhanced educational programs employed by school systems throughout the country had failed to produce higher achievement levels. Some *Milliken II* schools in Prince George's County made initial gains, but by the late 1990s, they were stagnating. Some observers attributed the lack of gains to *insufficient* funding; that is, in order to make gains, classroom sizes would have had to be reduced *significantly*[51] and much more fundamental changes would be required to counter the deleterious effects of poverty, inexperienced teachers, high student mobility, high crime rates, and poor school leadership that plagued the schools and neighborhoods in high poverty areas.

Apologists of the *Milliken II* schools argued that test scores would have been lower without those funds. However, desegregation expert Gary Orfield and other observers pointed to the lack of accountability as the primary explanation for little or no progress in *Milliken II* schools or other compensatory programs. Typically, little evaluation was required in recipient schools. Superintendent Clark pointed out that extra funding had never been contingent upon improved test scores. The purpose of *Milliken II* schools was merely to ensure that needy students received adequate funding, he claimed. In a surprisingly candid statement that evoked images of an entrenched bureaucrat, rather than the visionary who spoke of accountability when he assumed the position in 1995, Superintendent Clark declared, "There was nothing ever talked about regarding the quality of anything." Nevertheless, Clark said that by April 1998, the district would have completed a plan to establish new academic goals for the *Milliken II* schools.[52]

While Superintendent Clark may have been correct in asserting that compensatory funds did not come with *explicit* accountability requirements, given the *Brown* mandate of offering children an equal educational opportunity, and the *Milliken II* mandate of restoring victims to the educational level they likely would have attained

---

schools ranked below the others in achievement levels. Analysis indicated that three of the factors contributing to the lower scores in these schools were lower teacher experience, lower levels of teacher education, and high teacher turnover (telephone interview by author, 7 April 1998).

[51] Research shows that reducing classroom sizes to fifteen can make a significant difference, whereas in Prince George's *Milliken II* schools, the PTR (pupil-teacher ratio) was reduced to about twenty-four.

[52] Lisa Frazier and Michael D. Shear, "Extra Money Failed to Raise Scores in twenty-one County Schools," *Washington Post*, 26 October 1997, 1(A).

without segregation, the unmistakable *implicit* goal was improved achievement. Clearly giving school systems more money did not render victims of discrimination whole. However the nebulous concept of accountability was not something the courts were capable of overseeing effectively, particularly given the difficulty of separating race from poverty and other socioeconomic factors when addressing the achievement gap.

Gary Orfield stressed the "overwhelming odds" that challenged school districts with high poverty rates. "Schools that are in the concentrated poverty areas require radical reform, and people should realize that just spending more money is not likely to make any difference." The percentage of poor students in Prince George's County had increased in the previous two decades, and in 1997, about 44 percent of the district's 125,000 students qualified for free or subsidized lunches. At *Milliken II* schools, nearly two-thirds of the students qualified for the lunch program.[53]

On November 18, 1997, the trial regarding the resolution of the Prince George's County desegregation case began with Superintendent Clark testifying that changing demographics had rendered further desegregation within the district impossible. [54] The board of education wanted Judge Messitte to lift the busing order but continue to oversee the district and order the implementation of its $500 million plan to return to neighborhood schools. Attorneys for the county argued that the vestiges of prior discrimination had been eliminated from the district, that the county had prioritized school funding, and that the court's supervision should therefore end. The NAACP sought the court's continued oversight while the district addressed academic shortcomings and construction of new schools.[55]

Few observers attended the four-week trial; most of those in the courtroom were attorneys, school system administrators, and witnesses. Russell Adams, Chair of the Afro-American Studies Department at Howard University noted that major changes had taken place in the political landscape of Prince George's County in the previous twenty

---

[53] Ibid.

[54] William Clark, a demographer from the University of California Los Angeles testified at the trial that the number of white students in the district had dropped from 120,000 in 1970 to 20,000 in 1996 (Frazier, 28 November 1997, 3(D)).

[55] Lisa Frazier and Robert E. Pierre, "Schools Did All They Could, Superintendent Testifies," *Washington Post*, 19 November 1997, 1(B).

years, and black parents no longer felt that they were being discriminated against by a white dominated power structure.[56]   Dr. Alvin Thorton, Chairman of the Board of Education, agreed that the stakes were not perceived to be as high in 1997.   He observed, "In 1972 and 1985, everyone's eyes and ears were fastened on what Kaufman would say.   People were rallying.   City councils were bringing in their own experts.   The difference now is that the perceived consequence of a decision is not significant in the minds of most people."[57]

When the trial ended on December 19, 1997, Judge Messitte promised he would decide by June 1 whether he would end the order requiring busing to achieve racial integration.   In the meantime, he urged the parties to the suit to continue trying to work out a settlement before then.   In early March, the parties reached a tentative agreement that called for phasing out mandatory busing for desegregation while building as many as sixteen new schools and renovating others to accommodate students near their homes.   The plan called for the state's making an exception to its funding formula that required counties to pay at least 60 percent of school construction costs.   A week later, Judge Messitte telephoned attorneys for the three parties to the suit and indicated that he approved the proposed settlement agreement.[58]

The following week, Governor Glendening met with the three parties to the suit and promised that the state would pay 60 percent of the plan's school construction costs.   Traditionally, the state did not pay for such construction related expenses as architecture, engineering, and planning and permit fees, but Glendening agreed that it would do so in this case.   The governor and two other members of the state Board of Public Works could approve the funding formula.   However legislative approval was needed for several measures that would enable the county to meet its financial obligations under the plan.[59]

Following eight months of negotiations, on March 19, 1998, the parties reached a final agreement that would end busing for desegregation and implement the neighborhood schools plan.

---

[56] Frazier, "Debate on Busing Lacks Passion," *Washington Post*, 28 November 1997, 3(D).

[57] Ibid.

[58] DeNeen L. Brown and Jackie Spinner, "Judge Backs Pact to End Desegregation Lawsuit," *Washington Post*, 13 March 1998, 8(B).

[59] DeNeen L. Brown and Robert E. Pierre, "Md. Agrees to Terms in Pr. George's Busing Suit," *Washington Post*, 19 March 1998, 1(A).

Implementation would begin in the fall of 1998 and would be phased in over six years, by which time sixteen new schools were to be constructed. Governor Glendening's promise to seek $300 million over four years for the district, including $35 million per year for new school construction, induced the NAACP to accept the accord. The agreement called for closing the achievement gap between black and non-black students and gave the NAACP a role in monitoring performance. It required maintaining the magnet programs and providing extra resources in overwhelmingly black schools.[60]

The day after the historic agreement was reached, Superintendent Clark announced that strict new accountability measures would be put into place to improve student performance. These included expanding the Reading Recovery program that targeted first graders who were reading below grade level, and improving other intervention programs. The district would also consider expanding its summer school program and extending the school day for some students. Clark said that if the school system did not make dramatic improvements within the following three years, some top-level officials, including himself, could lose their jobs. Board of education Chairman Alvin Thorton concurred that the board would hold the superintendent accountable for improving academic performance in the schools and for dismissing poorly performing principals and administrators.[61]

Following two weeks of heated debate, the Maryland General Assembly approved a $140 million school construction plan for Prince George's County that would likely speed settlement of the desegregation case. The Senate amended the bill to withhold the funds if the parties to the lawsuit backed out of the settlement. A majority of the General Assembly had rejected the proposal for the state to pay construction costs for the architecture and planning fees. Hence, the funding package was expected to pay for only ten of the sixteen schools needed by the district.[62]

Full funding for the school construction plan had not been obtained, but settlement of the long standing desegregation suit in Prince George's County appeared imminent. The busing plan under

---

[60] Frazier, Final Accord Reached on Ending Pr. George's Busing,"
Washington Post, 20 March 1998, 1(C).
[61] Brown, "Schools Accord Pushes Changes," *Washington Post,* 21 March 1998, 1(B).
[62] Pierre, "Pr. George's School Money Okayed," *Washington Post,* 14 April 1998, 1(B).

which the district had been operating had long outlived its usefulness, and the district had technically been complying with the court orders for some time. The advisory panel appointed by Judge Messitte had concluded that the district had done what it could to desegregate and end discriminatory practices.

The district had technically met the requirements of the court, yet poor achievement levels and dwindling public confidence in the school system attested to the judicial system's inability to force school systems to provide the educational opportunity promised in *Brown*. School system administrators blamed poor student performance on insufficient funding and increasing poverty levels within the district, but others, including staff members, parents, community leaders, and education experts, pointed to poor management and faulty decision making. Though the district operated numerous impressive sounding special educational programs, it projected no cohesive overall plan that would promise to improve achievement. Following three reviews by a panel of national education experts, Maryland State Superintendent of Schools Nancy S. Grasmick, and a legislative task force, Grasmick told the legislature, "Prince George's County Public Schools has persistently failed to define any outcomes upon which its various programs may be assessed, or to evaluate those programs."[63]

These were not weaknesses that the judicial system could remedy. Resolution of such fundamental problems required energy, commitment, and determination on the part of the public. No court could eradicate bureaucratic malaise or public complacence or indifference. Courts could order remedial programs, but they could not imbue school district officials with the determination to make the programs work. Indeed, some administrators seemed to claim that court ordered compensatory programs conferred no other obligation than to spend the funds. Thus, while the court would likely soon determine that Prince George's County Public Schools had complied in good faith with the court orders and had done what it could to eliminate the vestiges of prior discrimination, it could hardly be claimed that the children of Prince George's County were receiving an education that would prepare them for success in life.

In 1988, *Washington Post* columnist William Raspberry reflected on the years of court supervision followed by an impending return to

---

[63]Eric Lipton, "Building Better Schools," *Washington Post*, 21 June 1998, 1(A).

neighborhood schools, "In a nutshell: Twenty-five years of often-bitter warfare has ended with little to show for it, either in racial integration or in academic performance."[64]

Conclusion

At the end of the twentieth century, Prince George's County's school system, like many others throughout the country was at a crossroads. Having met the court's requirements for desegregation and ending discrimination, it would now be directly responsible only to the community and to the state. Some indicators suggested that the population of Prince George's County would be more prepared to demand accountability from the school system, especially in terms of the educational service accorded minority children. Prince George's County was one of the nation's most prosperous predominantly black suburbs. Furthermore, whereas in the early 1970s whites filled most official posts, in the late 1990s, Prince George's County had a black county executive, a black school board chairman, a black superintendent of schools, and many other positions of influence were held by blacks. Thus blacks were in a better position to advocate for their children's education.

Yet, because of declining public confidence in the school system, more middle-class black parents were choosing to place their children in private schools. As criticism of the school district grew, some elected officials and school administrators suggested that middle-class black parents were not doing enough to force county officials to provide a high quality school system. Linda L. Waples, an African-American principal at Glassmanor Elementary School declared,

> I blame our people--black middle-class people. We are not doing it, not showing the amount of involvement. Too much of the time, we as a people are reactive--angry at maybe how a teacher treats our child--but not proactive when it comes to things like joining the school PTA. And it is an approach that has gotten us into trouble.[65]

---

[64] William Raspberry, "School Reforms to Nowhere," *Washington Post,* 27 March 1998, 25(A).
[65] Eric Lipton and Lisa Frazier, "Affluent parents Seek Wealth of Solutions," *Washington Post*, 24 June 1998, 1(A).

Samuel H. Dean, president of the Lake Arbor Civic Association, in the most affluent area of Prince George's County, echoed Waples' concern. "The school system, and the community at large, is failing our children. It is absolutely unacceptable. The community must demand better and expect more."[66]

The school system had made progress in the previous few years, in terms of strengthening the curriculum, eliminating low level tracking in math, science, English, and social studies. Also, board of education policy had been amended to include Algebra I and Geometry as graduation requirements. These steps were part of the school district's effort to address the disproportionate placement of minorities in low-level classes and the less than rigorous graduation requirements that left many graduates unprepared for the work force.

Superintendent Clark, board of education members, county leaders, and state legislators were all pledging that the school system and individual administrators and staff members would be held to greater standards of accountability. However, without grassroots support and pressure from parents and community members, such pledges would likely remain unfulfilled promises, just as the court order, the *Milliken II* schools, and the plethora of impressive sounding special programs had. Moreover, the future likely held even greater challenges for the district, whose population was rapidly increasing and flooding the severely overcrowded school system. The school construction funding provided by the state would allow for only ten additional schools, rather than the sixteen needed, and the tax cap, which county voters had repeatedly refused to lift, limited the county's ability to raise construction funds. Thus, overcrowding was likely to worsen. Furthermore, the gap between the rich and the poor was widening. The median income was rising, while the number of impoverished residents was also increasing, and poverty was a recognized impediment to achievement in school. Without a fundamental change in community attitudes, Prince George's County Public Schools appeared headed in the direction of impoverished inner city school systems, rather than the quality school systems characteristic of upwardly mobile suburbia.

The following case study of San Diego, California demonstrates some of the same limitations of the judicial system in rendering school systems accountable that have been seen in Wilmington and Prince

---

[66] Ibid.

George's County. Despite years of court supervision and relatively generous funding of schools, significant disparities in achievement existed among racial groups, and many community members complained of an unresponsive school system bureaucracy that continued to limit the achievement of minority children.

Epilogue

In the spring of 2002, Prince George's County school system was in turmoil, with the Board of Education threatening to fire Superintendent Iris Metts and the state legislature, clearly sympathizing with Metts, considering a bill to reconstruct Prince George's County Board of Education. The proposal would leave the school board with five elected members and four members appointed by the governor and the county executive. The bill also would create a chief financial officer for the school district.[67]

The upheaval followed nearly three years of tumultuous events following Superintendent Metts' taking the helm in July 1999. Within weeks of her arrival, Metts had made several controversial moves, including replacing the personnel director, placing a freeze on central office hiring, reassigning some experienced principals, and ordering an end to the hiring of uncertified teachers. She quickly developed a reputation for making unilateral decisions, rather than consulting with school board members, union officials, etc. Yet several of her actions were clearly aimed at accountability and turning around the troubled school district. In September 1999 she suggested evaluating teachers based on student scores on standardized tests. In June 2000, she demoted several principals in low performing schools. In September of 2000 she introduced a plan to send failing students to summer or weekend classes. Yet test scores did not improve under Metts' leadership. In January 2001 four Prince George's County schools were added to the state's take-over watch list, while one was removed, raising the list's total to fifteen schools. In May 2001 there was a glimmer of hope when county elementary schools realized their highest gains ever on the Comprehensive Test of Basic Skills. Thirrty-four percent matched or beat the national average, up from 21 percent the previous year. Metts was credited with the gains. However, in January

---

[67] Nancy Trejos, "Md. Panel Delays Pr. George's Bill on School Board," *Washington Post Online* (washingtonpost.com) 21 March 2002.

of 2002, the Maryland School Performance Assessment Program (MSPAP) scores registered a drop for Prince George's County and throughout the state. Only 28.3 percent of Prince George's County students passed the exams. Metts was blamed for the poor showing. Five county schools were added to the take-over watch list, bringing the number of Prince George's County schools on the list to twenty.[68]

Thus, the effects of poverty, public ambivalence, bureaucratic intransigence, and controversy between and among the superintendent and school board members continued to plague the public school system of Prince George's County. While the superintendent promised to produce results, her actions taken to hold building administrators and teachers accountable met with strong resistance from school system employees and unions representing them. The school board sought leadership from the superintendent, but her decisive actions led to bickering among school board members and charges that she was insufficiently collaborative. Chronically low achievement levels and the quarrelsome political climate in the district provided little reason for optimism that the school system would offer students a significantly improved learning opportunity anytime in the near future.

---

[68] "A Tumultuous Time in Prince George's," *Washington Post Online* (washingtonpost.com) 3 February 2002.

CHAPTER 8

Desegregation in San Diego, California

Introduction

The San Diego desegregation case differed from the other three cases in this study in several ways. San Diego was much more racially diverse than the other communities, and this diversity grew substantially over the thirty years from when the case was filed until the school district was released from court supervision in 1996. Secondly, the case never entered the federal court system, but remained in the California state court system. The courts did not find *de jure* segregation in the San Diego case. However, the state supreme court ruled that California's Constitution held school districts accountable for racial segregation *regardless of the cause*. Thus, the finding of racial imbalance and isolation within the district led to the court's call for desegregation. Thirdly, owing to concerns that mandatory desegregation, including busing, would engender strong public opposition and "white flight," the court approved a desegregation plan under which participation was completely voluntary. The program eventually garnered widespread public support and relatively high participation levels, especially by non-white students.

Thirty years following the filing of the desegregation case, however, many schools remained racially isolated, because San Diego itself was segregated. Nonwhites concentrated in the southern, especially southeastern areas of the city, while northern San Diego was overwhelmingly white. Nonwhite children who participated in the ethnic transfer program remained isolated within receiving schools.

Magnet schools in nonwhite neighborhoods attracted some whites, and nonwhite neighborhoods benefited by the enriched curriculum. However, the concept of magnets sparked controversy and resentment, with some minorities bristling at the fact that enhancement of such nonwhite schools was required to attract white children, whereas the schools had previously been deemed satisfactory for minority children. A significant achievement gap between whites and nonwhites persisted, and observers complained that integration (as opposed to desegregation) had never really taken place.

Two decades of court enforced desegregation and enrichment programs had produced neither meaningful desegregation nor a significant reduction in the achievement gap between whites and minorities. Despite a judicial remedy that included educational components, the quality of education in racially isolated schools suffered, as evidenced by lower test scores. Achievement levels among minorities who transferred to "white" schools remained lower as well. Various explanations for the persistent achievement gap included low expectations on the part of teachers, belief in stereotypes, segregation within receiving schools in the case of transfer students, lack of commitment on the part of the school district, and insufficient parental support.

These conditions and their results, unacceptably low achievement by minority children, belied the notion that courts could create quality public school systems. Beyond eradicating purposeful dual school systems, the courts had not been able to assure disadvantaged children equal educational opportunities. Courts could not install school boards, administrators, and teachers who were equally committed to the quality of education in minority areas. Only communities themselves could insure that children of all ethnicities and backgrounds were offered an equal opportunity to achieve and to prepare themselves for self-sufficiency as adults. Without pressure from parents and other community members, school boards, administrators, and teachers could remain unresponsive to the needs of disadvantaged children, and their achievement levels would reflect this indifference.

A Growing Mosaic

In the 1960s, San Diego, following the trend in the Sun Belt, was growing in size. Its population was becoming increasingly diverse as well. The San Diego City Schools never had an official racial segregation policy. However, owing to segregated housing patterns, many schools were racially identifiable. Because the United States Supreme Court distinguished between *de jure* and *de facto* racial segregation in public schools and held only the former unconstitutional, San Diego, like many other school districts in California and elsewhere in the nation, took no action to reduce racial isolation or segregation in its schools.

In 1965, the California Supreme Court issued a ruling based on the state Constitution that eventually would mandate a policy of racial integration in public schools that was more extensive than that laid down by the U.S. Supreme Court. The California Supreme Court held in *Jackson v. Pasadena* (1965) that racial segregation in schools deprived minority children of an equal opportunity to education and that it denied them the equal protection of the laws and violated due process. The Court further held that California school boards had a constitutional obligation to take "reasonably feasible steps to alleviate school segregation regardless of its cause." The ruling sparked widespread protest and left appellate court judges, educational experts, and legal experts wondering exactly what the court demanded.[1]

That same year, the Board of Education of San Diego Unified Schools created a Citizens Committee on Equal Educational Opportunity to study the impact of segregation on district school children and to "diligently and conscientiously seek facts on which educationally sound policies can be formulated to assure all children of an equal opportunity to acquire an education which will enable each child to achieve his maximum potential." A superior court judge, Byron F. Lindsley, chaired the committee, and Larry D. Carlin, a schoolteacher, served as its secretary. The committee consisted of members from all parts of the city and many occupations, and it included Caucasians, Hispanics, and African-Americans.[2] The committee held public hearings to gather data regarding the effects of racial and ethnic imbalance on San Diego's school children. It estimated that two thousand people attended the meetings, seventy-two of whom testified. The committee also consulted with educators and other authorities in the community, with similarly charged committees in other communities, and with available research in the field

---

[1] Michael Scott-Blair, "Welsh Order Only Beginning of Long Road," *San Diego Union*, 10 March 1977, 5(A).
[2] *Report of the Citizens Committee on Equal Educational Opportunities to the Board of Education, San Diego City Schools*, by Byron R. Lindsley, Chairman (San Diego: Board of Education of the City of San Diego, 1966), 1-2.

of school segregation and desegregation.[3]   In August 1966, the committee submitted its recommendations, commonly called *The Lindsley Report*, to the board of education.

The committee found "substantial" racial imbalance in the city's schools and reported that "too many" of the schools were "most seriously imbalanced;" that is, they were over 75 percent minority.   The district was approximately 10 percent black and 10 percent Hispanic at the time. Of the district's 114 elementary schools, 82 had less than 2 percent African-American enrollments, and only eleven fell within the "racially balanced" range, designated by the committee as 2.1 to 15 percent minority.   Though Hispanic children were dispersed more evenly throughout the district than African-Americans, they tended to be in attendance zones with a disproportionately high African-American enrollment and were concentrated in the southeast and Logan Heights areas. Furthermore, racial imbalance was increasing in the district.[4]

The committee declared that racial imbalance in the district's schools was detrimental to the education of all school children.   It urged the district to take affirmative action to reduce racial imbalance in the schools, including redrawing attendance zones, clustering schools in "education parks" where facilities could be shared, revising school site selections to enhance integration, encouraging voluntary transfers that would improve the racial balance of schools, ending optional transfer programs that increased racial isolation, and recruiting minority teachers and other personnel.[5]   The school district failed to implement any of the measures that would have resulted in some integration.[6] "They dragged their feet," recalled Chairman Lindsley.   Once the committee had submitted its report, its task was complete; neither the school board nor the administration was answerable to the committee.[7]

Some members of the public, including Larry Carlin, who were frustrated by the Board's inaction, formed a group called the Interorganizational Council for School Integration to pressure the board. In December 1967, still feeling that the board had made insufficient effort

[3] Ibid., 5-6.
[4] Ibid., 15-17.
[5] Ibid., 119-125.
[6] Shuford Swift, memo to author 20 May 1996; and Byron Lindsley, telephone interview by author, 19 August 1996.
[7]Byron F. Lindsley, retired judge and chairman of the Citizens Committee on Equal Educational Opportunities, telephone interview by author 19 August 1996.

to integrate the public schools, Larry Carlin and nine other parents filed a class action suit on behalf of their children, alleging that the schools were segregated in violation of the Equal Protection Clause of the Fourteenth Amendment of the United States Constitution and Article I of the California Constitution.[8]

Inspired by Civil Rights Era idealism, Larry and Kay Carlin eagerly placed their five-year old daughter Kari's name on the complaint. "We didn't know if anything was going to come of it. We just knew it was the right thing to do," reflected Kay Carlin twenty-five years later. This idealism was not well received within the school district. Larry Carlin was so ostracized that he quit teaching for a few years.[9] Cynics called the plaintiffs publicity-seeking bleeding heart liberals. Others appeared ambivalent.

The Reverend George Walker Smith, president of the San Diego Board of Education in 1967, claimed that San Diego's black community was not particularly concerned with racial integration. Irma Castro, former president of the local Chicano Federation recalled, "There was a division in the Chicano community. There were some who wanted their children to stay nearby and others who were willing to give that up to get their kids access to other programs." The ACLU argued the case, drawing support from the San Diego Urban League.[10]

After Carlin filed the suit in 1967, black and Hispanic students filed a class action suit against the Los Angeles school district, alleging that the 648,000 pupil school district was in violation of the California State Constitution for not taking affirmative action to desegregate the highly segregated school district. A class action desegregation suit was brought against the San Bernardino School District at about the same time. Because the Los Angeles and San Diego cases were very similar, the parties in *Carlin* agreed to postpone a trial pending the resolution of the Los Angeles and San Bernardino cases. The California Supreme Court ruled in June 1976 in both cases, clarifying its position in *Pasadena*, and holding that indeed, school districts were required to desegregate, regardless of the cause of the racial isolation.

---

[8] Larry Weiss, "Summary of Carlin v. Board of Education" (San Diego: San Diego City Schools, 185), 1 unpublished.
[9] Maura Reynolds, "Path to school integration has been rocky, winding," *San Diego Union*, 3 December 1992, 1 (A).
[10] Ibid, 13(A).

The Los Angeles Decision

The trial court found in the Los Angeles case that a substantial portion of the district's schools were segregated; that is, they had student populations of at least 90 percent minority or at least 90 percent white. The district-wide proportion of white to minority was 50-50. The Los Angeles Board of Education argued that the segregation within the school system was *de facto*, rather than *de jure*, and that the district was neither responsible for its occurrence nor for its elimination. Attorneys for the board of education argued that the state Supreme Court's statement in *Pasadena* that school districts were responsible for remedying *de facto* segregation was *mere dictum* and not central to the holding. Furthermore, argued the school district, it was not convinced that educational value of a desegregation plan would outweigh the financial costs.[11]

The trial court found that the board of education knowingly promoted racial and ethnic segregation through its neighborhood school policy, its site selections, its school attendance zones, its transportation policies and its use of transfers. The court found that the Board of Education had taken no actions to develop a plan or methods to promote racial balance in its schools, nor was it likely to do so unless it was so directed by a court.[12]

The state court of appeals reversed, holding that none of the trial court's findings of fact proved that the board intentionally discriminated against minority students by willfully promoting racial segregation in the schools. However, he state Supreme Court reversed the appellate court's ruling in *Crawford*, holding that the trial court's findings that the school district was segregated and that the school board had failed to undertake reasonably feasible steps to alleviate the segregation were sufficient cause for the trial court's ordering the district to implement a desegregation plan. Moreover, observed the Court, the trial court found that several steps taken by the school district had contributed to the segregation within the district.[13]

The Court conceded that its pronouncement regarding *de facto* segregation had not been central to *Jackson v. Pasadena*, in that the trial

---

[11]Crawford v. Board of Education of City of Los Angeles, Sup., 120 Cal. Rptr. 334, 335 (1975).

[12] Ibid., 338-39.

[13]Crawford v. Board of Education of City of Los Angeles, Sup., 130 Cal. Rptr. 724, 728 (1976).

court found *de jure* segregation in that case, but it noted that a series of subsequent cases "demonstrate(d) beyond dispute that the principles articulated (in) *Jackson* had been accepted as established constitutional law in this state." The Court elaborated:

> Wherever the origins or causes of school segregation may lie, we do not doubt that, under traditional constitutional doctrine, local school boards are so "significantly involved" in the control, maintenance and ongoing supervision of their school systems as to render any existing school segregation "state action" under our state constitutional equal protection clause. . . . Given the school board's pervasive control over and continuing responsibility for both the daily decisions and the long range plans which in fact determine the racial and ethnic attendance pattern of its district's schools, past authorities demonstrate that the state cannot escape constitutional responsibility for the segregated condition of the public schools.[14]

The Court held that in light of the detrimental effects of racial segregation in schools on minority children and California school boards' plenary authority over school governance, they were not "constitutionally free to adopt any facially neutral policy [they chose], oblivious to such policy's actual differential impact on the minority children . . .".[15] *Crawford* defined a segregated school setting as one in which "the minority student enrollment is so disproportionate as realistically to isolate minority students from other students and thus deprive minority students of an integrated educational experience."[16]

The Court noted that it previously had relied heavily on a study by the U.S. Commission on Civil Rights which found that the harm endured by minority children did not depend on whether segregation was *de facto* or *de jure*. The presence of racial isolation, rather than its legal cause, produced the unequal education.

> Given the fundamental importance of education, particularly to minority children, and the distinctive racial harm traditionally inflicted by segregated education, a school board bears an

---

[14] Ibid., 732.
[15] Ibid., 734.
[16] Ibid., 739.

obligation, under article 1, section 7, subdivision (a) of the California Constitution, mandating the equal protection of the laws, to attempt to alleviate segregated education and its harmful consequences, even if such segregation results from the application of a facially neutral state policy.[17]

The Court found fault with the trial court's language suggesting that a *racial balance* or specific mix was required. The Court held "rather, the constitutional evil inheres in the existence of *segregated* schools. It is the elimination of such segregation and the harms inflicted by such segregation that is the ultimate constitutional objective."[18]   Thus, the Court directed the trial court to refrain from requiring a specific racial mix, but upheld its decision to direct the Los Angeles Board of Education to prepare and implement a desegregation plan.

In attempting to alleviate the harmful effects of segregation in education, the California Supreme Court did not differentiate between the effects of a *dual school system,* which the United States Supreme Court had found harmful in *Brown v. Board of Education*, and the effects of racial isolation incident to community segregation. In so doing, the Court, like the U.S. Commission on Civil Rights, failed to recognize that it was not the racial isolation *per se* in the latter case that was harmful, but the indifference of school boards and administrators to the needs of socioeconomically disadvantaged children whose parents were less likely to vote and/or pressure the school system on behalf of their children. The educational needs of white children were much more likely to be met than those of minority children, because school boards, administrators, and teachers responded more readily to the demands of parents who were knowledgeable of the school system, and such assertive and efficacious parents were more often than not white.[19] This inequity would persist regardless of whether minorities attended school with

---

[17] Ibid., 735

[18] Ibid., 724

[19]Numerous people interviewed in San Diego, Wilmington, and in Cleveland noted the tendency of minority parents to be less comfortable in their children's schools and less knowledgeable of the procedures to follow if one had a grievance. For instance, Ebrima Ellzy-Sey of Wilmington noted many African-American parents had had negative experiences in school themselves, and they were disinclined to participate actively in their children's education, especially in terms of visiting the schools. Rashidah Abdulhaaq of Cleveland also noted that minority parents tended to be less engaged in their children's schools than were white parents.

whites, and it would persist where there was no viable remedy for racial isolation. It would persist until communities demanded accountability of teachers, administrators, and school boards on behalf of *all* school children.

Following the announcement of the decision in *Crawford*, plaintiffs reactivated *Carlin*, and it went to trial five months later, in November 1976. The California Supreme Court's ruling in *Crawford* destroyed the San Diego school district's defense that the segregation in the district resulted from residential housing patterns, rather than official policy, and that the district therefore was not constitutionally obligated to eliminate the segregation. School officials agreed that as a result of *Crawford*, their strategy would shift to trying to convince the court that it was making sufficient effort to reduce the segregation within the school system.[20]

The San Diego Trial

Nationally recognized desegregation experts, school district officials, and community activists testified at the lengthy trial. The plaintiffs and their witnesses stressed the inadequacies of the school district's desegregation efforts. The school district and many community activists emphasized their concerns that a mandatory desegregation plan, especially one requiring extensive busing, would be disruptive to the community and counterproductive, in that it likely would lead to "white flight" and result in higher levels of segregation. Curiously, public interest in the trial appeared to be quite low, despite the potential result of a mandatory busing plan that would affect virtually every family with school aged children in the district. Few people, besides members of the press, attended the trial. However, with the announcement of the March 1977 decision charging the district with devising a feasible and viable desegregation plan, public apathy gave way to heavy opposition to mandatory desegregation and widespread concern about the effects the final order would have on individual school children.

Throughout the trial, the plaintiffs argued that the school district had failed "to take reasonably feasible steps to alleviate school segregation regardless of its cause," which was the standard set in the Los Angeles and San Bernardino cases. Larry Carlin accused the board of education of

---

[20] Scott-Blair, "L.A. Ruling Felt Here By Schools," *San Diego Union*, 30 June 1976, 1(A).

neglecting to follow through on its promise to desegregate the school system. He said the school district had failed to correct the educational deprivation of students attending segregated schools and had lost its will to desegregate.   Carlin noted that in 1965 the Board had said it would "eliminate" segregation, whereas in 1967, it had said it merely would "retard" segregation. He rebuked the board for failing to act on the numerous suggestions made by the Committee on Equal Educational Opportunity that would have reduced segregation.[21]

The plaintiffs argued that 33 of the district's 121 schools were segregated and seven schools were "tipping;" that is, they had reached the 50 percent minority ratio, at which it was very difficult to attract non-minorities to the public schools, and they therefore steadily became more segregated. The plaintiffs charged that the district had been "intractable, recalcitrant and stubbornly opposed to desegregation," and they argued that only a mandatory desegregation plan that transferred minority and majority children from and to segregated schools would free minority children from their isolation.[22]

The school board countered that it had taken "reasonably feasible steps" to remedy the segregation in the district, that it had made substantial progress, and that it had demonstrated a commitment to doing more to end racial segregation in schools.[23] Superintendent of Schools Thomas Goodman testified that he felt that magnet and alternative schools could provide a workable voluntary desegregation program. The magnet schools would attract white students into minority neighborhood schools, and the alternative schools offered individualized programs for students who had rejected traditional schools. Goodman conceded that the number of students in segregated school settings had increased since he had taken the helm five years before, but he said that the problem lay with segregated housing patterns, not with school policies.[24]

San Diego Mayor Pete Wilson testified that he firmly opposed mandatory busing to desegregate San Diego's schools. In his words, it would "undermine and destroy" San Diego's policy for long-term growth management. Wilson said that the city had spent $1 million on plans to

---

[21] Scott-Blair, "Carlin Says City Schools Fail to Keep Integration Promise," *San Diego Union*, 5 November 1976, 3(B).

[22] Carlin v. Board of Education, No. 303800, slip op. at 3 (San Diego Super. Ct., 9 March 1977).

[23] Ibid.

[24] "Goodman Testifies at Trial, Suggests Desegregation Solutions," *San Diego Union*, 3 December 1976, 9(B).

foster an improved economic and racial mix within the central city. He explained that the city's managed growth plan made it more difficult to build outside the city and more attractive to build in the inner city. He claimed that this policy, combined with the district's voluntary transfer plan, would be sufficient to achieve desegregation within the schools. Mayor Wilson also predicted that forced busing would cause whites to flee to the suburbs. Outside the court, Wilson expressed resentment against the California Supreme Court, because it had gone beyond the United States Supreme Court in holding school districts responsible for desegregating when the segregated conditions resulted from forces other than state or school district policies.[25]

Desegregation expert David Armor predicted that mandatory busing for desegregation would drive white families from San Diego Unified School District to surrounding districts so fast that within five years, minority students would outnumber whites. Without busing, San Diego would experience a gradual decrease in the percentage of white students, which would result in San Diego's becoming a predominantly minority district by 1990. However, Armor predicted that within a year of a mandatory busing order, eleven thousand of the district's eighty thousand white students would leave the district, with another five thousand leaving the following year.[26]

Armor based his projections on studies of nineteen other U.S. cities with similar characteristics to San Diego which had been operating under court-ordered desegregation plans with busing. The studies included Denver, Boston, Dallas, Houston, Oklahoma City, and Nashville. These and the thirteen other cities studied resembled San Diego in that they were 20 to 50 percent minority before the busing orders, and they were surrounded by available alternative school districts to which families could move without giving up their employment or the general living area. Before the busing orders, these cities, like San Diego, had been losing their white student populations at a rate of 2.4 percent a year. In the two years following the mandatory busing orders, the rate of loss jumped to 10.2 percent. Armor concluded that mandatory busing led to such a high rate of white flight that the court orders became

---

[25] Scott-Blair, "School Chief Hits Integration Move," *San Diego Union*, 14 December 1976, 1(B).
[26] Scott-Blair, "Study Shows Whites Move From Busing," *San Diego Union*, 5 January 1977, 1(B).

counterproductive. He also noted that San Francisco and Pasadena had already passed the 50 percent minority mark, or the "tipping point."[27]

Oddly, though the public reportedly strongly opposed a mandatory busing plan, the trial itself appeared to spark little public interest in San Diego. Desegregation expert David Armor noted that this was not a "grass-roots" case and minority interest had been low since the case was filed. The *Carlin* case differed from most desegregation cases in that it was not initiated by the NAACP with intense local minority support. The ACLU, the organization backing this suit, was an "elite" group that oftentimes pursued its causes for plaintiffs without significant local backing. The two-month trial attracted few observers, despite the fact that the outcome could have such a profound impact on the community. Indeed, a "light-hearted" atmosphere seemed to surround the trial; yet, "[p]robably no other single event [could] have a greater impact on the life of a community than a school desegregation order," said Armor. He suggested that a ruling requiring busing would certainly spark public interest and concern, because at that point it clearly would affect individual children.[28]

As Judge Louis Welsh pondered his decision, Clarence Pendleton, Jr., executive director of the Urban League of San Diego, castigated local leaders for their indifference to the problem of segregation in the schools. He accused them of hoping the problem would just "go away." He declared, "In this city we have had no elected official speak out in support of full integration. It is time to look at the quality of our elected leaders on all levels." Pendleton also accused the media of unfair, biased, and sometimes "irresponsible" coverage of the trial, and of exaggerating the predictions of white flight and disruptions to the community by a mandatory plan.[29]

Several factors contributed to the apparent indifference of the community leadership observed by Pendleton. Whites, who comprised the vast majority of the population at the time, who were the more powerful constituents, and whose children were being well served by the present system, were understandably complacent. White leaders therefore would have been reluctant to call for unpopular change. Minority leaders may not have felt they had the backing of their constituents, either. As

---

[27] Ibid., 1(B), 4(B).

[28] Michael Scott-Blair, "Carlin Case Indifference is Assailed," *San Diego Union*, 23 January 1(A) and 9(A).

[29] Scott-Blair, "S.D. Leaders Assailed on Integration," *San Diego Union*, 16 February 1977, 1(B) and 4(B).

noted above, the African-American and Hispanic communities were divided over the issue of desegregation. Few parents relished the idea of sending their children on buses to distant and unfamiliar neighborhoods. Furthermore, many minority parents may not have been aware of the discrepancies between "white" and "minority" schools, and of those who were aware, many may not have known how to affect the system. The leadership thus reflected the ambivalent or apathetic views of the public, and this ambivalence and apathy would become a formidable impediment to integration. Judge Lindsley, chairman of the Citizens Committee on Equal Educational Opportunity, whose recommendations for desegregation went unheeded by the school board, said that he believed that the district never would have acted, had the lawsuit not been filed.[30]

Thus, before the decision was rendered, public attitudes seemed to vacillate between indifference to the growing segregation in the schools and opposition to any mandatory remedy. The community leadership failed to take a proactive position, waiting instead for direction from the court. The judge's March 9 memorandum decision brought an abrupt end to the calm, with the unsettling reality of school desegregation in the immediate future.

The San Diego Ruling

Judge Welsh relied heavily on *Crawford* in his memorandum decision of March 9, 1977. He found that eighteen elementary schools, three junior high schools, and two high schools were segregated, by the *Crawford* definition.[31] The court held that the San Diego City Schools had not taken sufficient "reasonable and feasible" steps to reduce the incidence of racial isolation and therefore determined that court supervision of a desegregation plan was necessary.[32]

Chastising Superintendent Goodman for failing to take affirmative action that could have alleviated the segregation in the district, Judge Welsh noted that although the district hired Thomas McJunkins, a black educator, to report to the superintendent with advice regarding

---

[30]Lindsley, *supra* note 2.

[31]*Crawford* defined a segregated school setting as one in which "the minority student enrollment is so disproportionate as realistically to isolate minority students from other students and thus deprive minority students of an integrated educational experience" (Crawford v. Board of Education of City of Los Angeles, *supra* note 5, at 723).

[32]Carlin v. Board of Education, *supra* note 22, at 7.

desegregation, the superintendent had never sought McJunkins' advice. In March 1972, McJunkins and his staff had prepared a report entitled "Desegregation and Integration of Schools," in which they had discussed the law and alternative suggestions for minimizing racial conflict and for increasing integration. Judge Welsh noted that none of the suggestions was adopted or considered seriously, though two of them would have reduced segregation while retaining the neighborhood school concept. In July 1974, at a gathering of citizens urging action to desegregate, the superintendent had proclaimed, "I will do nothing [concerning segregation] until a court tells me I must."[33]

The trial court conceded that the law regarding school districts' responsibilities to desegregate had not been settled and noted that district superintendents received conflicting messages from state education officials, as well as from the state legislature. Factions within the legislature had introduced numerous bills, ranging from a requirement for racial balance in all schools to the prohibition of busing for desegregation. An initiative banning the assignment of school children for purposes of desegregation had passed overwhelmingly, but the Supreme Court had rejected it as unconstitutional. Thus, Judge Welsh expressed some understanding for the board's inertia. The board's and the administration's ambivalence toward desegregation reflected the same public sentiments reflected in these legislative actions. This lack of public support would make it impossible for the court to change fundamentally the delivery of education services in San Diego.

The judge observed that the objective of desegregating San Diego's schools was complicated by conflicting district commitments and financial practicalities as well. For instance, the district operated a large bilingual program for non-English speaking Hispanic students, as mandated by state and national law. Hispanic children were relatively concentrated in certain schools, owing to housing patterns, and this concentration of the children requiring the bilingual program helped reduce operating costs. Dispersing Hispanic children for purposes of desegregation would make an effective bilingual program cost prohibitive. The Office of Civil Rights' requirement that faculty be integrated further complicated the bilingual program, which at the time

---

[33]Ibid., at 9-10.

placed Hispanic teachers where they were most needed, with Hispanic students.[34]

Furthermore, federal and state funds were allocated to schools on a priority basis. Schools received federal funding based on the percentage of students in poverty. State funds were allocated based on educational need, so that those schools with the lowest student achievement levels received the most funds. If disadvantaged children were dispersed throughout the school district, the district would lose much of the funds it received, and the children would be deprived of much needed remedial programs. Considering these and other mixed directives the district was receiving, Judge Welsh tempered his criticism of the board of education and the district. While the district's commitment had been less than satisfactory by current standards, Judge Welsh declared that it was "neither 'recalcitrant' nor 'intractable.'" [35]

Judge Welsh noted that while the district had no aggressive policy to combat segregation, racial *isolation* within the district had declined during the previous decade. By the time the court's opinion was delivered in 1977, San Diego was the second largest school district in California and the tenth largest in the nation. Its student population was 121,423 of which 34 percent was nonwhite. Though racial *imbalance* had increased (the percentage of minority children attending schools that were 50 to 90 percent minority had risen from 11 to 27 percent), the percentage of minority children who attended *racially-isolated* schools (90 to 100 percent minority) had fallen from 41 to 28 percent overall and to 15 percent among secondary students. The percentage of minority students attending imbalanced and isolated schools (50 to 100 percent minority) had fallen from 50 percent in 1966 to 42 percent in 1976, while the percentage of minority students within the school population had increased from 23 to 34 percent. During the same time period, the percentage of white students attending schools that were 90 to 100 percent white had fallen from 67 to 17.6 percent.

Judge Welsh attributed at least some of the improvement to the district's transfer program and to the creation of magnet schools. However, he castigated Superintendent Goodman for his apparent indifference to the recognized segregation within the district in the five months following the *Crawford* holding. He also criticized the school

---

[34] Ibid., 14-15.
[35] Ibid., 16-17.

board for not revising its policy that called for eliminating only *purposeful* segregation in schools.[36]

Quoting from *Crawford*, the judge explained his preference for allowing the district to design its own desegregation plan:

> [R]eliance on the judgment of local school boards in choosing between alternative desegregation strategies holds society's best for the formulation and implementation of desegregation plans which will actually achieve the ultimate constitutional objective of providing minority students with the equal opportunities potentially available from an integrated education.
> The key to judicial deferment to the judgment of a local school board . . . is [the board's] demonstration of its commitment . . . [to desegregation]. Faced with a recalcitrant or intractable school board, a trial court [may formulate and supervise its own plan].[37]

Judge Welsh noted that *Crawford* allowed school districts considerable discretion in designing techniques and programs to alleviate segregation and its detrimental effects. The main requirement was that the methods used be *effective and realistic*. "*Crawford's* dominant message is that school districts must embark on this project by implementing programs that focus on quality results, 'for the attainment of integrated public schools in our state.'"[38]

Thus, Judge Welsh ordered the school district to present a plan "to further alleviate racial segregation in those minority isolated schools identified in the [Memorandum Decision]" by June 13, 1977, and he specified that the plan be at least partially operable by the following fall.[39]

Judge Welsh indicated that he favored a voluntary or at least partially voluntary program, because no violation of the United States Constitution had been found and because a mandatory plan could conflict with the Equal Protection Clause of the Fourteenth Amendment. He noted that the United States Supreme Court had acknowledged several times that the Fourteenth Amendment's Equal Protection Clause protected the parents' right to raise and educate their children as they saw

---

[36] Ibid., 12-13.

[37] Ibid., 8 (quoting from Crawford v. Board of Education of City of Los Angeles) *supra* note 5 at 741.

[38] Ibid., 2.

[39] Ibid., 17.

fit. Thus, California's constitutional requirement for desegregation, regardless of the cause of the segregation, potentially conflicted with the United States Constitution.[40] Judge Welsh also suggested a possible Due Process Clause conflict. He observed that most Hispanic and many black parents objected to busing their children to unfamiliar neighborhoods. These parent groups had not been heard during the proceedings. Forcibly busing their children from their neighborhoods to attend integrated schools could infringe on these parents' rights. Judge Welsh allowed, however, that limited mandatory measures might be required if the desegregation plan were to be effective.[41] He noted other potential problems with an extensive mandatory desegregation plan, such as the trauma that might be experienced by the disproportionate number of lower income children who had severe emotional problems and who benefited at the time from bilingual and compensatory education programs. Such children would risk losing funding for those programs, as well as being uprooted from the culturally familiar and supportive settings of their neighborhood schools.[42]

Judge Welsh also acknowledged the "grave risk" of white flight's undermining the goals of a mandatory desegregation plan.[43] This concern with the possibility of white flight highlighted the constraints that a resistant public would place on the power of the courts to bring about social change. Judge Welsh clearly recognized the constraint of public opinion.

While he adhered strictly to *Crawford's* reiteration of the state constitutional requirement that school districts make reasonable and feasible efforts to desegregate, regardless of the cause of the segregation, Judge Welsh also emphasized the advantages of a voluntary plan. As the Supreme Court had done in *Crawford*, Judge Welsh stressed the importance of delegating the design of the desegregation plan to school district authorities, so that community advice could be sought, and community support for the final plan more likely would be achieved. The onus of fashioning a viable desegregation plan would fall on the school district, and the credibility of the plan would depend on the district's ability to secure community support.

---

[40] Ibid., 18-20.
[41] Ibid., 20-1.
[42] Ibid., 22-23.
[43] Ibid., 23-24.

Reaction to the Decision

Public indifference towards the desegregation challenge ended abruptly with the decision in *Carlin*. Both plaintiffs and defendants claimed limited victories. School district officials were pleased that the court had not required, and in fact had discouraged, a comprehensive mandatory busing plan for desegregation. They felt the judge's words of criticism for the district were "inaccurate and unfair," however. Carlin supporters were pleased that the court had finally acknowledged what they all along had seen -- that many of San Diego's schools were in fact segregated -- and that the district would finally be forced to act. Carlin supporters registered their disappointment, however, that Judge Welsh's ruling did not include stricter guidelines for the district, such as a busing order and firm deadlines for implementation.[44]

Janet Chrispeels, president of the League of Women Voters, which also supported Carlin, expressed regret that Judge Welsh had not included more specific remedies in the order. Attorney Nancy Reardon said she was "extremely disappointed" that the court had not ordered a stronger remedy. The Reverend George Smith, President of the Board of Education, as well as president of the National School Boards Association, strongly disagreed, however. He said that in the past year, as he had traveled in conjunction with his duties as national president, he had observed many failing mandatory desegregation plans and many successful voluntary programs. Immediate past President of the Board of Education Dorothy Edmiston also voiced her relief at the judge's rejection of a broad mandatory busing remedy. She termed Welsh's criticism of the school board's efforts and of Superintendent Goodman's failure to act to alleviate the segregation "harsh and unjustified." Goodman himself termed the judge's comments about his attitude regarding the segregation "grossly inaccurate," but he said he felt the decision was fair. Goodman said that in response to the judge's suggestion, the district would conduct a survey to determine which types of magnet or specialized programs would most likely encourage families to bus their children voluntarily.[45]

In response to the court's decision, county and state education officials complained that the educational system had been saddled with

---

[44] Scott-Blair, "Imbalance Found in 23 Schools," *San Diego Union*, 10 March 1977, 1(A), 4(A).
[45] Ibid., 4(A).

solving a "massive social problem it did not create." However, reactions of those outside the school administration were generally favorable, and people expressed relief that the court did not impose a mandatory busing plan. Charles Thomas, president of the San Diego NAACP appeared generally satisfied with the court's decision, saying that most people, black and white, opposed mandatory busing for desegregation. On the other hand, Thomas voiced some of the exasperation that other blacks and Hispanics had felt regarding the supposed necessity of integration for minorities to achieve. "The social institutions are telling us the same old story that blacks have to be in contact with Anglos to become competent. Our concern is that the board increase the quality of education in ghetto schools."[46] This sentiment would echo increasingly in subsequent years.

A poll commissioned by the board of education in response the court decision[47] showed that 81 percent of parents polled said that they would oppose a mandatory plan calling for two years of mandatory busing to achieve racial desegregation. Of that 81 percent, 52 percent said they would enroll their children in a different district or in private school to avoid such a program. Significant numbers of Hispanics and Asian-Americans were among those opposed to mandatory busing. Only blacks, who comprised 15.6 percent of the student population, supported mandatory busing, and 29 percent said they opposed a plan that would require two years of mandatory participation. Parents registered the strongest opposition to busing into the predominantly minority southeast section of San Diego in order to achieve integration. Even black parents from elsewhere in the city showed the same opposition to having their children bused into southeast San Diego. sixty-nine percent of the parents surveyed said they would oppose busing their children into southeast San Diego for even one semester. This opposition was registered by 72 percent of white parents, 62 percent of Hispanics, 62 percent of Asians, and 50 percent of blacks. There was less opposition to busing to areas outside of southeast San Diego. Almost 60 percent of parents said they would accept one semester of mandatory busing and only 56 percent said they would object to mandatory busing if it were to

---

[46]Carol Olten, "Reaction to Carlin Ruling on S.D. Integration Mixed," *San Diego Union*, 11 March 1977, 1(A).
[47] The poll was conducted by Oscar Kaplan, professor of psychology, San Diego State University.

schools outside of southeast San Diego. The majority of those polled favored integration if it did not require mandatory busing, however.[48]

The poll questioned six segments of the San Diego population -- voters, parents, teachers, classified school district staff, high school students in the eighth and tenth grades and sixth grade students. The vast majority of parents was willing to accept integration. Yet, all racial groups except blacks were generally satisfied with the status quo. These poll results supported indications during the trial that the public was generally indifferent to the segregation in public schools, but that it could accept integration if it were voluntary. The vast majority of the public strongly opposed mandatory busing, especially if it took children into the overwhelmingly nonwhite southeast section of San Diego. The polls also suggested that community members recognized that schools in the southeast area were inferior to those elsewhere in the district, and that support of a voluntary program lay in the fact that no one who did not desire change would be negatively affected.

Shortly after the announcement of the *Carlin* decision, the school district established a seventy-member Citizens Advisory Commission on Racial Integration (CACRI) to investigate options and alternatives for a viable desegregation plan and to gather public input. The school board charged the commission with advising the board and the district on 1) alternate plans for racial desegregation, including "reasonable and feasible steps to "further alleviate racial segregation," 2) how best to garner widespread public support for the plan, 3) how to ensure long term success of the plan, 4) how to stabilize the nineteen schools that were unbalanced but not yet deemed segregated, 5) how to develop programs that would assist students in learning to live and work in integrated environments. An eight member steering committee was formed from the Citizens' Advisory Commission to formulate proposals.[49]

When the first public hearings took place on May 11, thousands of area parents attended the meetings at ten local schools. Commission members who chaired each of the sessions informed the public of the progress made by the commission and listened to community concerns.[50] On May 19 when the steering committee presented its preliminary

---

[48] Scott Blair, "Parents Reject Forced Busing," *San Diego Union*, 20 May 1977, 1(A) and 21(A).

[49] Scott Blair, "School Integration Proposal Fails to Win Approval," *San Diego Union*, 20 May 1977, 1(A).

[50] "Thousands of Parents Attend Intense Integration Sessions," *San Diego Union*, 12 May 1977, 1(A) and 10(A).

proposals to the full Citizens Advisory Commission, the group voted to "receive" but refused to "approve" the steering committee's recommendations. Commission members found the recommendations "too bland and general" and lacking realistically workable solutions. Members asked for specific numbers of students and names of schools to be involved. Voluntary participation was emphasized, but the proposal said "any realistic program" to reduce racial isolation within the district "could not achieve its purpose without some mandatory assignment." Members complained that the proposals were no different from the transfer program under which the district had been operating for several years. They asked for specific target dates, which the court had demanded, and provisions for expansion of the program.[51]

Subsequently, CACRI submitted what members deemed was a workable plan for desegregation to Superintendent Goodman, but he rejected the committee's proposals and formed a new, smaller committee to devise a plan. Janet Chrispeels, Assistant Professor at University of California Santa Barbara in educational administration, was a member of CACRI. Chrispeels felt that the committee was "more of a symbol than it was a real force." Goodman's rejection of CACRI's proposal confirmed her impression that he and the board of education already had an idea for a desegregation plan, and CACRI was established merely to satisfy the court and the public that public opinion was being solicited. The general attitude of the administration was that they had no obligation to desegregate, "and (they) really treated it as a mockery." Following the announcement of the final order, the administration did comply in establishing the magnet schools because "they had to do something. . . . So did they do it as fast as the could have? Probably no. . . . Did they do it with any moral courage or purpose? No."[52]

Katie Klumpp, an activist Caucasian parent with children in the school district who strongly supported integration, spoke with several members of CACRI after the committee was disbanded. She recalled that several members of CACRI were angered by the Superintendent's dismissal of their proposal. Some of these committee members had been "rather conservative," and initially they had resisted proposals that would have treated all students equally. After having arrived at a proposal that

---

[51] Scott-Blair, "School Integration Proposal," 20(A).

[52] Janet Chrispeels, assistant professor at the University of California Santa Barbara and former member of the Citizens Advisory Committee on Racial Integration, telephone interview by author, 2 September 1996.

would do just that, they felt they had been "slapped in the face" when Goodman rejected their efforts.[53]   Thus ended the public input gathering phase of the process. With his hand-picked committee, Superintendent Goodman developed a proposal to submit to the court.

The San Diego Desegregation Plan

The parties returned to court in the summer of 1977 and the district presented its modest voluntary integration plan for the twenty-three racially isolated schools. Judge Welsh reviewed the plan to determine whether the district's proposal was "reasonable and feasible;" that is, whether it could be expected to effect integration. The plan approved by the court for the 1977-78 year included "a vigorous Racial Relations Program," including teachers, staff, parents, and students of all races throughout the district to prepare the students for "harmonious desegregation," and several specialized programs at various schools in the district, including an Inter-cultural Language Program at one elementary school.   Judge Welsh further ordered that all existing magnet schools and the VEEP program be maintained, and that the board of education initiate an evaluation of the entire voluntary desegregation plan, to be approved by the court each subsequent year.   The court directed the Citizens Advisory Commission on Racial Integration to continue assisting the board in implementing and evaluating the desegregation plan.[54]

In August 1977, following Judge Welsh's issuance of the final desegregation order, a coalition of business leaders and organizations formed San Diegans for Quality Education (SDQE), a group dedicated to the lawful and peaceful integration of the public schools. The group's founders, George Mitrovich, president of the City Club of San Diego, Gary Plantz of the San Diego Jaycees, and Charles Reid of the San Diego Community College Board of Trustees, said that they favored voluntary methods of desegregation, but urged the community to obey the direction of the courts.

The group's taking this position engendered strong opposition from the anti-busing group Groundswell, whose leader, Larry Lester, accused

---

[53] Katie Klumpp, parent activist in the San Diego City Schools, telephone interview by author, 31 August 1996.
[54] Final Order for 1977-1978 School Year at 1-3, Carlin v. Board of Education, (San Diego Super. Ct., 8 Aug. 1977) (No. 303800).

SDQE of favoring mandatory busing. Lester said that his group would oppose mandatory busing, even if it were ordered by the court. He said that Groundswell was attempting to effect changes in the state and U.S. constitutions that would prohibit mandatory busing for desegregation. SDQE leaders responded that integration was "a complex sociological issue and solutions (could) only be searched for in those terms." They refused to be coerced into focusing on the issue of mandatory busing.[55]

The school year opened smoothly on September 12, 1977, with widespread harmonious attitudes reported. Four magnet schools comprised the heart of the voluntary integration program the first year. These new magnet programs supplemented already operating model schools and the Voluntary Ethnic-Enrollment Program (VEEP), which transferred minority students to schools where their presence would improve the racial mix. Participation in the special education programs grew from three thousand students the previous year to four thousand in 1977-1978.[56] In 1978, Judge Welsh appointed community members to an Integration Task Force to monitor, analyze, and evaluate minority isolation in the public schools. The judge requested regular reports from the task force. Originally the group focused on five judicial recommendations: 1) raise minority isolated school students' CTBS (Comprehensive Test of Basic Skills) scores in reading, mathematics, and language to the national norm; 2) implement a race/human relations program for school employees; 3) implement race/human relations courses of classroom instruction for all students; 4) monitor the changing demographics in the area; 5) recommend staff reorganization.[57]

Dr. Harold Brown, professor of business administration at San Diego State University served as vice chairman of the task force its first year of operation, the 1979-1980 school year. He was elected chairman the following year. During its first year, the task force concerned itself primarily with ensuring that the Voluntary Ethnic Enrollment students felt comfortable and accepted at their receiving schools. The following summer, Dr. Brown approached Judge Welsh and suggested that what the court and the task force were actually trying to achieve was an *equal educational opportunity* for minority students. Brown met with Judge Welsh several times throughout the summer and "(I) finally convinced the

[55] Scott-Blair, "Debate On Busing Sought," *San Diego Union*, 19 August 1997, 3(B).
[56] Scott-Blair, "Bus Mix-Ups Only Hitch Here As School Integration Starts," *San Diego Union*, 13 September 1977, 1(A) and 4(A).
[57] Weiss, 8-9.

judge that the emphasis of the court's supervision should have been on quality education rather than just desegregation." The fact that the lawsuit as filed and litigated placed the emphasis on desegregation did not deter Judge Welsh. He charged the task force with focusing on quality education. "I consider that one of my greatest achievements," reflected Brown twenty years later."[58]

The task force was directly responsible to the court. The group tried to work with the administration and the board of education, but this was difficult. Judy McDonald, an Integration Task Force member, recalled Superintendent Goodman's resistance to desegregation. "Goodman [was] just panicked that there would be forced busing and so there was huge paranoia. I mean I can remember [he and a board member] would take me to lunch and say *please*, anything that you can do to keep this from going to court order." This attitude by the administration put members of the task force in a very difficult position; McDonald became convinced that the district was remiss in its duties to the children in the isolated schools. She thus found herself at odds with Goodman and with traditional businessmen within the community with whom he was aligned. Public support for desegregation increased over the years, as people's fears of a mandatory program were allayed.[59]

Cynthia Lawrence-Wallace, a retired instructor with the teacher education program at the University of California San Diego and a former monitor with the Integration Task Force, viewed the monitoring process as "very contrived." Monitors met principals who led them on tours of their buildings to see how well integration was taking place. Lawrence-Wallace visited classrooms on her own and was troubled by what she saw. For instance, at one school, all the Hispanic transfer students were held on their buses until the warning bell rang in the morning. She was informed that the practice was designed to reduce the potential for conflict between transfer and resident students. The program was always desegregation, based on numbers, rather than meaningful integration, she claimed.[60]

---

[58]Harold Brown, professor of business administration, San Diego State University and founding member of the Integration Task Force for the San Diego City Schools, telephone interview by author, 21 August 1996.

[59]Judy McDonald, former member of the San Diego Integration Task Force, telephone interview by author, 2 September 1996.

[60]Cynthia Lawrence-Wallace, retired instructor with the Teacher Education Program at the University of California San Diego, telephone interview by author, 23 August 1996.

Lawrence-Wallace, an African-American, noted that she had always been troubled by desegregation, especially busing, primarily for two reasons. First, schools in minority neighborhoods should have been just as attractive as any other school, she declared. They should not have required transformation into magnets solely for the purpose of drawing in white children. Second, she found offensive the notion that it should have been necessary to sit white children next to minority children so that they could learn. Lawrence-Wallace also expressed concern for the disruptive effects on neighborhoods when children (usually minority children, and oftentimes the brightest ones) left the neighborhood to attend school elsewhere. Finally, she reiterated her concern regarding the detrimental effects on transfer students, most of whom were minority students, when they were not well accepted in their new schools. Lawrence-Wallace pointedly disassociated herself from the anti-busing group Groundswell, however, noting that she believed their motives were quite different from hers.[61]

Judge Welsh's commitment to developing a workable desegregation plan that provided quality education would eventually lead to his resignation under a cloud of controversy. In 1980 attorneys in the case discovered that he was holding ex-parte meetings with members of the board of education and other groups. Judge Welsh wanted "a caring teacher in every classroom." His concern with educational, as opposed to mere equity, issues apparently led him to breech judicial procedure in holding the *ex-parte* meetings. Apparently in response to pressure from attorneys on both sides, Judge Welsh suddenly retired.[62] Thus, while Judge Welsh, Harold Brown, Cynthia Lawrence-Wallace, and certainly many others recognized that quality education was the ultimate goal, rather than desegregation, the judicial system was ill equipped to produce such a result. The adversarial relationship between the litigants, the resistance on the part of an administration and entrenched school system bureaucracy to change, and an ambivalent community, all worked against the vision of a quality school system for all of San Diego's children. The court could require that various organizational and programmatic measures be adopted and that certain overt discriminatory practices cease, but it would not be able to rid the system of more subtle inequities, nor

---

[61] Ibid.

[62] Christina Dyer, legal counsel for the San Diego City Schools, telephone interview by author, 3 May 1996.

could it provide the qualitative educational components that would improve achievement.

Judge Franklin Orfield replaced Judge Welsh, and he continued to require annual hearings during which the district's annual integration plans were reviewed. The plaintiffs accused the defendant school district of failing to aggressively combat segregation, claimed it was exaggerating the likelihood of white flight if a mandatory plan were applied, and claimed that segregation was in fact increasing. The school district continued to defend its efforts, contending that it was making reasonable and feasible efforts, that progress was taking place, that a voluntary plan was the only method that the community would accept, and that changing demographics -- the increase in minority population -- rather than recalcitrance on the part of the district, was resulting in increases in minority enrollment in some schools.[63]

Despite the continued officially adversarial relationship, the tenor of the meetings changed soon after the arrival of a new superintendent, Tom Payzant in late 1982. With a new judge, a new superintendent, and new school district counsel, Payzant seized on an opportunity to forge a new relationship. One of the most contentious issues between the parties had been the school district's refusal to comply with the plaintiffs' demands that it provide data on student performance disaggregated by race. Payzant, who had been accustomed to providing disaggregated data in his former position as Superintendent of Oklahoma City Schools, readily agreed to produce the requested information. In this and other ways Payzant attempted to send a signal to the court that he was interested in conciliation.[64]

Payzant sensed that Judge Orfield planned to oversee very carefully the district's efforts to meet the court's goals. Uncomfortable with such obtrusive oversight, he arranged for a meeting with the judge during which he explained his reorganization plan for the district and asked the court's indulgence in allowing him time to demonstrate to the court "that it was going to be a new day with respect to the relationship." Judge Orfield complied, and a much more cooperative relationship among the parties and the court ensued.[65]

---

[63] Shuford Swift, "History of the *Carlin* case," November 1994, *passim.*
[64] Tom Payzant, former superintendent of the San Diego City Schools, telephone interview with author, 21 October 1996.
[65] Ibid.

In May 1985, Judge Orfield issued a final decision holding that substantial and meaningful progress toward integration had occurred. He noted that the board of education and the superintendent "were dedicated to the desegregation of all schools in the School District; and that the thrust of the program in San Diego should continue in the direction of voluntary desegregation and the continued improvement in the quality of education of students in the minority-isolated school . . .".[66] He observed that while some of the desegregation plan's goals and objectives had not been met, meaningful progress had occurred, and he ended the requirement for annual integration plan submission to the court prior to district implementation of any revisions. Judge Orfield required that the district continue to submit annual written reports to the court.[67]

The final order included several additional requirements of the school district, perhaps most notably, certain requirements directed at minority achievement, rather than mere integration. For instance, the court directed the district to investigate why Voluntary Ethnic Enrollment Program (VEEP) students scored lower on standardized tests than their resident ethnic counterparts, as well as their ethnic counterparts in the sending schools, and to take action to raise the achievement levels of the VEEP students. The order incorporated several other aspects of earlier desegregation plans, including the goal that 50 percent of the students in racially isolated schools should achieve at or above the national norm on standardized tests in reading, mathematics, and language.[68] These requirements suggested that Judge Orfield, like Judge Welsh, was concerned with the quality of education in minority schools, yet neither requiring the district to investigate low achievement nor setting achievement goals would ensure the improved delivery of education.

Judge Orfield disbanded the Integration Task Force that had monitored district integration since 1978. However, he maintained the court's jurisdiction in the case, along with specific requirements for continued performance.[69] In 1985, steadily improving achievement scores in the racially isolated schools, as well as increasing participation

---

[66] Achievement levels in racially isolated schools as measured by standardized tests had improved significantly since the implementation of the desegregation plan. They leveled out in the mid 1980s and by the late 1980s were declining. This topic is discussed in the following chapter.

[67] Final Order at 2-3, 13, Carlin v. Board of Education (San Diego Super. Ct., 21 May 1985) (No. 303800).

[68] Ibid., 3-5.

[69] Ibid., 12-13.

in the VEEP and magnet programs provided grounds for optimism. Many options were available to students and families who sought educational alternatives.

In May 1989, Judge Arthur Jones (Judge Orfield retired in October 1987) amended the final order to reflect the changing demographics within the district. The court redefined the district's Already Balanced Community Schools program to include schools whose resident populations were 35 to 50 percent majority (white), and it ordered the establishment of an Academic Enrichment Academy program in all schools whose resident student populations were less than 35 percent white and which previously had not been designated as minority isolated. The Amended Final Order also directed the district to report on the VEEP program, including "specific steps being taken to raise test scores of VEEP students" and to analyze significant gaps in achievement between white and nonwhite groups.[70] By this time the court was stressing achievement relatively more than it had in the past, but the court's supervision of the district was increasingly relaxed, and achievement levels, which had never reached the court's target levels, had declined since the mid 1980s.

Conclusion

At the close of the 1980s, San Diego City Schools' voluntary program had grown and diversified. The voluntary nature of the program and the appearance of a relatively high level of community involvement in shaping the plan seemed to have contributed to its acceptance with the public. The court deemed that the district had demonstrated an ongoing commitment to desegregation, and its oversight of the desegregation plan was quite unobtrusive. The court recognized that changing demographics had rendered the task of keeping the schools integrated increasingly difficult. Nevertheless, it maintained the pressure to vigorously pursue integration goals, with particular emphasis on reducing the achievement gap between whites and nonwhites.

As the following chapter reveals, however, despite the court's vigilance, scores continued to decline during the 1990s, and many earlier supporters of desegregation grew weary of the effort that they now

---

[70] Final Order As Amended May 1989 at 5, Carlin v. Board of Education (San Diego Super. Ct., 4 May 1989 (No. 303800).

deemed misdirected. Magnet schools, though popular, engendered resentment, because it should not have taken a court order to provide minority children with quality educational programs. The insinuation that minority children had to "sit next to white children in order to learn" evoked indignation. The fact that most of the burden of busing fell on minority children also incited resentment. The three primary factors at the heart of the dissatisfaction of former proponents appeared to be increasing levels of racial imbalance in the district, along with a significant achievement gap, and the perception of a clear difference in the quality of education delivered in minority isolated schools.

CHAPTER 9

San Diego in the 1990s

Introduction

In December 1990, San Diego City Schools hosted the National Integration Conference, the theme of which was "Integration at a Crossroad -- From Compliance to Commitment: Investing in Our Nation's Future." Educators and desegregation experts from across the country discussed differing views on racial integration in public schools. Primary goals were identifying alternatives for achieving equity in education and discussing and considering choices. The symposium focused on "third generation" problems that contributed to the *achievement gap*, the lower achievement levels of minority children, particularly African-Americans and Hispanics. The symposium brochure noted "There are few, if any, school systems in America--whether they describe themselves as desegregated or integrated--that can truly claim to have resolved (these) third generational challenges . . .."[1] Indeed, despite the progress that San Diego City Schools had made towards desegregation in its voluntary program, the school system faced challenges typical of school districts long under court supervision for desegregation. By the mid-1990s, frustration over the achievement gap overshadowed the initial goal of increasing the level of racial integration.

---

[1]Kevin W. Riley, Ed.D., "National Integration Conference Symposium: Integration at a Crossroad: From Compliance to Commitment; Investing in our Nation's Future," San Diego City Schools, 5.

The demographic mix in San Diego's schools had shifted dramatically since the desegregation suit had been filed in 1967. At that time, 78 percent of San Diego public school students were Caucasian. African-Americans comprised 11 percent, Hispanics comprised 9 percent, and all other minorities combined were less than 2 percent of the student population.[2] In 1997-98, San Diego City Schools was the eighth largest school district in the nation. The vast majority of the students were nonwhite; 34.8 percent were Hispanic, 29 percent were white, 16.8 percent were African-American, and 19.3 percent were Asian.[3] Students spoke at least fifty-six native languages and about thirty-five thousand students had limited English proficiency, a 28 percent increase in ten years.[4]

Following the implementation of the court ordered integration plan, which included a wide array of enrichment programs directed at improving achievement levels, achievement among children in racially isolated schools, as measured by standardized tests, improved through most of the 1980s, but it leveled out in the late 1980s and early 1990s and then declined. Initially, the district had been using the Achievement Goals Program that stressed test-taking skills and shaped the curriculum around the subject matter covered by standardized tests. The program worked; improvement was quite pronounced in the early to mid-1980s.[5] However, the district found that it could not raise student achievement above the 50th percentile in court-identified racially isolated schools. Administrative assessment of the curricula determined that too much emphasis had been placed on rote learning and test-taking skills, rather than higher order thinking skills coupled with alternative assessment such as portfolios. Complaints from

---

[2] Maura Reynolds, "integration's failures shake schools' faith: 25 years after Carlin suit," *San Diego Union*, 2 December 1992, 1(A).

[3] "District Totals" (San Diego: San Diego City Schools, Schools Services, 1998), unpublished. I have consolidated figures for Alaskan/Indian, Asian, Filipino, Indochinese, and Pacific Islander in the category "Asian."

[4] "Fast Facts and other information about San Diego City Schools" (San Diego: San Diego City Schools, Public Support and Engagement, 1995), unpublished.

[5] "Testing Results For Court-Identified Racially Isolated Schools: Spring 1995: (San Diego: San Diego City Schools, Planning, Assessment, and Accountability Division, 1995), 19, unpublished.

employers in the community that graduates lacked thinking skills corroborated this finding.[6]

In an effort to increase achievement, the district refocused on developing higher level thinking skills in students and jettisoned the Achievement Goals Program. In the mid-1990s, certain teachers and schools were again stressing test taking and teaching content areas that they knew would be addressed on standardized tests, but this was not yet a district-wide policy.[7]

Shuford Swift, a parent who had actively followed the case since it first went to trial, suggested that the lack of full and meaningful integration lay at the root of the achievement gap. That is, teacher attitudes towards resident and transfer students differed in terms of expectations and the encouragement they offered children. Swift declared, "Where the school accepts (the transfer students) and welcomes them and the teachers welcome them and treat them as if they have just as much ability as the resident students, you'll get achievement." From its inception, this had been a primary concern and focus of the Integration Task Force. Yet, in 1985 it was found that nonwhite students who transferred to more racially balanced schools were performing less well than their ethnic counterparts who remained in racially isolated schools. This discovery led to more aggressive action on the part of the district to ensure that the transfer students were treated well in their receiving schools.[8] Achievement improved, and in the mid 1990s, it was relatively equal between nonwhite transfer students and their ethnic counterparts remaining in racially isolated schools, with the former performing slightly better. San Diego City Schools operated an integration-monitoring program that strongly emphasized improved achievement and the promotion of meaningful integration in academic, co-curricular, and extracurricular activities.[9] Swift observed that despite some complaints about the school system in general and the desegregation program, the high levels of voluntary participation evidenced satisfaction on the part of many residents.[10]

---

[6] Pat Trandal, School Services Division, Area III, San Diego City Schools, telephone interview by author, 18 March 1996.

[7] Ibid.

[8] Shuford Swift, telephone interview by author 18 May 1996.

[9] San Diego Plan for Racial Integration, 1995-1996" (San Diego: San Diego City Schools, School Services Division, Area III, 1996), 23-24, unpublished.

[10] Swift, *supra* note 8.

Jimma McWilson, an active African-American parent in the district and the founder of We the Collective, a parent group that petitioned to enter the case as intervening plaintiffs in 1995, gave the school district an A+ for public relations, but a D- for achievement. He argued that the district should drop the current curriculum and return to the programs that had improved achievement in the 1980s. Referring to the district's efforts at improving student achievement, McWilson observed:

> So I have to say that they're duplicitous in the way that they present themselves. . . . You know there are some really simple basic issues here, and they're trying to say it's complicated. Achievement is not complicated. Slaves learned to read by candlelight and became scientists. They learned to speak different languages. They learned to do higher order mathematics. So I don't buy into all this . . .. You know at first we thought it was a matter of the *Carlin* case and racial discrimination, but we found that as many black students failed in schools headed by black principals as in schools headed by white principals. So what's the answer there? It's competency.[11]

While some critics blamed segregation and discrimination within schools, others suggested that too heavy a burden had been placed on the schools to effect integration. Studies from the 1990s showed that housing segregation in San Diego was growing, especially in the west and among Hispanics.[12] Cynthia Lawrence-Wallace, a former monitor with the San Diego schools Integration Task Force reflected,

> I'm not sure [integration] could ever be done by the schools. We have a segregated city here. We have a racist city here. So as long as housing is segregated and as long as communities are segregated and people's attitudes towards each other are racist, there's no way that you are going to integrate the schools.[13]

---

[11]Jimma McWilson, telephone interview by author, 22 March 1996.
[12] Reynolds, 1(A).
[13]Cynthia Lawrence-Wallace, retired instructor with the Teacher Education Program at the University of California San Diego, telephone interview by author 23 August 1996.

Tom Payzant, Superintendent of San Diego City Schools from late 1982 through mid 1993, also suggested that the court had placed unrealistically high demands on the school system. "No other social institution has been asked to take on such a major societal change as schools have since *Brown v. Board of Education* in 1954. And I think it's pretty clear that schools can't do it alone. But that doesn't mean that we won't continually be asked to try."[14]

The United States Supreme Court held in June 1995 in *Missouri v. Jenkins* that school districts could not be held responsible for the achievement gap because there were many factors outside the control of the school systems that appeared to contribute to students' achievement levels. Two months later, in the Wilmington, Delaware case,[15] federal district court Judge Sue Robinson released the state and the school districts from supervision, despite the plaintiffs' arguments that the achievement gap constituted proof of continued racial discrimination. In that case, the Judge Robinson relied heavily upon the testimony of desegregation expert Dr. David Armor,[16] who presented evidence regarding the socioeconomic factors that he claimed explained 80 to 96 percent of the achievement gap. Judge Robinson wrote, "Because the environment outside school is so strong, cumulative, and varied, schools cannot overcome such environmental/differences (sic) among children."[17] In August 1996, Judge Arthur Jones released the San Diego School District from supervision based on long-term compliance with the court order. He required the district to continue operating the Voluntary Ethnic Enrollment Plan (VEEP) and the magnet schools.

The judicial trend of releasing districts from supervision after years of compliance with desegregation orders, despite what many viewed as the unfulfilled promises of *Brown*, belied the confidence of those who had relied on the courts to guarantee children of all races an equal and quality education that might eventually eliminate not only the achievement gap, but the socioeconomic gap between white and nonwhite Americans. Forty years after *Brown*, notwithstanding rare exceptions such as Kansas City, where vast sums were expended in an

---

[14]Reynolds, 1(A).

[15]See Chapters 6 and 7.

[16]Dr. Armor had testified in the San Diego case regarding white flight in response to court-ordered desegregation plans including mandatory busing.

[17]Coalition To Save Our Children v. State Board of Education, 901 F. Supp. 784, 819 (D.Del. 1995).

attempt to equalize programs and facilities, the rule of stark disparities between minority isolated schools and predominantly white schools persisted. And across the nation, regardless of the funds expended, the achievement gap persisted. Some school boards and administrators undoubtedly would interpret the Supreme Court's pronouncement in *Missouri v. Jenkins* (1995) as absolving the school system of responsibility for the achievement gap. What it actually signaled was the end of the *Brown* era, during which the judicial system had played the primary role in educational equity, and it placed the responsibility back in the hands of local policy makers, which had traditionally overseen the provision of public education. With the courts having reached the limits of their authority, advocates for quality and equity in public education would have to look inward, making demands of themselves, of other parents and community members, of teachers, administrators, school boards, and legislatures; that is, those who had the authority and the capacity to deliver the desired results.

In the mid-1990s San Diego's Plan for Racial Integration included magnet schools, a popular ethnic transfer program, enrichment programs for children in racially isolated schools, along with special programs for students with limited English proficiency, African-American males, and Hispanic females, who were at greater risk for failing or dropping out of school. In addition, the district encouraged meaningful parental participation in the school system through various programs. It was expected that these programs would continue, despite the court's release of the school district from supervision.

Education and Integration Programs in the 1990s

During the 1994-1995 academic year, the school district implemented a new program aimed at closing the majority/minority achievement gap, entitled "A Plan to Improve Student Achievement and Organizational Effectiveness." For the 1995-96 academic year, the schools planned to redouble their efforts to bring all children to the level of reading mastery by the end of grade three, in accordance with the California Reading Task Force recommendations. By 1996-1997 each of the schools receiving integration funding had established accountability expectations with regard to integration and achievement.[18]   Schools

---

[18] "San Diego Plan for Racial Integration, 1995-1996," 2.

were required to assess and report annually on the effectiveness of integration funds aimed at reducing the achievement gap.[19]

Each year since the issuance of the 1977 order, the school district revised its plan for racial integration to meet the evolving needs of the district's school children. The integration program emphasized the "elimination of discriminatory, attitudinal, and behavioral practices which foster racial/ethnic isolation" and this focus was a "fundamental component of all district activities."[20]

In the mid-1990s increasing emphasis was placed on strengthening the district's academic offerings and attempting to reduce the achievement gap between whites and minorities. San Diego City Schools offered specialized and enhanced academic programs in its 31 elementary and fourteen secondary magnet schools. The magnet schools, along with the Voluntary Ethnic Enrollment Program (VEEP, described below), formed the core of the voluntary integration program in San Diego schools. The majority of magnet schools attempted to attract students to schools in predominantly nonwhite neighborhoods, where their enrollment would improve the racial balance. "Mirror magnet" schools attempted to draw nonwhite students into schools that were disproportionately white. All students within the district were eligible to apply to magnet programs where their participation would bring the racial/ethnic balance within the school closer to that of the overall district balance. Most magnet schools recruited their nonresident students, though some racially isolated schools were "packed" with neighborhood children, so recruitment was not a priority for these schools. Nor was it an issue for magnets such as the language immersion programs and the San Diego School of Creative and Performing Arts, which had long waiting lists that parents signed well before their children were ready to enter the schools. Nonetheless, the task of those schools that sought to recruit whites became increasingly difficult in the mid 1990s as the proportion of white students in the district dipped below 30 percent.[21]

In 1997-98, 38,315 students were enrolled in magnet schools. In 1998, the Voluntary Ethnic Enrollment Program (VEEP) was the second largest integration program in the district. The program transferred a total of 9,853 students, the vast majority of whom were

---

[19] Ibid., 8.

[20] Ibid., 1.

[21] Trandal, *supra* note 6.

African-American and Hispanic students who were bused from south of Interstate 8 to schools north of the freeway. Participation in both programs had decreased because elementary school space had declined with Governor Wilson's August 1996 initiative to reduce classroom size in grades one and two from thirty-two to twenty.[22]

The number of students in the VEEP program had grown steadily since its initial year when three thousand students participated until the late 1990s when class size reductions created space limitations. The district provided transportation, including that for before and after school activities twice a week.[23] Because the school system served a large number of students identified as English learners (thirty-five thousand limited English proficiency -- LEP), the district offered several second language education programs. The programs included English as a Second Language (ESL) or English Language Development (ELD), which helped students attain proficiency in English as quickly and effectively as possible, and bilingual programs in Spanish and Vietnamese which included ESL and instruction in the primary language in reading, language, and mathematics.[24]

Owing to the fact that Latinas (female Hispanics) had the highest dropout rate in the district, the board of education commissioned a study in 1989 to determine the contributing factors to this phenomenon and to determine how the district might better serve its Latina students. The study[25] found several factors to be important to the academic achievement levels of Latinas, most of which were confirmed in published literature on the subject. Of particular interest were findings that Latinas were much more responsive to teachers and counselors who seemed caring and personally interested in their progress. The research showed that Hispanic females responded better to positive reinforcement by teachers than did female Caucasians and male Hispanics.[26] The study therefore recommended faculty development in such areas as listening skills, cross-cultural communications, and

---

[22]Ibid.

[23]:San Diego Plan for Racial Integration 1996-1997," 136.

[24] Ibid., 133-34.

[25]Davis, Donna G., "Empowering the Hispanic Female in the Public School Setting, Part I," and Rafaela M. Santa Cruz and Maria Nieto Senour, "Empowering the Hispanic Female in the Public School Setting, Part II" (San Diego: San Diego City Schools, Planning, Research, and Evaluation Division, 1989), unpublished.

[26]Ibid., 59 (Part II).

motivational techniques, to enable teachers to better meet the needs of Latina students. The study also recommended teacher training to develop skills toward more effective and positive communication with parents of Latinas.[27]

In 1992, the board accepted a series of proposals that included the establishment of the Latina Advocacy Program whose purpose it was to try to help Latinas to perceive themselves as capable and successful students and encourage them to remain in school and go on to higher education. Irma Castro, Director of the Latina Advocacy Program, explained that based on the Santa Cruz and Senour study's findings that Latinas perceived themselves as unsuccessful in school, especially after the sixth grade, the program attempted to build their self-esteem, raising their self-expectations in order to promote higher achievement in school, as well as higher rates of college matriculation.[28]

Owing to the finding that African-American males were the most "at-risk" group within the school system, the district initiated a special program called "Improving the Academic Achievement of African-American Male Students" (IAAAAMS) in 1989. The district began the program at four demonstration schools. All schools in the district were encouraged to adopt the program's school board approved objectives which included: 1) increasing the achievement levels of African American males, 2) improving their school attendance rates, 3) reducing the number of suspensions from school, 4) reducing the number of African American males who were referred for learning handicapped classes, 5) decreasing the number of dropouts and increasing the number of graduates, and 6) increasing the number of African American males who met college entrance requirements.[29]

In addition to these academic and counseling programs, the San Diego City Schools operated a well developed *Parent Involvement and Support Program* which promoted a collaborative home-school relationship to ensure student academic success. The district had committed to involving parents in 1988 and had thoroughly researched the literature on parent participation in their children's education, aiming to develop the most effective policy possible. Based on the research, Jeanna Preston, director of the Parent Involvement and

---

[27]Ibid., 64.
[28]Irma Castro, director, Latina Advocacy Program, San Diego City Schools, telephone interview by author. 19 March 1996.
[29]"San Diego Plan for Racial Integration 1995-1996," 21-22.

Support Program, established a policy whose goals included parent partnership in governance, shared decision making, and participation at the school site and district levels. The program stressed the responsibility of schools to make community resources available to parents and to provide assistance in promoting the home-school relationship for the benefit of students.[30]

Thus, the San Diego City Schools Plan for Racial Integration included an impressive array of programs intended to increase integration, to improve the achievement levels of minority students, and to keep students in school. Furthermore, the district had an institutionalized parent involvement policy to help improve home-school communication and to assist parents in supporting their children's education. Yet, despite what appeared to be an aggressive integration and academic program, the achievement gap stubbornly persisted in the 1990s, to the growing frustration of parents. Calls for accountability mounted, and many parents, such as Jimma McWilson, blamed the school district. Lower expectations, tracking, and other manifestations of racial prejudice held minority students back in school, they claimed.

The district, on the other hand, appeared to be drawing support from the Supreme Court's holding in *Missouri v. Jenkins* that school districts could not be held responsible for the achievement gap. Society demanded too much of an already overburdened school system; socioeconomic conditions and parental support or lack thereof explained the achievement gap. After nearly twenty years under court-ordered desegregation, the lacuna between equal educational opportunity and equal achievement levels among ethnic groups confirmed that *Brown* could not eradicate racial segregation in schools any more than *Shelley v. Kraemer*[31] could eliminate racial segregation in housing. The Court's pronouncement that all American children had the right to an equal educational opportunity could not produce that equality. Nor could expensive, judicially inspired enrichment programs eliminate the achievement gap between the generally more

---

[30]Jeanna Preston, director of the San Diego City Schools Parent Involvement and Support Program, telephone interview by author, 22 March 1996.

[31]In Shelley v. Kraemer, 334 U.S. 1 (1948) the Supreme Court unanimously held that judicial enforcement of racially discriminatory restrictive covenants constituted state action which violated the Equal Protection Clause of the Fourteenth Amendment.

privileged white American children and less privileged minority children. The impetus for quality education would have to emanate from the community, from parents and other community members who demanded dedicated teachers and administrators, along with effective educational programs in every school and for every child. Without such commitment, the courts were powerless to eliminate inequities or to render school systems effective.

Release from Court Oversight

On December 15, 1995, the parties in the San Diego desegregation case returned to court to address two motions. One was a motion to intervene brought by a group of African-American and Hispanic parents, called *We the Collective*, which had filed a motion in September 1995 to become a party to the case. The group, which was represented by the United States Justice Foundation, included about thirty parents, five of whom presented declarations that their children's educational needs were not being met by the school district. The group informed the court that if they were allowed to intervene, they would request that the twenty-three schools that were deemed racially isolated be turned over to the county board of education or the state board of education, or that they be allowed to become a charter school district.[32]

These were radical measures the group was requesting, but founding member of We the Collective, Jimma McWilson, explained afterwards that the group wanted the judge to make a clear decision, informing the community that he was prepared to enforce the existing court orders. He insisted that the issue was no longer desegregation, but quality education. We the Collective argued that the court should not continue to require desegregation, which was costing the state $48 million, when the money was not providing a quality education. Spending such funds actually demeaned minority children and hurt them economically in the long run, the group maintained, because the same dominant social structure that denied minorities a quality education later would have to provide affirmative action programs when minorities could not compete on an even playing field.

---

[32] Christina Dyer, legal counsel for the San Diego City Schools, telephone interview by author, 13 March 1996.

We wanted to put a stop to (affirmative action programs) where it's supposed to be, and that's when they graduate. They should be qualified, and then the law of the land protects them so that if they're discriminated against, then they just can file suit . . . they can say "I'm qualified, I'm knowledgeable, and this is the reason [that I didn't get hired,]" not "I'm sorry, but they didn't teach me to read, so now you have to let me into college, even though I can't read at a college level."[33]

A second motion was filed by Groundswell, an intervener in the case since 1980. This group had filed a motion in 1994 asking the court to end the voluntary busing program. Groundswell relied heavily on the *Bakke* case, taking the position that student assignments should not be race or ethnicity conscious. The school district had opposed Groundswell's 1994 motion and the court had rejected it, but the judge had said that Groundswell could return to the court if it had new evidence or new issues. The group acted upon that invitation in 1995, again asking the court to end its supervision.[34]

The district, the plaintiffs, and the ACLU, which had brought the suit on behalf of the plaintiffs, opposed the motions of both groups. The district opposed the first motion because it felt that the plaintiffs already represented the class that We the Collective represented, African-American and Hispanic students and families. Secondly, the motion was not timely. Furthermore, if We the Collective were allowed to intervene, the remedies that they were seeking were beyond the purview of the court, argued the school district.[35]

School district counsel Christina Dyer observed:

The county board does not run the Kindergarten through twelve schools, nor does the state board of education. . . . and the charter school statutes were not meant for this type of judicial intervention. They were meant for a grassroots group of teachers to redesign a school and sign a charter. It was not

---

[33]McWilson, *supra* note 11.
[34] Dyer, *supra* note 32.
[35] Ibid.

appropriate for the court to circumvent the charter parameters.[36]

Furthermore, argued the district, some of We the Collective's allegations regarding student achievement were rejected by the Supreme Court in *Missouri v. Jenkins* (1995), when the Court held that socioeconomic factors beyond the control of school districts contributed to unequal student achievement and that the achievement gap did not represent a constitutional violation on the part of the district. Nevertheless, the district opposed Groundswell's motion for release from court supervision, because it found the court's minimal supervision and the reporting requirements and meetings helpful.[37]

Judge Arthur Jones denied the motion to intervene, saying it was not timely, and holding that the plaintiffs represented the class that We the Collective sought to represent. On the second motion, the court granted Groundswell's motion to end supervision and told the parties to present a final order to the court by June 1996. The judge made comments to the effect that the district had been operating in good faith, and he found no evidence of constitutional violations. The judge noted that the schools seemed to be quite equal; that is, students who remained in their racially isolated schools did nearly as well as those who voluntarily transferred through the VEEP program, which indicated to the judge that the school district had been successful in its efforts to equalize the schools in the district and there was no longer any significant disparity between the racially isolated schools and those that were integrated. Progress may not have been what many, including the court, had sought, but the judge did not believe that continued court supervision was necessary.[38] Thus, the court interpreted the similarly lower achievement levels between minority children who remained in their neighborhood (racially isolated) schools and their ethnic counterparts who transferred out as evidence of *equality* (between isolated schools and more balanced schools), rather than *disparity* (between the educational programs provided white and minority children).

After the court indicated that it would grant Groundswell's motion for release, the district sought an order recommending that it maintain

---

[36] Ibid.
[37] Ibid.
[38] Ibid.

the voluntary desegregation program under which it was operating, including the magnet schools, voluntary ethnic enrollment, and human relations programs. According to Dyer, this was a financial, political, and judicial strategy.[39]   In the spring of 1996, the prospect of the California Civil Rights Initiative, which would prohibit race and gender conscious affirmative action programs in the absence of a court order, loomed. The initiative, which was promoted by Governor Pete Wilson, would be placed on a ballot in November 1996.[40] Thus, if the district did not have a court order requiring it to operate the voluntary integration programs, the initiative could preclude their continuation. In 1995-1996, the district received $48 million from the State for use in its voluntary desegregation plans, and the initiative jeopardized the district's receipt of those funds.[41]

Loss of funding for the desegregation programs would have multiple ramifications for the district. There was insufficient space in many of the neighborhood schools for all of the transferred students to return there. Moreover, residents of the receiving school neighborhoods favored continuation of the transfer program, because their schools needed the transfer students. Many schools in receiving neighborhoods likely would have been closed if the transfer program ended. Consequently, Shuford Swift concluded that the majority of San Diegans would support the continuation of the desegregation programs even after the release of the district from court supervision.[42]

Though the parties were unable to reconcile the issue of responsibility for the achievement gap, Dyer characterized the San Diego public school system as a success story:

> The district is fiscally sound. We just got the highest bond rating for a bond issue from Moody's Investors (a Wall street company that rates municipalities for purposes of bonding) . . . The achievement level of our kids is right at the 50 percent level district wide for math, reading, and language arts. For

---

[39] Ibid.

[40]California's liberal use of initiatives allows for a high level of direct citizen participation in policy making. Its use of initiatives dates back to the Progressive movement of the 1910s and 1920s, which called for direct citizen participation in legislating. The California Civil Rights Initiative, also known as Proposition 209, passed in November 1996.

[41]Dyer, *supra* note 32.

[42] Swift, *supra* note 8.

an urban district (70 percent nonwhite) that's phenomenal. The drop out rate is very [low] compared to . . Chicago and other urban districts with 30 and 40 percent of the kids dropping out . . . Ours is about 5 percent at the most.[43]

Dyer believed that one major advantage the school district enjoyed was that San Diego was not a city with urban decay. Furthermore, besides its urban area, the district included suburban middle class and upper middle class areas such as LaJolla, Point Loma, and Scripps Ranch. These affluent areas strongly supported the San Diego public school system, with about 90 percent of the area children attending public schools.[44]

Indeed, compared to other large urban school districts such as Philadelphia, Chicago, and Cleveland, and to the more rural Prince George's County, Maryland, San Diego had many factors weighing in its favor as it confronted the problem of the achievement gap. Though 70 percent of its student population was nonwhite and over 25 percent had limited English proficiency, the district operated numerous programs to strengthen simultaneously the students' English and their mother tongues, to engage parents in their children's education, and to strengthen basic academic skills. Furthermore, the district was well funded and the city was economically strong and growing. Despite these positive indicators, a crisis that shook the school district in early 1996 revealed parental discontent with the student achievement level, with the district's openness to parental participation in school policy making, and with the district's failure to communicate effectively with parents.

Teachers' Strike

A highly contentious teachers' strike in early February 1996 brought widespread parent frustration with the school system to the surface, with some people calling for a parents' union to work for greater parental influence in district policy making. Because of a near complete breakdown in communication between the school district and the public, the San Diego Center for Parent Involvement in Education played a vital role in disseminating information and bringing parents

---

[43]Dyer, *supra* note 32.
[44] Ibid.

together during the strike.   Parental dissatisfaction transcended racial/ethnic and socioeconomic lines, and it focused on three issues: low student achievement, district resistance to substantive parental participation in decision making, and the teachers' union's attempt to gain 50 percent control of school governance teams.[45]

The issue of unsatisfactory achievement levels, especially among African-American and Latino students, came to the forefront during the strike.   Walter Kudumu, Director of the Center for Parent Involvement in Education, noted that while the district had issued a number of policy statements regarding improving achievement levels, no strong position statement with any "teeth" had emanated from the district administration or the board of education.[46]   As tempers flared during the strike, a new sense of urgency characterized parental calls for accountability on the part of the school district.

Judith Williams, president of the San Diego Council of PTAs (Parent Teachers Associations) had sensed dissatisfaction with student achievement levels within all ethnic groups. "(Parents) want to look at all children and see that they are achieving higher than we achieved, and when they don't see that happening, as private sector people, they want accountability."   Engaged parents, who were overseeing their children's education and whose children were doing their schoolwork, were dissatisfied with their children's achievement levels. Williams stressed that these parents did not seek to control school administrators or teachers; they merely were concerned about their children's education.[47]

Dr. Francine Williams, director of Race and Human Relations for the San Diego City Schools suggested that the district could have been doing better in consulting with nonwhite parents and students to determine how the curriculum could better meet the students' needs. She suggested that both content and teaching techniques needed reassessment to better meet the needs of nonwhite students, but noted that the Race and Human Relations office tended to work with crisis intervention, rather than curriculum development, except for social studies.   From her contacts with nonwhite students, Dr. Williams found that several factors appeared to contribute to lower achievement

---

[45] McWilson, *supra* note 11.

[46] Walter Kudumu, director, Center for Parent Involvement in Education, telephone interview by author, 22 March 1996

[47] Judith Williams, president of the San Diego Council of PTAs 1995-1996, telephone interview by author, 22 March 1996.

in school, including access to challenging classes, teacher expectations, and attendance problems which correlated with lower achievement and which oftentimes derived from difficulties at home which nonwhite children experienced more often. Dr. Williams said that she often perceived a strong fear of failure in students who were not performing well in school. Nonperformance was a mechanism to maintain self-esteem, she explained; it was much easier for a student to claim that he or she *chose* not to do an assignment, rather than admit that he or she was unable to complete it. This observation coincided with other evidence of low self-esteem in non-achieving students.[48]

Shuford Swift suggested that the achievement gap stemmed, at least partially, from the fact that *real integration* had not taken place. "The students go to school together, but they still aren't truly integrated, . . . there are still teacher attitudes that work against that and students attitudes that work against it."[49]

Pat Meredith, a middle school assistant principal in an upper middle class VEEP receiving school in the early 1990s, witnessed the effects of negative teacher attitudes toward minority VEEP students. Meredith, an African-American, was surprised to discover negative attitudes toward the transfer students fourteen to fifteen years after the VEEP program had been in place. Teachers declared that they would not lower their standards for the transfer students, and there was much resistance on the part of teachers and parents to the administration's policy of aiming for greater minority participation in the honors classes and gifted and talented program. Teachers complained that the minority students were "mouthy," yet Meredith had witnessed minority teachers in other schools being nonplused by bright, "fresh" white students. Thus she viewed the problem as cultural. As the assistant principal and disciplinarian, she saw many minority students being referred to her office for being "mouthy," whereas white children exhibiting similar behavior were rarely referred.[50]

Meredith spoke of the oftentimes-unconscious racism that resulted in such discrimination:

---

[48]Dr. Francine Williams, director of Race and Human Relations, San Diego City Schools, telephone interview by author, 28 March 1996.
[49]Swift, *supra* note 8.
[50]Pat Meredith, assistant principal at Balboa Park Elementary School, San Diego, telephone interview by author, 2 September 1996.

It's very subtle, but it's still there, and if you're looking, you see it. Minorities see a whole lot of things and other people think they're not paying any attention to this. . . . That's why I used to say to the teachers all the time, "the kids know. Even though you're saying you like everybody in this classroom, the kids know, just by the way you don't smile or by the sharp tone that you use or you don't want them to stand by you or whatever, your own body language tells the children, and they're very perceptive. Of course, they pick these things up and then the act out. So you say something and they take it personally, and then they retaliate."[51]

Meredith related an anecdote that confirmed her assessment of the palpable racism at this middle school. Some time after she took another position, she met a former male student at a conference. "Oh, Mrs. Meredith," he said, "we missed you at _____." When she asked what he meant, he replied, "Well, there was nobody there who really liked us." Meredith concluded, "And I felt, you know, at least he knew that I did like 'em. I liked the kids."[52]

Asked why minority students nevertheless participated in the VEEP program at relatively high rates, Meredith responded that safety was an important factor. "Everybody knows that the schools in the southeast aren't safe. There are drugs and there are drive-bys and all those things," so parents felt their children were safer in middle class neighborhood schools.[53]

Former superintendent Tom Payzant spoke of the continuing challenge of setting high expectations for all students as opposed to accepting a two- or three-tiered system with lower expectations for socioeconomically disadvantaged children. As superintendent of public schools in Boston, 80 percent of whose student population qualified for free or reduced lunch, he faced the same problem. "It wasn't particularly unique to San Diego."[54]

Kenji Ima, professor of sociology at San Diego State University and a former member of the Integration Task Force, said that the common practice of addressing the achievement gap in terms of race

---

[51]Ibid.

[52] Ibid.

[53] Ibid.

[54]Tom Payzant, former superintendent of schools, San Diego City Schools, telephone interview by author, 21 October 1996.

impeded resolution of the problem, especially in the case of Asians. The stereotype was that Asian students performed equally well as Caucasian students, or even better in the case of math. In fact, vast disparities existed among groups of Asians, and it was language that caused the problem, Ima explained. Third and fourth generation Chinese and Japanese students performed very well academically. Asian newcomers, on the other hand, especially refugees, experienced severe difficulties in school, owing to language and cultural barriers. In fact, Asians were much more likely to be language deficient than Latinos, though due to their greater numbers, more Latinos participated in ESL programs.[55]

Ima noted that the court's tendency to rely on the African-American experience in addressing the achievement gap was "a mistake, because historically they have a different set of needs." Nor did "putting bodies of one group next to another" address the linguistic and cultural needs of Asian students. Thus, the court's perception of Caucasians and Asians as higher achievers and African-Americans and Hispanics as lower achievers did not sufficiently address the complexity of the demographics in San Diego, explained Ima. Nor were the needs of newcomer Asians addressed through the political system, owing to their low political efficacy.[56]

The Reverend George Walker Smith voiced his frustration with misdirected judicial remedies:

> Putting a black kid beside a white kid does not mean achievement. That's the fallacy of this whole thinking. . . . My contention now is that our kids get as good an education as the parents and the teachers provide for them. Schools can't do it without the parents and vice versa. The teachers need to be held accountable. So my whole attitude towards this issue . . . (is that) we need caring teachers and supportive parents.[57]

Many San Diegans expressed similar sentiments.

---

[55]Kenji Ima, professor of sociology, San Diego State University, telephone interview by author 29 September 1996.
[56] Ibid.
[57]The Reverend George Walker Smith, former president of the San Diego Board of Education, telephone interview by author, 26 August 1996.

The second issue around which parental resentment centered during and after the strike was the feeling of alienation on the parts of many parents, especially minorities. This was at first glance puzzling, given the institutionalized parent involvement and the shared governance programs in the district. Yet, the disjunction between official school district policies and parent perceptions was striking. "San Diego Unified School District is probably viewed as one of the most progressive urban districts in the nation in terms of (official) policies, . . . and that's good, but then we have to get to those bottom lines, and that's where our problem starts," observed Walter Kudumu. As the parents of five children, all of whom attended San Diego City Schools, he and his wife had long been actively involved in their children's education. Though sometimes less than receptive school personnel did not put off the Kudumus, he understood that many parents felt uncomfortable in their children's schools.[58]

PTA Council President Judith Williams observed that despite well-intentioned efforts on the part of the district, parents from all racial and ethnic groups had legitimate concerns about the school system and were frustrated by their inability to make themselves heard.

> What we want is to have more distinct guidelines of where we can enable and empower parents to have a voice in implementing change in school and participating in that implementation and decision making process. I would say that it has been there in a limited form, but I think that parents realized during the strike that their voice was a very loud voice and a voice that should be heard. . . .   What parents want to do is to participate in a very important part of their children's lives, their education. They want to be able to have a voice in what is right or wrong about education. . . .[59]

Jeanna Preston, director of the school district's Parent Involvement and Support Program, conceded that the district's "systematic" effort to involve parents, had fallen short of its goals. "It was to be the best of all worlds," said Preston. Yet, tension that surfaced during the 1996 teachers' strike demonstrated that the program had not produced the results that its framers had intended. Preston observed:

---

[58]Kudumu, *supra* note 46.
[59]J. Williams, *supra* note 47.

I think that if we are enlightened, it is only because we are aware of the problems and we admit to them and we understand that there is a disconnect between what we want to have happen and what actually happens at the schools. . . . The strike was awful. . . . Our district leadership got so distracted by what was happening with the teachers [that we communicated very poorly to the parents]. . . . We were really remiss in that . . . [60]

Preston added that the strike brought the severity of the communication problem to the attention of the district, and she expressed hope that the airing of concerns that occurred during the strike would produce positive results.[61] PTA Council President Judith Williams said that if a strike or similar crisis were to occur again, the PTA would be better prepared to step in and facilitate communication, as well, so that parents and other community members would be advised of all parties' positions.[62]

The third major source of contention during the strike, the teachers' union's demand for 50 percent representation on the school governance teams, seemed to be the most easily resolved. The governance teams were an outgrowth of the district's site-based management policy developed in the early 1990s. They included representatives or "stakeholders" in the school communities. Walter Kudumu explained that parents sought an equal one-third partnership with teachers and the school district on these governance teams, but there had been a "tilt toward the nonparent interests." The teachers' union's attempt to secure 50 percent control epitomized the type of action and attitudes that left parents feeling unwelcome in the schools, according to Kudumu.[63]

Three days before the strike began, the Center for Parent Involvement in Education convened a forum which allowed parents to pose questions regarding unresolved issues in the teachers' contract to union representatives and board of education member Dr. Shirley Weber. Though seemingly open dialogue ensued, parents felt, according to Kudumu, that vital aspects of the negotiations were being

---

[60]Preston, *supra* note 30.
[61] Ibid.
[62]J. Williams, *supra* note 47.
[63]Kudumu, *supra* note 46.

kept from parents. "[Parents] felt disenfranchised. . . . They didn't like being informed after the fact. . . . The one greatest issue that secured the notion of disenfranchisement on the part of the parents was the fact that the teachers were negotiating for 50 percent representation on all governance teams as a collective bargaining issue . . .." Kudumu emphasized that parents' participation rights were being challenged and diminished within contract negotiations of which they were not a part. This grievance lay at the center of the parents' attempt to organize into a collective voice for future negotiations. [64]

Judith Williams concurred with Kudumu's assessment:

> When the teachers' union decided to put certain things in the contract and then go on strike, and then the district wasn't talking, the parents were saying, "Wait, you can't do this! It's our kids!" And if you have children, you know how it is--you can say anything in the world to me; you can do anything in the world to me, but you don't do it to my kid! . . . We felt that our children were being held hostage by both the district and [the] union, and by the news media. An so that's where the frustration came from. . . . The teachers had a right to strike, but when it affected the children, then the parents had a right to stand up and say "get this thing settled."[65]

With the Center for Parent Involvement in Education serving as a communication hub, parent groups coordinated their activities directed at bringing an end to the strike. The Center operated phone banks, organized groups of people to pass out leaflets in neighborhoods, shopping malls and churches. The Center organized two candlelight vigils, and residents of Scripps Ranch, an affluent neighborhood in northeast San Diego, held a rally at the same time to call for an end to the strike. "We were in touch with each other; as a matter of fact, we were supporting each others' efforts. The announcements that we put out made reference to each other," explained Kudumu. He emphasized that the Center was by no means a nerve center. The effort was grass roots, and the Center merely served as a communication link for parents.[66]

---

[64]Ibid
[65]J. Williams, *supra* note 47.
[66] Kudumu, *supra* note 46.

Following months of negotiations, in late November 1996, the board of education, with the consensus of community members, PTA representatives, and school district representatives, approved an accountability program which called for governance teams which would evaluate student achievement in the district. Five sub districts or clusters within the San Diego City Schools were created, each with its own assistant superintendent, and each with a governance team consisting of seven community members and six school district employees.[67] The settlement of the conflict regarding participation on the governance teams was a major accomplishment.

Thus, the school district and the community appeared to be moving towards conciliation and a more cooperative relationship. The teachers' strike had united various parents groups, as well as concerned community members together in common cause, raising the quality of education for all the district's children. After nearly two decades under a court ordered plan that had failed to produce meaningful integration or correct the achievement gap, the people of San Diego were applying *political pressure* to the school system and demanding both quality and equity in public education.

Two years after the contentious 1996 teachers' strike, the district and the teachers' union negotiated a new contract that reflected parent and community concerns and which clearly prioritized student welfare and achievement. The school community had come a long way since the acrimonious process of two years earlier. The PTA petitioned to be nonaligned observers during the contract negotiations process. While that request was not granted, the district held five community forums during the negotiations process, in which it solicited parents' and other community members' concerns and their views on the issues the district should prioritize. The overriding theme expressed by parents was that the children should remain the center of the negotiations. Parents and community members had felt strongly that during the 1996 negotiations, the children's interests had been ignored.

The atmosphere during the 1998 negotiations was fundamentally different, reflecting the progress the community had made in the previous two years with regard to communication and understanding among the "stakeholders" in the public school system. The facilitator informed Judith Williams, former president of the San Diego Council of PTAs and the communications vice-president for 1997-1998, that

---

[67] Swift, *supra* note 8, on 4 December 1996.

the parties had taken the parent's plea as a "guiding point." The facilitator informed Williams that each time the parties sat down to negotiate, the word "children" was written on the butcher paper.[68]

Two pieces of the contract directly reflected parent concerns. Parents felt that having eight faculty and staff development days during the school year hindered student achievement. They asked that at least some of these staff development days be placed outside the traditional school year. The final contract reduced the number of faculty/staff development days during the school year by two and the removal of an additional two days the following year.[69]

A second parent concern was that high teacher turnover and insufficient teacher experience in the "hard-to-staff" schools south of Interstate 8, where most of the minorities lived in San Diego, contributed to the lower achievement levels in those schools. In response to this concern, the new contract included a stipulation that mentor teachers[70] would be required to accept placement in hard-to-staff schools for three years. This requirement would ensure that more experienced teachers would remain in the schools with overwhelmingly minority student populations, where they could guide new teachers through the challenges of the first years of teaching.[71]

In addition to the gratifying results of the teacher contract negotiations, the community of San Diego developed an accountability process, called Process Accountability Review (PAR) which reflected successful collaborative effort by teachers, administrators, and parents in the district. The district had had an accountability program since the early 1990s, but the frustrations that surfaced during the 1996 teachers' strike provided new impetus for developing an effective program. A task force with equal representation of parents and community members, administrators, and teachers, with the help of six

---

[68] J. Williams, *supra* note 47, on 13 June 1998.

[69] Ibid.

[70] Mentor teachers serve as advisors to new teachers. They receive compensation for serving as "sounding boards" for inexperienced teachers and offering advice on everything from discipline issues to alternative lesson plans to communication with parents. Williams noted that some schools in the district whose faculties had, on average, many years of experience had several mentor teachers. Yet, hard-to-staff schools with inexperienced teachers had virtually no teachers with sufficient experience to serve as mentor teachers.

[71] J. Williams, *supra* note 68.

facilitators, constructed PAR. The accountability process would require every school in the district to examine its own performance, identify shortcomings, and institute plans for improvement.[72]

PAR was designed as an approximately 3_-year process that involved reassessments to ensure that improvement was taking place. The plan included standards and assessments of students, accountability by all involved parties, and professional development. The district had developed standards for language arts and math and was working on standards for the other subject areas. The standards were higher than the state standards. For example, eighth grade, rather than ninth grade, students would be taking algebra under the new standards. The district had already implemented a requirement of a cumulative 2.0 grade point average for graduating seniors. The district was in the process of developing appropriate assessments to accompany the new standards.[73]

PAR also included a compact which was to be signed by a board member, a school administrator, each child's teacher, the child's parents, and the child him or herself. The compact outlined the responsibilities of the board of education, the superintendent, the principals, the teachers, the staff, the parents, the community, and the students. Some schools had already begun using the compacts during the 1997-98 school year.[74]

Both the new teachers' union contract and PAR reflected the emphasis within the community on achievement. Judith Williams observed, "Right now, as far as everybody is concerned, education is the by-word in California."[75] While the voluntary desegregation programs remained popular with a minority of the population, the overwhelming emphasis was on student achievement. Shuford Swift confirmed this assessment, noting that even the minorities, though of course he couldn't speak for all of them, were primarily concerned with the children's obtaining an education.[76]

---

[72] Ibid.
[73] Ibid.
[74] Ibid.
[75] Ibid.
[76] Swift, *supra* note 11, on 8 June 1998.

Release from Oversight

On August 16, 1996, Judge Arthur Jones issued the final order terminating court jurisdiction. The release order included numerous requirements of the school district, most notably that it continue to operate the Voluntary Ethnic Enrollment Program and the magnet school programs, and that it aggressively recruit students for participation in these programs. Further, the court required that the district continue to measure student achievement and that it devise programs for improving the achievement levels of any racial/ethnic groups whose performance, as measured on standardized tests, fell significantly below the highest scoring group. The court also required that the district monitor the achievement levels and general well-being of participants in the VEEP program and take steps to remedy any shortcomings. The court required that the district maintain a race and human relations program at each grade level to promote the integration effort.[77] The order included a sunset provision that declared that after January 1, 2000, the district would not be held in violation or contempt of the order if it failed to comply with any of its provisions.[78] Thus, the district's integration programs would continue for at least four years, and with the court order requiring them, state funding was likely to continue. Community support for the programs remained high, despite their shortcomings. Moreover, owing to rapid population growth in southeast San Diego, neighborhood schools could no longer accommodate the students who participated in VEEP.

In the late summer of 1996, Governor Pete Wilson approved a measure to reduce class size in grades one and two from the previous average of thirty-two students to twenty students. Since the 1980s, California had had the largest class sizes of the fifty states, with the possible exception of Utah,[79] and Governor Wilson was apparently responding to growing public pressure and negative press regarding inadequate funding of public schools. The legislation provided funding for the class size reduction, but only if the pupil/teacher ratio (PTR) were in fact reduced to twenty.[80] This significant reduction in class size in the first two grades offered hope that achievement levels,

---

[77]Final Order Terminating Court Jurisdiction at 3-6, Carlin v. Board of Education (San Diego Super. Ct., 16 August 1996) (No. 303800).
[78]Ibid., 9.
[79]Payzant, *supra* note 54.
[80]Trandal, *supra* note 6, on 3 December 1996.

at least among children *entering* the San Diego school system, could rise dramatically. Whereas compensatory educational programs in the form of remediation or placing teacher aides in classrooms had shown little if any lasting positive effects on achievement levels, lowering the PTR had had a significant effect on achievement.[81] Reducing the PTR in the first two grades was especially important because research had shown that children who were not reading at grade level by the third grade are at high risk for failing in school.

In 1996, as the San Diego school district was released from court supervision after nearly twenty years, many close observers who applauded the court's goal of providing an equal educational opportunity, recognized that the court lacked the capacity to produce such results. Many people acknowledged significant improvements in the school district's commitment to providing quality education, particularly since Tom Payzant's arrival in 1982. Superintendent Bertha Pendleton, Payzant's successor, received generally favorable ratings, as well. However, the complexity of the issues involved, including residential segregation, poverty, language and cultural barriers, conscious and unconscious racism in schools and classrooms, insufficient teacher training, community indifference, and political factors rendered the overall problem of unacceptably low achievement levels too onerous for the court to remedy. Virtually no one called for returning to pre-*Carlin* school district policies, but residents understood that further substantive improvement in the quality of education delivery would come about only as the result of community commitment and unrelenting pressure on the school system.

Judge Lindsley, Chairman of the Citizens Committee on Equal Educational Opportunity, which had first suggested to the school board several steps that could be taken to alleviate racial segregation in 1966, observed that the schools remained segregated because the community was segregated. Yet he applauded Judge Welsh's efforts and said that he believed that no desegregation would have taken place had the lawsuit not been filed.[82] Former Superintendent Payzant felt that the voluntary aspect of the program had resulted in a relatively positive experience with desegregation in San Diego, as compared to the

---

[81]See Chapter 3 on compensatory education..
[82]Lindsley, Byron F., retired judge and chairman of the Citizens Committee on Equal Educational Opportunities, telephone interview by author, 19 August 1996.

traumatic experiences of Oklahoma City and Boston, which had undergone mandatory desegregation.[83]

Judy McDonald, former Integration Task Force member, agreed that while virtually no one called for returning to the rigid boundaries of the pre-desegregation era, neither were residents satisfied with the accomplishments of the desegregation plan. Echoing the disappointment expressed by many others, she said there was a time when she had been quite optimistic about the potential for improving race relations and the quality of the educational program. Some programs were worthwhile, "but a lot of it was just going through the motions. Maybe it was because it was forced on people and they didn't really engage in it or embrace it . . . but I just don't think that the whole overall effort -- it didn't really get us where we wanted to go."[84]

The Reverend George Smith, former president of the San Diego Board of Education, was even more direct:

> You have to change folks' attitudes. The attitudes of this nation are basically racist and you just cannot create a phony situation whereby you're going to force me to love you or you to love me. . . . I don't waste my time talking school integration anymore. I thought the judge did a beautiful job when he lifted that order. Why waste all this money when we could be using it for something else?[85]

Pat Meredith suggested that teacher-training programs focusing on multicultural teaching strategies would reduce the inequities and subconscious racism in schools. "Most teachers don't know how to teach minority kids. They don't learn that in the colleges." Teachers tended to blame the non-achieving child, rather than examining the education delivery system, she claimed.[86]

Kenji Ima stressed the complexity of the language, race, and socioeconomic diversity in assessing the limited success of the desegregation plan. "I think the legal system seems to be overly simple about solutions, and I think that reality is much more complex

---

[83]Payzant, *supra* note 54.
[84]Judy McDonald, former member of the integration talk force, San Diego City Schools, telephone interview by author, 2 September 1996.
[85]Smith, *supra* note 57.
[86]Meredith, *supra* note 50.

than the legal system could possibly envision. Probably the legal system is (a) vehicle, but not a total solution (and) to rely on the legal system as a total solution is an error."[87]

In July 1997, interveners Groundswell asked Judge Jones to end court jurisdiction by discharging the writ of mandate, arguing that it violated Proposition 209. The school district opposed early termination of the desegregation order, arguing that it could jeopardize state funding of the district's voluntary desegregation programs.[88] On September 5, 1997, Judge Arthur Jones denied Groundswell's request, but he accelerated the end of supervision by one and one half years, setting the final release date at July 1, 1998, in the event that Proposition 209[89] was upheld as constitutional.[90] The district immediately appealed the modification of the release order, asking the appeals court to clarify that it was unnecessary to vacate the order early, because court-ordered race-based programs were excluded from Proposition 209's ban on discriminatory programs. [91]

In February 1998, the state court of appeals held that Judge Jones had not erred, that he had not given undue emphasis to Proposition 209, but that he had merely considered it, along with other factors, and had determined that continued supervision of the school system was no longer necessary.[92] The appeals court noted that the superior court was "mindful the ultimate goal was to return [the school district] to local control," but that it would be available if the district "engaged in activities that warrants (sic) a new writ of mandate."[93]

Although the appeals court upheld the lower court's decision, the school district was generally pleased with the decision, because the appeals court said that the writ of mandate requiring the desegregation programs remained in effect. The appeals court said that the lower court released the district because it was doing a good job and was expected to continue to do so without court supervision. Regarding

---

[87]Ima, *supra* note 55.

[88]Board of Education v. The Superior Court (Carlin), 71 Cal.Rptr.2d 562 (Cal.App. 4 Dist. 1998), 564-65.

[89]Proposition 209 became article I, section 31 of the California Constitution.

[90]Board of Education v. The Superior Court (Carlin), *supra* note 89, at 565-66.

[91]Jose Gonzales, acting general counsel for the San Diego City Schools, telephone interview by author, 8 May 1998.

[92] Board of Education v. The Superior Court (Carlin), *supra* note 89, at 563.

[93] Ibid., 567.

state funding for the programs, the appeals court said that the state should treat San Diego no differently than it had been treating Los Angeles. Furthermore, by the time the decision was rendered, Governor Wilson had indicated that funding for the desegregation programs would be forthcoming for the 1998-99 school year, and there had been no indications that the funding would be terminated the following year. Jose Gonzales, acting general counsel for the San Diego City Schools, observed that following the appeals court decision, the school district was in the same position it would have been, had Judge Jones not accelerated the end of supervision of the district. On November 3, 1997, the United States Supreme Court denied certiorari on the appeal of the Ninth Circuit's upholding of Proposition 209.[94]

Thus, the future of the San Diego's desegregation programs looked secure in 1998, although fewer students were able to participate, owing to space constraints resulting from the state mandated lower classroom sizes for the primary grades. The state provided much of the funding for the lower class sizes, but not the full costs. Some California school systems had placed bond issues on the ballot for building new facilities, but with the California requirement of a two-thirds vote for passage of a bond issue or tax raise, it was difficult to obtain passage of such proposals. The fact that the majority of San Diego voters did not have children in the public school system rendered passage of such a bond issue even more doubtful.[95]

In March of 1998, the board of education named U.S. Attorney Alan D. Bersin, the Clinton Administration's California "border czar," superintendent of schools, effective July 1, 1998. Superintendent Bertha Pendleton had announced her resignation the previous fall. Bersin was one of several "nontraditional" superintendents recently appointed to head large school districts, including Seattle, the District of Columbia, and Chicago. Mr. Bersin had a reputation as a strong leader with excellent organizational skills.[96] Besides some initial reservations from some Chicano groups, owing to Bersin's immigration policies, public reaction to his selection was very positive. Beginning in April, Bersin met with community members in

---

[94] Gonzales, *supra* note 91.
[95] Trandal, *supra* note 6.
[96] Bess Keller, "San Diego's New Chief an Unlikely Pick," *Education Week*, 18 March 1998, 1 and 18.

each of the board members' areas, and initiated an additional meeting with parent and community leaders to listen to people's concerns regarding the school system.[97] Bersin made it clear that his primary concern was improving student achievement. Shuford Swift described Bersin as very open ("he wants everybody to call him Alan") and energetic. Two board members reported that virtually everyone with whom they had spoken who had heard Bersin, including teachers and parents, was hopeful and encouraged. By June of 1998 it appeared that even most of the concerns among Chicanos had subsided.[98]

Conclusion

In the summer of 1998, with the end of court supervision of San Diego's voluntary desegregation plan looming, there were many hopeful signs in the school community. Little evidence suggested that desegregation or court supervision had improved achievement in the school system. Yet, it appeared that the voluntary desegregation programs would continue because many San Diego families appreciated the choices they offered and because California's Constitution, required school districts to take steps to reduce racial segregation, regardless of the cause.

While the desegregation programs were well entrenched, the community appeared to be much more focused on student achievement than on desegregation. An accountability program was in place, new standards for higher achievement had been developed, and appropriate assessments were being designed to ensure the effectiveness of the accountability process. Following a very acrimonious teachers' strike two years earlier, the administration, the teachers' union, and parents and community members were communicating much more effectively and working collaboratively toward the shared goal of improving student achievement and reducing the achievement gap between white and nonwhite students. The grassroots efforts of committed parents from all sectors of San Diego appeared to have been the most significant catalyst for transforming the relationship among the administration, the teachers' union, and the parents and community. The prospect of a new, highly energetic superintendent with strong organizational skills and a commitment to raising student achievement

---

[97]J. Williams, *supra* note 68.
[98]Swift, *supra* note 3, on 8 June 1998.

contributed to the positive outlook for the district. Governor Wilson's class-size reduction program for the early grades reflected the pro-education political climate within the state, and San Diego's children were sure to benefit from this redirection of state funding, as well. While it was too soon to tell how much these changes would affect student achievement, it appeared that the future held the promise of a much-improved educational opportunity for San Diego's children.

Epilogue

In the spring of 2002, San Diego was one year into a reform program entitled *Blueprint for Student Success*, which was highly rated by an independent review team, but viewed with skepticism by many teachers and parents. Superintendent Alan Bersin and Chancellor of Instruction Anthony Alvarado initiated the program, which focused on raising student performance in reading and math.[99] The plan used three strategies: 1) *prevention*, which included well-defined curriculum, content standards, and professional development to raise the proficiency of all students, 2) *intervention* through increasing the instructional day and year for students who were well below grade level, and 3) *retention* of students who were significantly below grade level, to give them a chance to catch up in their early school years. The plan included extra instruction in math and especially in reading for students lagging in those subject areas, and extra funding for enhanced materials in schools with the largest percentage of low performing students.[100] Though the Palo Alto based independent review team American Institute for Research praised the program, its report noted that the administration had not communicated effectively to teachers and parents the purposes of the program and what was expected of them. Educators feared they might lose their jobs based on poor student performance, and they resented a perceived loss of authority in their classrooms. The report said teacher responses to a survey conducted by the research team indicated that teacher morale had declined since the implementation of the reforms and "educators feel undervalued and disrespected."

---

[99] Maureen Magee, "School 'blueprint' saluted," *San Diego Union-Tribune* (SignOnSanDiego.com), 13 February 2002.

[100] San Diego City Schools Institute for Learning, "Executive Summary, Blueprint for Student Success in a Standards-Based System: Supporting Student Achievement in an Integrated Learning Environment," 14 March 14, 2000, *passim*.

Considering the potential value in the plan for improving student learning, the review team urged all stakeholders to "'lay down the rhetoric' and give the reform a chance to gain a foothold."[101]

In January of 2002, the state released school-by-school ratings on its Academic Performance Index (API), which also offered some validity to San Diego's reforms, particularly in elementary schools and to some extent in middle schools, though less progress was seen in San Diego high schools. Five San Diego City schools were ranked in the highest categories when compared with all California schools and when compared with schools with similar demographics. Eighteen percent of San Diego City's schools scored at or above the state's goal of eight hundred on the API, whereas more than 20 percent ranked in the two lowest categories.[102]

Superintendent Bersin's emphasis on accountability resulted in the school board's proposing to abolish the magnet programs at five under performing schools. The $1.1 million allocated to their magnet programs would be dispersed among fifteen schools, including the five magnets in question, for their literacy and math programs. Parents protested the rescinding of the popular magnet school programs, but board members noted that the magnet program goals of racial integration and academic achievement were not being met in these schools. The five schools were ranked either two or three on a scale of ten on the state's API, whereas most of the city's twenty-nine magnet schools placed in the four to seven range.[103] Thus, it appeared that the costly and popular magnet programs were being held to the same standards as other district schools. The magnet schools would have to justify their costly programs through acceptable achievement levels.

---

[101] Magee, "School 'blueprint' saluted."

[102] Chris Moran and Jill Spielvogel, "Ratings show how schools measure up," *San Diego Union-Tribune* (SignOnSanDiego.com) 17 January 2002.

[103] David E. Graham, "Five S.D. magnet schools get reprieve," *San Diego Union-Tribune* (SignOnSanDiego.com) 28 February 2002.

CHAPTER 10

Desegregation in Cleveland, Ohio

Introduction

In the mid-twentieth century, the city of Cleveland was strikingly racially segregated, with virtually all the black population living on the east side of the Cuyahoga River. Several strong ethnic communities of European descent were also located on the east side of the city. These communities had traditionally resisted encroachment from the growing black population. Cleveland public schools reflected the racial segregation within the community, owing to the Cleveland board of education's official "neighborhood school" policy. The board, responding to public pressure, long supplemented its official neighborhood school policy with numerous unofficial policies that resulted in profound racial segregation within the school system.[1]

Racial segregation characterized the metropolitan area, as well. Like many other metropolitan areas in the United States in the 1930s through 1950s, Cleveland had experienced the in-migration of blacks to the city and the out-migration of whites to the suburbs. By 1960, 98 percent of all the nonwhite public school children in the greater Cleveland area were enrolled in Cleveland city schools, while nearly 70 percent of the area's white children attended suburban schools. The Catholic school system also contributed to the racial isolation within the school system. In 1950, 30 percent of the white school aged population in Cleveland

---

[1] Willard C. Richan, *Racial Isolation in the Cleveland Public Schools: A Report of a Study Sponsored by the United States Commission on Civil Rights* (Cleveland: Case Western Reserve University, 1967), 5-7.

attended Catholic schools.[2] A study conducted by the Urban League of Cleveland showed Greater Cleveland to be the most segregated community in the United States in 1960.[3] Ninety-eight percent of all blacks in metropolitan Cleveland lived east of the Cuyahoga River within the city, and ninety percent lived in five areas: Central, Hough, Glenville, Mt. Pleasant, and Kinsman. The rapidly growing black population was expanding northeast and southeast, encroaching on formerly all white mostly eastern European ethnic communities.[4]

Dissatisfaction within the black community with school system policies which served to concentrate blacks within inferior and often severely overcrowded schools began in the 1930s and reached a violent peak in the early 1960s as the fervor of the Civil Rights Movement fueled long simmering frustration within the black community. Ironically, between 1954, the year of the Supreme Court's landmark *Brown v. Board of Education* decision, and 1963, the percentage of Cleveland's black school children who attended totally segregated schools more than quadrupled.[5]   Finally in 1973, several African- Americans brought a class action suit against the school system and the state board of education, charging that Cleveland had operated a *de jure* racially segregated school system in violation of the Fourteenth Amendment. A liability finding on the part of the school district and the state resulted in one of the most comprehensive remedial orders of the time. Rather than implementing the plan, which could have revitalized a declining urban school district and improved the quality of education offered all students, the district employed delay tactics to challenge the court's authority and spent years and millions of dollars appealing the decisions, at the expense of funds and energies which could have been used to improve educational programs. Thus, owing to a mixture of factors, including administrative incompetence, irresponsible board of education practices, public fears regarding the negative effects of desegregation, and flight of the middle class to the suburbs, the school system declined throughout the next two decades by virtually every standard of measurement.   This chapter addresses the events and forces leading to the main desegregation case and subsequent litigation and educational reforms. The following chapter

---

[2] Ibid., 5-6.

[3] *The Negro in Cleveland, 1950-1963; An Analysis of the Social and Economic Characteristics of the Negro Population* (Cleveland: The Urban League of Cleveland, 1964) 6.

[4] Ibid., 3.

[5] Richan 1-2.

addresses the challenges facing the district at the turn of the twenty-first century, with analysis of the legal, political, and socioeconomic factors that limited the success of the remedial order.

History

During the ante-bellum era, Cleveland had a reputation as a liberal northern city, many of whose residents gave refuge to fugitive slaves. Heavy immigration from Europe during the latter half of the nineteenth century contributed to rapid population growth in Cleveland. By 1890, three of four residents were European immigrants or their descendants. As a consequence, the city became increasingly segregated.[6]

Policies promulgated by the Federal Housing Administration (FHA) contributed to the racial segregation that would define the Cleveland metropolitan area. The FHA underwriting manual of the 1930s warned appraisers against any "infiltration of inharmonious racial or nationality groups" into neighborhoods. Only neighborhoods with zoning regulations and restrictive covenants that effected racial segregation received high FHA ratings. Despite the U.S. Supreme Court's ruling against such covenants in *Shelley v. Kramer* (1948), the FHA recommended restrictive covenants until 1950. Restrictive covenants continued to be a factor in the public financing of housing until a 1962 executive order regarding equal opportunity in housing effectively ended their use. Moreover, the Cuyahoga Metropolitan Housing Authority (CMHA), whose policies also promoted racial segregation, worked closely with school officials, securing their assurances that schools would be provided for public housing estates before construction of the housing was approved. Thus, schools were built to serve racially segregated public housing projects, and the racial composition of the schools mirrored that of the projects.[7]

In 1940, approximately 15 percent of Cleveland's public school students were black. Just over half of those students attended ten one-race schools that were located in central Cleveland. The remainder of Cleveland's black school children was enrolled in the district's fifty-eight other elementary schools, with very low percentages of blacks in each school.[8] During the 1950s, Cleveland's school population increased

---

[6] Ibid., 31-32.
[7] Reed v. Rhodes, 422 F. Supp. 708, 788-90 (N.D. Ohio 1976).
[8] Ibid., 718-19.

dramatically owing to the post war "baby boom". Due to in-migration of blacks and out-migration of whites to the suburbs, the black student population was increasing much faster than the white student population. The school district allowed black schools to become severely overcrowded. When it finally approved new schools in black neighborhoods, it typically chose sites that concentrated black students, rather than shifting some of them from overcrowded schools to nearby underutilized predominantly white schools.[9]

In 1953, the Ohio legislature placed ultimate responsibility for public education with an elected state board of education that was bound by the Ohio Constitution. In June of 1956, the state board requested an opinion of the attorney general regarding its responsibilities to ensure that Ohio school systems were not segregated. The attorney general informed the board in writing that according to state law, it was required to investigate whether school districts were complying with the law, *including providing a desegregated learning environment.* Furthermore, the board was obligated to withhold funds from any district that did not conform to applicable laws, rules, and regulations. Thus, the state board knew without a doubt in 1956 of its legal responsibility for any purposeful segregation within Ohio school districts. Yet, despite the obvious and growing racial segregation within the Cleveland school district, the state board never acted on its duty.[10]

In the Hough-Dunham area on the east side of Cleveland, school district policies served to contain the rapidly growing black student population in Hough and Wade Park schools. The board allowed severe overcrowding in schools with appreciable black student populations, while adjacent all-white schools remained significantly under enrolled.[11] The schools in the Beehive area were clearly racially identifiable well into the 1960s, when the school district knew of the suspect nature of maintaining black schools and white schools side by side.[12] Multiple opportunities existed for integrating students at the schools, often times requiring the students to walk shorter distances and/or traverse less hazardous routes. School district officials instead used numerous measures that were completely inexplicable, other than through their obvious purpose, to maintain the racial identifiability of the schools in

---

[9] Richan, 31-36.
[10] Reed v. Rhodes, *supra* note 7, at 792-93.
[11] Ibid., 753.
[12] Ibid., 738.

the area.[13] In the Glenville area, to the north and east of the Hough area, the rapidly growing black student population was contained in certain schools, as well. The school board eventually placed severely overcrowded predominantly black schools on a relay class schedule to relieve severe overcrowding, rather than redraw attendance zones and place some of the black students in nearby underutilized predominantly white schools.[14]

Glaring disparities existed between the predominantly black and the predominantly white schools. "The best teachers were on the west side and the not-so-good teachers were on the east side. The west side--the white schools--would get the best equipment, and the black schools got what was left," recalled Stanley Tolliver, an attorney who became active in the movement for integration.[15]

The district tracked students academically, separating students into learning groups from the brightest students, to strong students, to average learners, to slow learners, to various categories of children with learning disabilities. Mrs. Charles (Dr. Mareyjoice) Green, professor of sociology at Cleveland State University and an actively involved parent in the school district at the time, recalled that there were perhaps as many as nine tracks. Advanced tracks or classes were offered in schools with large percentages of white students. As schools became increasingly black, advanced classes were pulled from those schools. Black children of single parents tended to be placed in slow learning classes, apparently because administrators anticipated that children in single parent homes would have more learning difficulties.[16]

Furthermore, black students were often placed in slow learning tracks for disciplinary reasons. Following a minor disciplinary incident with Mrs. Green's eight-year-old son, he was recommended for a slow learning class. The school psychologist called Mr. and Mrs. Green in for a consultation regarding their son's placement. In an unusual move, the

---

[13] Ibid., 742.

[14] Ibid., 768-69.

[15] Stanley Tolliver, attorney at law, former member of the Cleveland board of education and original member of the advisory board to the Office on School Monitoring and Community Relations, telephone interview by author, 15 July 1997.

[16] Mrs. Charles (Dr. Mareyjoice) Green, professor of sociology at Cleveland State University, telephone interview by author, 12 July 1997. Owing to her sensitivity to the stereotype of African-American women being single mothers, Mrs. Green asked to be cited as Mrs. Charles Green, rather than by her professional title.

psychologist advised the couple to remove their son from the school immediately. He informed the Greens that the child did not belong in a slow learning class, but if he remained in that school, he would eventually be placed in a low track. The Greens placed their son in another school.[17]

Thus, the Cleveland public school system was operating separate and unequal schools for whites and for nonwhites. Disparities included the quality of the facilities, the number of students occupying the school buildings, the use of relay classes in severely overcrowded black schools, equipment and supplies, and the experience of the teachers. Although there was a small group of very vigilant minority parents who vociferously advocated for better service and facilities for their children, the district, for the most part, ignored these pleas. A very effective tactic used by the district to maintain its dual school system was to control information provided to the public. The district administration systematically denied parents and the general public access to information regarding financial issues, student assignment, facility use, and virtually all aspects of the district's operations. Despite the district's campaign to diffuse criticism, public awareness grew.

The Seeds of Unrest

Disparities in the school system mirrored socioeconomic disparities between blacks and whites in Cleveland. In 1959, the median family income for white residents of Cleveland was $7,350. The median family income for blacks was $4,768.[18] Cleveland's economy centered on heavy industry, which was on the decline. Blacks were increasingly concentrated, not only in such declining heavy industries as steel mills, foundries, and machinery manufacture, but in the less skilled positions at these factories. Advances in technology would eliminate many of these positions within a decade. Blacks comprised 13.8 percent of the labor force, but represented 31.5 percent of the unemployed in Cleveland in 1960.[19] Because of housing discrimination, blacks were not only segregated in restricted areas of east Cleveland, the housing quality was far inferior to white housing which commanded the same rent.[20] As in

---

[17] Ibid.

[18] *The Negro in Cleveland, 1950-1963, supra* note 3, at 10-11.

[19] U.S. Census of Population, Ohio, 1960, Ibid., Table 11.

[20] Ibid., 19.

countless other American cities, racial discrimination resulted in substandard education, underemployment, unemployment, and substandard living conditions for African-Americans.

Frustration grew within Cleveland's black community. Not only were black students concentrated in certain schools, but all the district's black teachers were assigned to the east central area. The board's transfer policy continued to rankle black residents.[21] The inequitable service provided black children reflected both the political impotence of the black community and their supporters, and the school board's susceptibility to public pressure from Cleveland's white community.[22] Racial segregation within the district was increasing. Between 1958 and 1965, the district built twenty-one new schools. All opened either nearly all black or nearly all white.[23]

The placement of increasing numbers of black children in relay (half day) classes to relieve overcrowding in their schools, while whole classrooms sat empty in white schools, brought frustration within the black community to a head in the early 1960s. In the fall of 1961, in response to the demands of parents, the school board jettisoned relay classes for busing classes of black students *intact* to white schools.[24] The transported students were kept segregated from white students in the receiving schools.

In the early 1960s, the Civil Rights Movement began to move out of the deep South and border states to the North. In 1963, the approximately fifty area organizations supporting civil rights formed a federation called the United Freedom Movement (UFM). They were an eclectic collection of organizations, which ranged from conciliatory and moderate to militant, and this diversity hampered their working effectively together over an extended period of time. Yet, their unity on the school integration issue provided momentum for the movement and brought the entire community into conflict.[25]

In August of 1963, on the eve of the historic March on Washington, the UFM presented the Cleveland board of education with seven demands

---

[21]Apparently, schools honored transfer slips written by *city councilmen* (who had no legal authority over the school system), evidence of the politically charged nature of school district operations. (See testimony of Superintendent Paul Briggs in Richan, 18).

[22] Richan, 38-39.

[23] Ibid., 8.

[24] Reed v. Rhodes, *supra* note 7, at 732.

[25] Ibid., 735.

all related to integration and ending discriminatory practices. The most controversial was that bused classes be integrated in their receiving schools. Besides segregating the black students in separate classes, administrators allowed black students to use the restrooms only once a day, when white children would not be using them. They also prohibited black students from participating in extra-curricular activities, from viewing the annual Christmas program, and from using the playground. In a move that reflected the white receiving community's influence with the board, it finally responded to the UFM's demands with vague assurances that the children would be integrated where doing so was deemed "educationally sound."[26]

Following additional protests, the board finally agreed to integrate the bused classes as "fully as is educationally sound" by January 1965. It also established a Citizens' Council on Human Relations to assist with meaningful integration. When integration of the bused classes had not taken place by January, the UFM and the Hazeldell Parents Association, which represented the interests of the Glenville area, began picketing the host schools. Angry residents of the host neighborhoods heckled and shoved the picketers. Violence broke out at Murray Hill School in "Little Italy." As over one thousand men terrorized the neighborhood, attacking blacks and newsmen, smashing cars and throwing rocks and bottles at policemen and priests, the mayor merely appealed for calm and asserted that law and order would be maintained; the police made no arrests. The board of education refused to take further action on the integration issue until they received a full report from the Citizens' Council on Human Relations.[27]

Following another demonstration, the board, the mayor, leaders of UFM, and the Hazeldell Parents Association agreed to a plan calling for the immediate diffusion of transported students at their receiving schools. On March 9, the classes were fully integrated, without incident except for higher than usual absenteeism. Meanwhile, the board began a crash construction program in Cleveland's ghetto, despite the adequate space in the receiving schools for the black students.[28]

The Citizens' Council on Human Relations submitted its recommendations in April 1965. The council recommended redrawing attendance zones to increase integration, selective use of transfers to

---

[26] Ibid., 735-36.
[27] Ibid., 736-38.
[28] Ibid., 740.

promote integration, and the pairing of nearby white and black schools. The board immediately shelved the council's recommendations, which were much more radical than the demands of any of the civil rights groups, and proceeded with its own construction plan which would resegregate the students.[29]

The Hazeldell Parents Association and the UFM began picketing the construction site of one of the three new ghetto schools. Picketing evolved into civil disobedience when the demonstrators began throwing themselves into excavation ditches and in front of construction machinery in order to halt construction. The Reverend Bruce Klunder threw himself down behind a bulldozer as another protester lay in front of the machine. Unwittingly, the driver backed over Klunder, killing him. Blacks from the neighborhood, who had watched in anger as police dragged demonstrators away, exploded in rage when they realized Klunder had been killed. They attacked police and vandalized and looted area stores late into the night. Within the city, state, and nation, the Reverend Klunder's death wrought mixed reactions. Many middle class blacks who had not yet joined the cause felt compelled to join the battle for which a white minister had given his life. Some viewed Klunder's action as a reckless and futile gesture, typical of the civil rights activists. Some news reports blamed the activists for the violence that followed the accident. Others viewed Klunder as a martyr.[30] The UFM reasserted itself, staging a sit-in at City Hall the following day, but the school construction continued, with the district eventually erecting construction fences around the sites to keep demonstrators away.[31]

In 1964, a lawsuit entitled *Craggett v. Board of Education* was filed to prevent the construction of additional schools for the purpose of containing black children in black neighborhoods. The Court of Appeals for the Sixth Circuit declined to issue an injunction against the school district, however. The court's denial of an injunction provided a green light for the school district to continue its segregative site selection policies with impunity.

Though civil rights activists failed in their effort to integrate Cleveland's schools, they brought attention to the poor educational service provided by the school system and to mismanagement by the

---

[29] Ibid.
[30] The Reverend Klunder's death would not soon be forgotten. Of the over twenty Cleveland residents interviewed for this case study in 1997, virtually every person mentioned the death of the pastor.
[31] Richan, 66-68.

board of education that bordered on abdication of responsibility. Superintendent Levenson resigned in the spring of 1964 amidst the turmoil.   Dr. Paul Briggs, appointed superintendent following Levinson's resignation, took on a school district driven by social conflict. The board of education acquiesced in his demand that he be given full authority to act, rather than serving as the board's puppet. Briggs brought energy to the office and seemed to bring the community together by stressing a theme of quality education for all children. His success in bringing federal War on Poverty funds to Cleveland increased his popularity.   The fight for integration had illuminated gross deficiencies throughout the school system, including long kindergarten waiting lists, elementary schools without libraries, a lack of vocational classes in most high schools, unfilled staff vacancies, antiquated and dilapidated buildings, and seemingly insurmountable financial woes.[32]

Given the severity of the deficiencies within the school system as a whole, the pervasiveness of the racial segregation, and resistance from within the white community and the power structure, Briggs chose concentrating on quality rather than integration issues.   Riots in the summer of 1964 and calls for black power had brought to the surface lingering and deep-seated racial tension, hardening opposition to integration, especially in Cleveland's ethnic enclaves.[33]

In an effort to reduce racial tension, a group of seventy community leaders, thirty-five white (mostly businessmen) and thirty-five black, met at Case Western Reserve University and signed an agreement giving Superintendent Briggs a six month "grace period" in which to begin correcting racial inequities in the schools before they would take any action.   This group eventually formed the Businessmen's Interracial Committee on Community Affairs, which kept Briggs apprised of their concerns during the next ten years.   With the committee's advice and support, the support of the extended business community, as well as that of the local newspapers, whose editors had also agreed to allow Briggs a "grace period," Briggs largely transformed the school district in the following ten years.[34]

---

[32] Ibid., 83.
[33] Ibid., 42.
[34] Frank Kuznik, "The Politics of Desegregation," *Cleveland Magazine*, September 1978, 84.

With $200 million approved by taxpayers,[35] Superintendent Briggs embarked on an ambitious building program, replacing approximately one third of the district's buildings within a relatively short period of time. Attorney James Hardiman recalled, "The community loved him, because of the fact that he was building schools, people were working, architects were making money, builders were making money, everybody was making money." Very few people questioned the fact that the school system was becoming increasingly segregated. Following the dismissal of the *Craggett* case, it appeared that the district had a "carte blanche" for building segregated schools. "The few dissenting voices were drowned out."[36]

Superintendent Briggs surrounded himself with loyal subordinates, and the board of education rubber-stamped his policies without question.[37] In fact, Briggs would become a "community icon," whose stellar reputation allowed him to resist the court's authority when the district was found liable for system-wide racial segregation twelve years later.[38] "The system's public image was positive, its alliances with the private-sector leadership were strong, its portrait in the media was glowingly affirmative"[39] at the time the court found it guilty of unconstitutional discrimination against black students.

In the early years of the Briggs administration, blacks rose for the first time to positions of significant power within the educational system. By the mid 1970s, more than 40 percent of Cleveland's teachers were black, giving Cleveland perhaps the highest percentage of black teachers of any urban school district in the nation.[40] However, pledges to integrate the faculty were not fulfilled. The district and the

---

[35] Kay Benjamin, "A Case Study of an Urban Superintendent: Paul Briggs, 1964-1978" (Ph.D. diss., Cleveland State University, 1995), 237.

[36] James Hardiman, counsel for plaintiffs in Reed v. Rhodes, telephone interview by author, 18 July 1997.

[37] Benjamin, 237-38.

[38] Leonard Stevens, former director of the Office on School Monitoring and Community Relations, telephone interview by author, 18 July 1997. Following the announcement of the remedial order, the judge named Dr. Stevens director of the Office on School Monitoring and Community Relations, the "watchdog" agency he established to assist him in overseeing the implementation of the remedial order.

[39] Leonard Stevens, *More Than a Bus Ride: The Desegregation of the Cleveland Public Schools* (Cleveland: The Office on School Monitoring and Public Relations, 1985), 21.

[40] Ibid.

administration reflected the political atmosphere in Cleveland. It was a city divided by race and one in which the power structure, which included the business community and the media, accepted and perpetuated a positive image of the district, which was purposely segregating children by race, long after the practice had been declared unconstitutional by the United States Supreme Court.

In 1967, a report based on a study made by the United States Commission on Civil Rights concluded:

> It seems clear from all that has been said thus far that the Cleveland Board of Education is a political institution in a political environment which does not support racial integration in the schools. School officials would have to be willing to court tremendous opposition in order to initiate any serious attempt to reverse the trend toward complete racial isolation. And, as of 1967, they have few visible signs of support from any major quarter.[41]

The school district pursued its racially segregative site selection policies well into the 1970s, even after a class action suit that relied heavily on such policies had been filed in federal district court.

Reed v. Rhodes

In December 1973, ten school children, including Robert Anthony Reed, III, and their parents brought suit against the governor of Ohio, the attorney general, the state board of education, the superintendent of public instruction of the Ohio Department of Education, the Cleveland superintendent of schools, and the Cleveland board of education. They charged them with pursuing policies that had promoted the racial segregation of children in Cleveland's public schools. In other words, the plaintiffs charged the state and school system with *de jure* segregation. They noted as evidence such actions as boundary changes, the creation of optional attendance zones, the use of rented classroom space, additions of temporary and permanent classroom space and other facilities, and the construction of new schools and closing of schools, all

---

[41]Richan, 89.

of which contributed to the increasing racial segregation within the school system.[42]

The defendants countered that the segregation resulted from housing patterns over which they had no control. Yet, the evidence showed that numerous school district policies, especially those related to student assignment and measures taken to accommodate the growing student population, defied explanation other than that they purposely perpetuated a racially segregated school system. Furthermore, school officials appeared to have collaborated with city officials on an ongoing basis through various home construction and urban renewal projects to delineate Cleveland neighborhoods based on race. The district coordinated its activities with public housing authorities whose decisions on placement of projects depended on the cooperation of other public agencies providing services, including public school authorities. Testimony at the trial indicated that real estate agents offered black consumers housing in certain areas only.[43] Thus, the school district's neighborhood school policy reinforced the segregated housing patterns.

The board defended its actions, claiming it had adhered to a neighborhood school policy. Superintendent Briggs conceded that he could have altered attendance zones to increase racial integration, but that he had acted in the best interests of the city in not doing so. Massive reassignment of students to integrate the schools would have resulted in white flight and resegregation, he said.[44]

In his 1976 opinion establishing the school district's liability, Judge Frank Battisti wrote, "At some point, the failure of the Board to deviate from its 'neighborhood school policy' can be viewed only as a conscious and deliberate choice to contain the black school children of Cleveland in racially identifiable schools."[45] Judge Battisti relied heavily on *Keyes v.*

---

[42]Reed v. Rhodes, *supra* note 3 at 716.

[43]Ibid., 718-19.

Norman Krumholz, director of city planning during the 1970s in Cleveland and later professor in urban studies at Cleveland State University, explained that both black and white realtors benefited from the segregated residential conditions in Cleveland, because each had his or her own territory. Furthermore, block busting practices had been fairly well established; realtors colluded to instigate panic selling as neighborhoods began to "tip" from predominantly white to predominantly black (interview by author, 25 July 1997).

[44]"Judge Battisti Must Sift Mountain of Evidence to Render His Verdict," *Cleveland Plain Dealer*, 14 February 1976, 1(A).

[45]Reed v. Rhodes, *supra* note 3, at 756.

Denver School District No. 1 (1973), the first "northern" case where the Supreme Court rejected the "neighborhood school policy" defense and refused to distinguish between *de jure* and *de facto* segregation where school district policies had manipulated neighborhood school policies to further racial segregation.

Judge Battisti held that the school district actively contributed to the segregated nature of the Cuyahoga Metropolitan Housing Administration's projects by consenting to build schools to serve the projects, knowing that the schools, like the projects, would be racially segregated. Thus, the district's "neighborhood school" policy was not racially neutral. "The natural, probable, foreseeable, and actual effect of the local school board's application of the neighborhood school policy was to create or perpetuate a segregated school system."[46] Battisti found the district and the state board of education liable for the segregated state of the system.

James Hardiman, counsel for the plaintiffs, recalled that while the evidence against the district was overwhelming, the NAACP had been far from certain of the outcome of the case, especially in light of the dismissal of *Craggett* in 1964. "It was a lot less than a slam dunk," he observed. Once the liability order had been issued, however, Hardiman assumed that the most difficult task was over. This was not to be the case, however. The crafting of the remedial order proved much more challenging than proving liability.[47]

Following the court's finding of liability on the part of the Cleveland board of education and the state board of education, the defendants quickly appealed. On July 20, 1977, the Court of Appeals for the Sixth Circuit remanded the Cleveland case to the district court for reconsideration of its findings in light of *Dayton Board of Education v. Brinkman* (1977), wherein the Supreme Court required that the court determine the consequence(s) of the constitutional violation and fashion a remedy accordingly. In *Dayton*, the court had found *de facto* segregation, but it found "no present segregative effect" from the defendants' "past intentional segregative actions." In stark contrast, in the Cleveland case, Judge Battisti found that the defendants' actions had contributed to the segregated housing patterns and that they continued to contribute to the segregation within the school system.[48]

---

[46]Ibid., 790.
[47]Hardiman, *supra* note 36.
[48]Reed v. Rhodes, 455 F. Supp. 546, 551 (N.D. Ohio 1978).

Again finding the district and the state liable, Judge Battisti cited over two hundred instances of intentional segregative actions, not only in the Central area, but in numerous other areas, the cumulative effect of which was system-wide segregation. "Intentionally segregative conduct pervaded the entire system in Cleveland, dictating the legal conclusion that defendants were purposefully operating a dual system. . . . Their actions impacted on every school in the system by racially identifying every school and by signaling to all residents, black and white, which schools were theirs."[49] To illustrate his findings, Judge Battisti listed fifty-three instances of boundary changes, three instances of converted board owned facilities to other than classroom uses, thirty-eight instances of optional zones, twenty-one instances of reassignment of students, twenty-seven instances of construction of new school facilities, sixteen additions to existing schools, seventeen instances of busing in which cases black children were kept segregated from the white children in their receiving schools, seven instances of school closings followed by reassignment of students, eleven instances of erecting portable classrooms, two instances of transfer and annexation of school territory between school districts, four instances of changing the grade structure of schools, seven instances of the use of private rented facilities, six instances of conducting relay classes (for six years at one school), and two cases of deliberately keeping schools under utilized while nearby schools were severely overcrowded.[50] The judge emphasized that the foregoing was "*not* an exhaustive list of the massive amount of evidence of constitutional violations presented and considered by this Court prior to arriving at a final decision."[51]

The school board's defense consisted of three major arguments: 1) that there had been no intent to violate the rights of minority children, 2) that it had racially neutral, educationally sound explanations for all of the plaintiff's allegations of racial segregation, and 3) regardless of intent, its actions were not responsible for the pervasive racial segregation within the school district. In response to the first defense, the court declared that while the defendants may have thought that their actions were well motivated, they were nevertheless unconstitutional. Furthermore, said Judge Battisti, few of the school district's segregative acts could be construed in such a positive light. Regarding the second defense, school

---

[49]Ibid., 552-53.
[50]Ibid., 558-565, *passim.*
[51]Ibid., 558.

district officials argued that their site selection, boundary, and optional zone decisions were prompted by concerns for the children's safety or were aimed at relieving overcrowding; that is, they tried to avoid railroad tracks and busy thoroughfares. However, in the over two hundred instances of intentional racial segregative actions cited by the judge, these explanations "were not credible or were not legally permissible."[52]

Judge Battisti rejected the district's third line of defense as well. The school district built schools in racially segregated housing estates or built schools to serve such projects, thus contributing to the racial segregation in housing and incorporating known residential segregation in the schools.   Battisti held that the school system "had been and was a causal factor in the residential segregation which is rampant in the city."[53]

The state board of education denied any responsibility for the racial segregation in Cleveland public schools, claiming that the state board had no authority over site selection, attendance zones, transfer policies, pupil and teacher assignments, and other acts that had contributed to racial segregation. Unmoved, the court noted that the state board had failed to explain why it had ignored the attorney general's 1956 advice that the board was obligated to investigate whether racial segregation existed within Ohio school districts, and once found, the board was legally obligated to take measures to eliminate racial segregation. "Because of their consistent record of default in their official duties, the state defendants became a part of the problem, not part of the solution."[54]

Judge Battisti ordered the defendants to submit to the court a desegregation plan which would restore the plaintiffs "to substantially the position they would have occupied had (the segregative actions) not occurred" and which would reduce the racial imbalance in the system as much as was feasible. He appointed a special master, Daniel McCarthy, and two experts to help him evaluate the plan.[55]

The plan eventually adopted by the court was based on the third proposal submitted by the school district, with revisions recommended by the special master and following public testimony. The desegregation plan consisted of pairings, clusterings, boundary changes, grade structure changes, and feeder pattern changes to effectuate pupil desegregation.[56] All areas and grade levels were to be desegregated in September 1978.

---

[52] Ibid., 555.
[53] Ibid., 567.
[54]Ibid., 557-58.
[55]Reed v. Rhodes, 455 F. Supp. 569, 571-72 (N.D. Ohio 1978).
[56]Ibid., 573.

The judge estimated that approximately fifty-two thousand students would require transportation to their newly assigned schools.[57]

In addition to the desegregation of pupils and faculty, the remedial order included nine educational components and other ancillary relief, which were designed to eliminate the deleterious effects of years of racial segregation. These included:

a) Prohibition of testing and ability tracking if they resulted in racial segregation, as long as the judge believed that under achievement of certain racial groups resulted from prior segregation;

b) Institution of an "affirmative reading skills program" to improve the reading skills of minority students whose poor reading skills the judge blamed, at least in part, on the effects of disparate treatment in schools;

c) Institution of counseling programs to ease student stress related to desegregation and to provide all students with nondiscriminatory career guidance;

d) Development of a comprehensive plan for magnet schools and programs;

e) Development of a comprehensive plan to involve universities, business, and cultural institutions in cooperative educational ventures;

f) Development of a plan to assure equal access to extracurricular activities;

g) Staff development and student training in human relations;

h) Clarification of student rights and responsibilities to avoid discriminatory treatment of students;

i) Development of a plan for community involvement in the desegregation plan to engender support for its smooth implementation.[58]

The remedial order was replete with references to the school system's lack of cooperation with the special master and the court, poor record keeping, financial incompetence, and general lack of good faith prior to and throughout the development of the desegregation plan. The judge observed, "the record clearly demonstrates that the Cleveland defendants

---

[57]Ibid., 602.
[58]Ibid., 598-602.

presently lack either the capability or the desire to implement and administer a desegregation program in the Cleveland public schools." He cited the defendants' "lack of expertise" to address the complexities that would arise during implementation of the desegregation plan, the defendants' incompetence in management and financing, and their "lack of commitment in carrying out the letter and spirit of the Courts' orders. While asserting they will obey this Court's orders 'cheerfully', the defendants have consistently resisted them."[59]

As was the rule in desegregation cases, the court resisted imposing a desegregation plan of its own design on the school district, instead encouraging the district to devise its own plan, which would be examined by the special master and the court to ensure that it incorporated the court's basic requirements. Yet, as of the date of the remedial order, the district had not submitted a plan for pupil reassignment to the court. Based on this resistance and the history of incompetence displayed by the district, Judge Battisti ordered the establishment of a Department of Desegregation Implementation and the hiring of a deputy superintendent to oversee the enforcement of the desegregation plan. Judge Battisti allowed the administration and the board of education time to appoint someone to the position. However, when neither the administration nor the board did so, the judge eventually appointed Dr. Charles W. Leftwich to the position.

Both the Cleveland board of education and the state board of education appealed Judge Battisti's ruling. In the meantime, Judge Battisti forged ahead. On April 21, 1978, exasperated with the defendants' recalcitrance regarding the desegregation order and general incompetence, he placed all school system departments engaged in or related to the desegregation process, including business, computer, research and development, and community relations, under the direct supervision of Deputy Superintendent for Desegregation Leftwich. Dr. Leftwich was a well known expert in desegregation implementation who had testified about his experience with the Boston desegregation case during the trial. Judge Battisti authorized him to hire whatever staff he needed to ensure that desegregation took place. In a memo explaining his action, Judge Battisti said that he found that "the Cleveland defendants

---

[59]Ibid., 605.

do not possess either the expertise, experience, or willingness to comply with this court's orders without outside assistance."[60]

The board of education quickly appealed Judge Battisti's order of April 21, claiming that it was "unwarranted, improper, and exceeded the equitable power of a district court in a school desegregation setting for the reason that not only was there no showing of necessity for such order, but no such necessity exists."[61] On April 27, Superintendent Briggs, who had taken his position in 1964, in the midst of the civil rights crisis, resigned. Briggs had held the position of superintendent longer than any other contemporary large-city school superintendent, and much longer than the district's average of 2.5 to 3 years. The appointment of Charles Leftwich as Deputy Superintendent of Desegregation, followed by the Judge Battisti's ordering the hiring of Leftwich's hand picked staff, after Briggs had refused to hire them, had evidently been the final straw that drove Briggs to resign. After more than a decade as the heralded savior of the school system, Briggs could no longer accept the indignity of having his accomplishments belittled and his authority usurped by the court. As Frank Kuznik put it in the *Cleveland Magazine*, "Paul Briggs resigned and left town a bitter and broken man."[62]

Local supporters of school desegregation applauded both Battisti's order empowering Leftwich and Superintendent Briggs' resignation.[63] Supporters were few, however. The majority in Cleveland was so convinced of the contributions that Briggs had made to the school system that they were unwilling to accept his guilt in intentionally promoting segregation in the school system or his duplicity, as he repeatedly denied the segregative intent of school district actions and thwarted the implementation of the remedial order. In the eyes of the community, Briggs was a hero who saved the school system and Judge Battisti was a villain who was out to destroy it.

Owing to his ambitious building projects, which affected the east side of Cleveland more than the west side and his hiring of black teachers and administrators, Briggs had won considerable support not only from whites, but from many blacks in Cleveland. The *Call and Post*, the

---

[60]Robert G. McGruder and Thomas H. Gaumer, "Board appeals; slow to obey orders, judge says," *Cleveland Plain Dealer*, 28 April 1978, 1(A), 9 (A).
[61] "Obey Battisti, board lawyers advise," *Cleveland Plain Dealer*, 24 April 1978, 1(A).
[62]Kuznik, 88.
[63] "Obey Battisti," 10(A).

newspaper of the black community, was owned by a black Republican who supported Briggs because of the numerous schools Briggs had built on the east side. He was apparently unconcerned about the segregated conditions of the schools. Besides segregation, Briggs had been very generous to blacks. Arnold Pinkney, the black president of the board of education, was strongly supportive of Paul Briggs, and openly opposed the suit against the school system. Pinkney was also closely associated with the *Call and Post*. While Pinkney's vocal opposition to the plaintiffs' efforts might have been expected, given his position as president of the defendant board of education, it was nevertheless ironic, given his status as board member emeritus of the NAACP. James Hardiman noted that the desegregation case produced numerous curious alliances.[64]

In 1997, Blanche Wallace, a black activist who followed school politics for years and strongly advocated for equity for black students and quality educational service for all students, explained the sentiments of many blacks for Paul Briggs:

> Now Paul Briggs wasn't all bad. He wasn't perfect, but Paul Briggs did things for us that nobody else had done previously. He didn't integrate the schools, but to me, he shared more (equitably) than some people are doing today. . . . We had almost everything, but we didn't have everything. When you find anybody (who can give everything), that's the person I want to meet. But he was more fair with the black children than anybody has been since he left.[65]

Public Reaction to the Remedial Order

As the board of education and administration remained intransigent, public apprehension regarding the impending desegregation of the schools increased. Prior to the release of the remand opinion, the district had operated on a "business as usual" basis, issuing no official statements regarding the case, claiming that that was the only prudent course of action until the final court decision was known. Following the release of Judge Battisti's remand opinion, the district continued to conduct its

---

[64]Hardiman, *supra* note 36.
[65]Blanche Wallace, community schools activist, telephone interview by author, 21 July 1997.

business behind closed doors out of the public eye. The administration and board of education refused to inform the public of what could be expected, increasing public anxiety.

Since the inception of the case, the administration's and board of education's pointed official policy of silence had contributed to community apprehension regarding the outcome. The Reverend Donald Jacobs, head of the Inter-church Council, his assistant, the Reverend Joan Campbell, Bishop Hickey of the Catholic Diocese, Bishop John Burt of the Episcopal Diocese, and Rabbi Daniel Jeremy Silver had been meeting on a regular basis to select courses of action to help inform their constituents of the law of the land pertaining to racial desegregation in public schools, as well as to urge people to do what was "morally right."[66] Having learned from the violent upheaval following the busing order in Boston that violence was more likely to occur when there was a void in community leadership, the Cleveland Foundation and the George Gund Foundation[67] gave the Greater Cleveland Inter-church Council funds to establish an entity that would provide positive leadership and disseminate accurate information regarding desegregation. "It was a peacekeeping grant," recalled Leonard Stevens, who was brought to Cleveland and given a one year grant from the Inter-church Council to "do something" to promote peaceful desegregation. Thus, Stevens with the help of religious leaders and others founded the Greater Cleveland Project, which was a federation of sixty to seventy church-related and community social service agencies committed to peaceful desegregation.[68] Daniel Elliott and Stanley Tolliver, two local attorneys, one white and one black, co-chaired the advisory commission to the Greater Cleveland Project.

The mission of the Greater Cleveland Project was *very controversial*, explained Stevens. Owing to the politically charged atmosphere surrounding the subject of desegregation and Superintendent Briggs' well cultured and highly positive public image, any group that would entertain the idea of accepting or complying with the court order, any group that would propose looking into how the task could be accomplished *peacefully*, was viewed as anti-Paul Briggs. The district took the

---

[66]Dr. Aileen Kassen, former deputy director of the Office on School Monitoring and Community Relations, telephone interview by author, 10 July 1997.

[67]These were the largest and second largest philanthropic organizations in Cleveland, respectively.

[68]Stevens, *supra* note 38.

position that the accusation that the Briggs Administration, which was known to have done so much for the black community, could have committed unconstitutionally discriminatory acts was *preposterous and heretical*. The boards of directors of most social agencies (who represented the political and social power structure of Cleveland) strongly discouraged the agencies from participating in the Greater Cleveland Project.[69]

In many people's views, the media also contributed to the confusion. The media had sabotaged desegregation even before the remedial order was released, suggested Len Stevens. "By failing to do investigative reporting on Briggs, they built up this community icon," and that image was difficult to dispel once the judge made the decision to desegregate. The media never questioned the Briggs administration, no matter how obvious its failings.[70]

Just as the business community's and the media's support for Briggs preceded the court battle, the business community's dislike for Judge Battisti preceded the liability finding and the remedial order. Prior to the desegregation case, Judge Battisti had rendered some antitrust decisions that had created a negative view within the business community of Battisti as a judicial activist. Attorney Daniel Elliott felt that the business community tended to confuse what were very sound school desegregation decisions with Judge Battisti's rather aggressive antitrust decisions. "To an astonishing degree, (the business community) had their feet set in cement on this issue, and they did not want to be persuaded as to what the law was on these subjects. And Battisti was pointed out as some kind of a maniac, when in fact, his liability finding and his remedial order are I think to this day viewed as some of the great writing on school desegregation cases."[71]

Neither the mayor of Cleveland, George Voinovich, who would later become governor of Ohio, nor the black City Council President George Forbes, who was extremely influential within the business community, showed leadership by voicing support for the court orders. Elliott recalled a meeting between Voinovich, Forbes, Stevens, and himself, wherein Voinovich and Forbes appeared incredulous that Stevens and Elliott would ask for their support. They indicated that supporting the

---

[69]Ibid.

[70]Ibid.

[71]Daniel Elliott, first co-chairman of the steering committee for the Greater Cleveland Project, telephone interview with author, 30 July 1997.

decision would not only be poor business judgment, but politically disastrous. "So . . . everybody ran for cover. . . (There was) no political courage on the subject. . ."[72]

The Greater Cleveland Project's emphasis was education of the public regarding the law and what the people could expect, given the experience of other school districts. The level of anxiety in Cleveland was very high. Parents fretted about how their children would be affected. Teachers wondered how the remedial order would affect them. Many people worried that violence would erupt. The Greater Cleveland Project sought to fill the information void left by the school system and provide a voice of calm. The Project was the only accurate and objective source of information on the case.[73] The Project established a resource center to provide copies of the court orders and other information to the public. Teachers and principals came to the resource center to obtain copies of the court order. The Project began training people from the membership agencies and organizations so that they could disseminate information to their respective clients and inform them of the materials available at the resource center.[74] The Project also began a program called Building Parent Power, whose purpose it was to teach parents about the law in the case and the implications, as well as teaching parents what types of questions they should be asking the school system.

One of the many ironies in the Cleveland case was that the district so vehemently denied any wrongdoing, in spite of the mountain of evidence, and it so adamantly opposed the implementation of the remedial order, that it stymied the efforts of Greater Cleveland Project to insure that the desegregation process would be *peaceful.* Gloria Aron, a parent who became actively involved in the Greater Cleveland Project's efforts, through her work at the West Side Community House,[75] recalled that the Project had to "fight" to obtain information so that they could assist parents in cooperating in the desegregation process.[76]

---

[72]Ibid.
[73]Stevens, *supra* note 38.
[74]Dr. Frances Hunter, former director of the Greater Cleveland Project and later professor at Cleveland State University in the College of Urban Affairs, telephone interview by author, 23 July 1997.
[75]Cleveland had approximately twenty community centers at the time. These were settlement houses or social service agencies which served the various geographical areas of Cleveland and coordinated their efforts through the Neighborhood Centers Association.
[76]Gloria Aron, community activist with children in the Cleveland school system, telephone interview by author, 12 July 1997.

Opponents of the order held anti-busing rallies during which they exploited people's anxieties and prejudices. On April 25, 1978, an angry crowd of two thousand people filled a west side dance hall to protest forced busing for desegregation, after congressional candidate Norbert Denerell Jr., a former city councilman had advertised the meeting on local radio stations all day. Denerell denounced Judge Battisti and the NAACP, to the enthusiastic cheers of the crowd.[77] Denerell established the anti-busing group called Citizens Opposed to Rearranging Kids (CORK). Leonard Stevens described Denerell as the most bizarre, but not one of the most politically efficacious opponents of busing.

In many communities undergoing desegregation, parents had sought refuge from busing orders in private schools, especially Catholic schools. In Cleveland, however, Bishop Hickey announced that the Catholic schools would not become havens for people escaping desegregation. "Now that was a powerful thing," recalled Dr. Aileen Kassen, who worked with the Greater Cleveland Project and was deputy director of the Office on School Monitoring and Community Relations. "As far as I know, no other Catholic bishop or leader across the country has ever made such a statement, and it held true." The Catholic schools had served a large percentage of Cleveland's children prior to desegregation, greater than other large northeastern cities, recalled Kassen, who suggested that the reason for the large Catholic school enrollment may have been the strength of Cleveland's ethnic communities and the fact that the churches were the anchors of those communities.[78]

On May 4, 1978, Judge Battisti established the Office on School Monitoring and Community Relations to monitor the implementation of the desegregation order and to provide a credible, independent source of information for the court. Battisti appointed Leonard Stevens director, and he appointed twenty-one residents of Greater Cleveland to serve on an advisory commission to the OSMCR. Commission members were respected members of the community, ranging from business to education leaders, professionals, and "members of the public at large," and in accordance with Judge Battisti's order, they were known to be committed to desegregation. Ten commission members were white, nine were black, one was Hispanic, and one was American citizen born in India.[79] The

---

[77]Joseph L. Wagner, "Busing jeered by more than 2,000 here," *Cleveland Plain Dealer*, 26 April 198, 2(A).
[78]Kassen, *supra* note 66.
[79]Christopher Jensen, "Battisti names twenty-one to panel to monitor desegregation," *Cleveland Plain Dealer*, 24 June 1978, 12(A).

judge appointed Daniel Elliot as chairman of the advisory commission and included Stanley Tolliver on the commission.

Many observers of the desegregation related tensions experienced in Cleveland felt that the law firm representing the board of education did the school system and the community a great disservice by encouraging resistance and the filing of numerous appeals. Daniel Elliott suggested that attorneys for Squire, Sanders, and Dempsey were being dishonest with their clients and with business community. Attorneys appeared to encourage resistance to (what they characterized as) "this totally irrational judicial edict," implying that Judge Battisti had "woken up and invented new law one morning." Squire-Sanders attorneys publicly ridiculed the ruling, declaring it would eventually be overturned, when, according to Elliott, the defendants' "never had a chance of overturning the decision." The law firm's poor legal advice not only cost the district millions of dollars, observed Elliott, but it prolonged the legal battle for years.[80]

The law firm's and the district's ability to inflame the community, delay the litigation process, and deny blacks and other school children the benefits of the remedial order demonstrated the court's weakness in the face of community resistance, especially when the political power structure opposed the court's decision and mocked its authority.

In Cleveland, as in so many other communities where courts challenged the social structure of the community, the court's ability to desegregate the schools was severely limited by the determined resistance of the school system and the community. Judge Battisti's broader goal of eliminating the vestiges of prior discrimination by improving the *quality* of public education would prove much more daunting. In fact, the courts were completely unequipped to bring about such educational reform.

Implementation

As desegregation and the opening of the school year loomed, community activists worked feverishly to reduce tension among community residents, particularly school children, and to ensure that no incidents would mar the first day of school. One group, called Welcome--West Side and East Side Let's Come Together--focused on the students, endeavoring to make them feel welcome in their receiving schools on the "other side of town." Michael Charney, founder of the organization,

---

[80]Elliott, *supra* note 71.

explained that Welcome sought to reach an entirely different sector within the community than that reached by the Greater Cleveland Project. While the Greater Cleveland Project's message resonated somewhat with the intellectual community in Cleveland, it was unable to reach working class Cleveland, where resistance stood directly in the path of effective *integration* of students. Therefore, Welcome directed its efforts at the children, in the hope that this emphasis would diffuse some of the hostility engendered by the remedial order and increase the likelihood that the desegregation process would be a positive one for all Cleveland school children.[81]

On August 20, 1978, shortly before school was to open, the group orchestrated a Welcome Walk as a show of support for the children and to demonstrate the determination of the participants to work together for the benefit of the children. Residents from each side of Cleveland marched, holding hands toward the center of the Detroit-Superior Bridge, which connected east and west, and the leaders of each contingent joined hands in a symbolic gesture signifying solidarity of purpose. On the banks of the river below, opponents of desegregation heckled the marchers. Stanley Tolliver, a professionally trained vocalist, led the singing. Welcome memorialized the euphoria of the walk and its symbolism in its logo, which superimposed hands joined over the image of a bridge.[82]

On August 23, 1978, less than two weeks before school was to open under the desegregation plan, Judge Battisti delayed the implementation of desegregation for up to one year, primarily because the school system had done virtually nothing to secure the buses needed to transport students and because of the general financial disarray in which the school district found itself. Judge Battisti repeatedly condemned the board of education and the administration for their transparent delay tactics, for their refusal to make use of the expertise of the deputy superintendent of desegregation, and for their financial irresponsibility in failing to close any of the 31 schools that were operating at far under capacity.[83]

On August 23, 1979, the Court of Appeals for the Sixth Circuit, citing "massive evidence of intentional discrimination," upheld Judge Battisti's liability finding and the remedial orders based thereon.[84] Four

---

[81]Michael Charney, founder of West Side East Side Let's Come Together (Welcome), telephone interview by author, 20 August 1997.

[82]Tolliver, *supra* note 15.

[83] Reed v. Rhodes, No. C73-1300, slip op. (N.D. Ohio 25 August 1979).

[84]Reed v. Rhodes, 455 F. Supp.546 (N.D. Ohio 1978) *aff'd* 607 F2d 714 (6th Cir.1979), *cert. denied* 445 U.S. 935 (1980).

days later, Judge Battisti ordered the school system to implement the remedial order that fall.

On September 9, 1979, the day before Cleveland Public Schools opened under the court ordered desegregation plan, Welcome held its second walk across the Detroit-Superior Bridge, again emphasizing the theme of welcoming the children to their assigned schools on opposite sides of the city and promoting peaceful and meaningful integration. About twelve hundred people participated in the walk, including several prominent community members, such as Congressman Louis Stokes, Bishop Hickey, Bishop James Lyke, the Reverend Don Jacobs, Stanley Tolliver, and Daniel Elliot. Only one school board member, Berthina Palmer, participated and neither the superintendent of schools nor the deputy superintendent for desegregation participated.[85] The school district mailed no information whatsoever to parents explaining the remedial order. It did mail school reassignment notices and bus route information a few days before school opening.[86]

On September 10, forty-three schools, including thirty-six elementary schools, four junior high schools, and three high schools opened desegregated.[87] No significant race-related incidents were reported until October 12, when a fight broke out between white students who had been heckling black students on a bus near John Marshall High School. The following day white students picketed the school carrying signs protesting busing, the remedial order, the judge, etc. Protests continued until October 18 when the Cleveland teachers went on strike. The OSMCR report on the first phase of implementation noted that virtually nothing had been done by the school district administration to prepare the students or the staff for fostering meaningful integration of the students. Not surprisingly, notable polarization of the students had developed at John Marshall High School.[88]

Phase II of the implementation of the remedial order began on March 19, 1980, the first day of the second semester. With this phase, all of the junior high schools in the district were desegregated. The atmosphere in most schools was calm and relaxed, although harassment by parents and

---

[85] *OSMCR Report to Judge Frank Battisti on Phase 1 of Desegregation Implementation* (21 November 1979), 29.
[86] Ibid., 20.
[87] Ibid., 1-2.
[88] Ibid., 6.

students of busloads of students manifested the racial tension in some schools and neighborhoods.[89]

In the spring of 1980 court hearings on the second phase of desegregation revealed what Judge Battisti described as "systematic maladministration, a form of resistance quite different from 'standing in the schoolhouse door', but equally effective in impeding desegregation." The judge appointed a desegregation administrator to oversee the implementation of the remedial order for two years. The "dual administration" that was created resulted in deep controversy within the community and fractious relations within the administration.[90]

In Phase III Implementation, the remaining seventy schools in the district were desegregated when school opened on September 29, 1980. Phase III involved the closure of eighteen schools due to declining enrollment. The overwhelming majority of schools in the district remained significantly underutilized. With the final phase of desegregation having been completed, OSMCR's report to Judge Battisti on Phase III Implementation focused on the unfulfilled obligations from the remedial order, primarily the educational components and the administrative/ organizational shortcomings and financial woes that continued to plague the school district.

Though hindered by divisiveness and a lack of continuity within the administration and on the school board, the system made some progress toward fulfilling its court-mandated obligations under the dual administration in the following two years. The atmosphere in the schools appeared calm; however, the community remained bitterly divided over the desegregation issue.

Judge Battisti became the target of most people's anger and frustration. He received numerous death threats, often in the form of letters, as well as volumes of other hate mail. For one to two years he was under twenty-four-hour guard by federal marshals who sat in the lobby of his apartment building at night.[91] Dr. Aileen Kassen recalled:

> Battisti was a unique man. He was very bright. He was unafraid of anybody else, and he did what he felt was the right thing. And, as far as I'm concerned, it's the best remedial order that's ever been written in America, because it contains all these

---

[89]*OSMCR Report to Judge Frank Battisti on Phase II Implementation*, 37-38.
[90]Stevens, *More Than a Bus Ride*, 29-30.
[91]Stevens, *supra* note 38.

educational components, which no other order did (at the time). I think he was a wonderful man, but he was pilloried. He was pilloried by the press and . . . by the business community who thought that all he was doing was wrong. And because he was the kind of a man he was, he didn't try to defend himself. And he was hated. He really was. It was as though everything was dumped on the judge and cross-town busing. They became the two sort of swear words of the city. [92]

During the trial and following the release of the remedial order, there had been dire predictions of white flight if the court ordered desegregation of the city's schools. However, no substantial white exodus took place as a result of desegregation. Enrollment in the Cleveland schools had begun to decline in 1967, and it continued to decline in the years following the desegregation order. The primary cause of the decline was lower birth rates.[93] Other causes were suburbanization by middle class Clevelanders beginning prior to desegregation, a decline in Cleveland's industrial based economy with consequent loss of employment opportunities,[94] and desegregation of the public schools. During the two years following the implementation, OSMCR estimated that a maximum of 20 percent of the loss could have been attributed to white flight owing to desegregation.[95]

Although the initial litigation process was lengthy and acrimonious, and several delays preceded the implementation of desegregation in Cleveland, by September 1980, the system was substantially desegregated. Advocates of desegregation were hopeful that achievement among Cleveland's students would improve and opponents would recognize the benefits of desegregation, especially the numerous educational components of the court ordered plan. In November of 1985, OSMCR reported to the court that reading scores in the district had improved for both white and black students since 1981, when the court had approved and adopted final standards for the implementation of the remedial order. OSMCR reported, however, that despite gains among students of both races, parity had not been achieved, except in first and second grades. By the third grade, a gap developed, and each subsequent

---

[92]Kassen, *supra* note 66.
[93]Stevens, *Enrollment Decline and School Desegregation in Cleveland: An Analysis of Trends and Causes* (Cleveland: Office on School Monitoring and Community Relations, 1982), 20.
[94]Ibid., 17-18, 24-25.
[95]Ibid., 25-26.

year, the gap increased to 25 percent in twelfth grade, with 71.4 percent of white students and 46.2 percent of black students achieving above the 34th percentile rank.[96]

The dropout rate for the Cleveland Public Schools, which had long been higher than the national average,[97] rose dramatically in 1984 to 49 percent and remained there for the following year as well. Contrary to the national trend, white students in Cleveland dropped out at higher rates than black and Hispanic students. Furthermore, students who walked to school dropped out at higher rates than those who were bused to school. OSMCR attributed the high dropout rate to poor academic achievement, which began in elementary school and continued into high school.[98] Most students who dropped out were eighteen years old and had reached the tenth grade, but were not likely to be promoted to the eleventh grade.[99]

Many people blamed the incompetence of the school system on a combination of community ambivalence and board politics. According to many observers, board members either used the position as a stepping-stone or as a route to obtain monetary benefits for relatives and friends. Indeed, descriptions of board politics approximated machine politics. Dr. Aileen Kassen recalled, "The school board people were political hacks and used that position to further their own political position to put their relatives on the payroll." The unions were exceedingly powerful, as they had been traditionally in Cleveland, and school board members placed their relatives and friends in positions with the trade unions. School board members' commitment to education was so dubious, recalled Kassen, that "(M)y main memory of the school board is that each two years when there was an election, we prayed, we hoped, that the people who would win would care about the children. And they never did. And that was one of the things that wore me down."[100]

OSMCR Advisory Board Member Martha Smith surmised that the court's disclosure requirements were what engendered the greatest

---

[96]Stevens, *Reading Parity in the Cleveland City School District* (Cleveland: Office on School Monitoring and Community Relations, 22 November 1985), 10-11.

[97]The national average was 25.9 percent in 1984, as reported by the U.S. Department of Education.

[98]Stevens, *Dropouts in the Cleveland Public Schools,* OSMCR Report to Judge Frank Battisti, 7 August 1997, 2-3.

[99]Ibid., 7.

[100]Kassen, *supra* note 66.

resistance from the school board and administration. When the district came under court supervision, everything the district had managed to keep hidden in the past, from the abysmal performance of the students to the disparities in funding for schools, to the names of the people who were awarded contracts with the school district, suddenly became a matter of public record. The Cleveland schools were essentially a fiefdom, with the largest budget in the county, and there was virtually no accountability regarding the spending of those funds.[101] Neither board members nor the administration would willingly cede that power.

Michael Charney, on the other hand, felt that board politics played a minimal role in the poor performance of Cleveland students. He stressed the disadvantages that a majority of Cleveland's school children experienced at home, circumstances of poverty that hampered parents' ability to contribute to their children's education. He also spoke of the continuing racism within the district and within society that held minority children back in school. Charney differentiated racism from discrimination. He referred to the conscious and unconscious stereotyping and lower expectations that teachers harbored and exhibited toward minority children. Charney noted that he had observed a remarkable improvement in overt attitudes among teachers towards minority children in the years since desegregation, and a much more enlightened attitude in general regarding racial tolerance and sensitivity. Yet the pervasive racism within American society could not help but invade the school system, he said, and color teachers' expectations of minority children as well as children's self-expectations.[102]

The validity of Charney's observations notwithstanding, board and administration politics clearly misdirected efforts and funds that could have benefited Cleveland's public school children before, during, and after the trial. The most common frustration expressed by the people who were interviewed for this research project was that people who had been entrusted with the education of Cleveland's children had sacrificed the education and futures of a whole generation through their petty and often self-serving bickering.

---

[101]Martha Smith, former member of the advisory commission to the Office on School Monitoring and Community Relations and former member of the Cleveland board of education, telephone interview by author, 14 July 1997.
[102]Charney, *supra* note 81.

Ten Year Assessment

As was common in desegregation cases, the lack of positive leadership among Cleveland's school administration, board of education and the community's political elite, severely hampered implementation of the desegregation plan. In 1988, Leonard Stevens, director of the Office on School Monitoring and Community Relations (OSMCR) wrote, "The court order was endorsed by few elected officials, openly opposed by a vocal number, and generally shunned by Cleveland's leadership. Early support came only from grassroots groups and agencies serving them, religious leaders, and two local foundations." The public readily accepted and repeated dire predictions of school violence, population flight, and the loss of local control of the schools, none of which materialized. However, the public's obsession with such prognostications resulted in the efforts of those in a position to facilitate the enforcement of the plan being directed instead towards resisting the court's authority and thwarting the implementation of beneficial educational programs.[103]

In addition to the lack of resolve on the part of the leadership, the board of education and administration were plagued by instability and inconsistency. Between 1978 and 1988, twenty-two people filled the seven seats on the school board. Board member Ralph Perk observed in 1988, "Such a turnstile operation could only result in a series of misdirections for the district in its efforts to comply with the court's order. Motivations varied, agendas changed, interpretations differed-- progress was impeded." Perk declared that Superintendent Alfred Tutela and the current board were committed to the implementation of the remedial order. He noted, however, that not just board, but community, support was essential to the successful implementation of all the components of the order.[104]

Franklin B. Walter, state superintendent of public instruction also placed blame for the lack of progress in the Cleveland desegregation case on divisiveness and a lack of commitment on the part of members of the Cleveland board of education. In 1988 he wrote:

---

[103]Stevens, "Cleveland shrugs off applause it deserves," *Cleveland Plain Dealer,* 16 February 1988, 3(B).
[104]Ralph J. Perk, Jr., "Why did school board have to go to court?" *Cleveland Plain Dealer*, 17 February 1988, 13(A).

There is no excuse that Cleveland schools are still under the jurisdiction of the court in the desegregation case. The court has given the Cleveland board and administration every opportunity to extricate themselves from the court's jurisdiction. Yet, virtually every opportunity has been lost because of either the divisiveness or irresponsibility of the board and administration. During the past decade there have been seven superintendencies filled by six different individuals. Sustained leadership has not been a hallmark of the Cleveland schools.[105]

Edward Mearns, Jr., a law professor at Case Western Reserve University Law School and one of the two court-appointed experts who examined the school district's proposals for desegregation attributed the problematic implementation of the desegregation plan to the community's enthusiastic embracement of the myth that school segregation merely reflected residential segregation. The pervasiveness of this myth allowed the school district and the community to avoid responsibility for the desegregation plan's implementation. In 1988, many people in Cleveland stubbornly clung to that myth, as well as the myth that the school system's financial problems resulted from, rather than long predated, the desegregation order.[106]

Mearns attributed, at least in part, the persistence of these myths to the media's coverage of the desegregation case. The media failed to present the facts of the case: the massive evidence of purposeful segregative actions on the part of the school district, the overwhelming evidence of unequal educational services offered black and white children by the school system, the shocking evidence of financial mismanagement and incompetence which resulted in such a precarious fiscal state that the district was able to continue operations only because it convinced many of its major tax payers to pay their property tax in advance, and the complete lack of organizational structure which rendered the school district incapable of designing an acceptable desegregation plan, all of which policies and conditions predated the implementation of the desegregation plan. Instead, the media presented the case as "a clash of personalities with the focus on board members, superintendents, the

---

[105]Franklin B. Walter, "Only Cleveland can solve Cleveland's problems," *Cleveland Plain Dealer*, 15 February 1988, 11(A).
[106]Edward A. Mearns, Jr., "The city didn't want to believe it, *Cleveland Plain Dealer*, 16 February 1988, 3(B).

parties, and the judge. . . . The matter was treated like an athletic contest with winners and losers. The media searched for someone to blame rather than analyze the intractable issues facing the schools. None of this raised the community's level of understanding to where it needed to be." Mearns posited that the persistence of the myths inhibited collaboration among people who had the energy and ability to facilitate the effective implementation of the desegregation order and to improve the quality of education in the Cleveland school system.[107]

Mearns later elaborated on his analysis of the critical role of the media in desegregation politics. He observed that the communities, rather than the school boards and administrators, were the actual defendants in desegregation cases. The culture and the society of the community were on trial, and the media reinforced the sentiments of the community and upheld its social structure. He observed that the press was willing to crucify any individual, "but they seem not to take on the great beast, . . . the public. The public (was) not condemned for what it (had) done by the seller of newspapers to (that) public." A few nationally prominent newspapers, such as the *Los Angeles Times* and the *Atlanta Constitution* had criticized Cleveland for its handling of the case, but the Cleveland press never did so.[108]

Conclusion

In the late 1980s, the Cleveland public schools were desegregated, but the school system was in financial and organizational disarray, and test scores and drop out rates were abysmal. The school population was 70 percent black and predominantly poor, and a significant achievement gap between whites and nonwhites persisted. Although busing had become relatively routine, desegregation and related legal issues tended to flare up and polarize the community during elections.

The community had rejected the court's finding of *de jure* racial segregation in the public schools, clinging steadfastly to the myth that the segregation within the city and the school system had occurred "naturally." The board of education and the school administration, with pressure from the community, had stubbornly resisted the court's jurisdiction and thwarted what many people viewed as one of the greatest

---

[107]Ibid.
[108]Edward A. Mearns, Jr., professor of law at Case Western Reserve University Law School, telephone interview by author, 11 July 1997.

desegregation orders in the country in terms of the hope that it offered the victims of segregation. The community lashed out in anger at Judge Battisti and at the busing element of the remedial order. As lawyers battled in court and politicians exploited the issue of desegregation to win electoral support, the general public appeared to lose sight of the educational components of the remedial order and of the children themselves. The district spent millions of dollars to challenge the court's authority, rather than applying the community's and the school system's energies and resources to improving the education offered by the school system.

Cleveland's struggle with desegregation thus provides stark evidence of the limited power of the courts to bring about educational reform in the face political resistance. The following chapter examines the school system through the 1990s, as it underwent a series of crises until the court eventually approved a legislative move to place the school system under the control of the mayor of Cleveland. The tumultuous events of the 1990s demonstrate the need for community or political pressure to engender responsibility within a school system.

CHAPTER 11

Cleveland at the Turn of the Century

Introduction

At the turn of the century, Cleveland remained a very troubled school system. The financial and organizational disarray in which the district found itself, along with its dubious legal status, and most importantly, the exceedingly poor performance of its students, provided compelling evidence of the limits of the courts to bring about social change and to offer poor and minority children an equal educational opportunity. The remedial order under which the school system had been operating since 1978 was one of the most far reaching in the country with numerous components designed not only to desegregate the system but to raise the students' performance, especially in reading. Believing the lower test scores of Cleveland's minority children were a vestige of previous discrimination, Judge Battisti had ordered the district to devise and operate a remedial reading program and numerous other programs aimed at improving the performance of African-American students and eliminating the achievement gap between minority and white students. However, the promise of the remedial order had gone unfulfilled.

During the nearly two decades the district was under court supervision, it spent millions of dollars and focused much of its energies on challenging the court's authority, rather than taking advantage of the opportunity to reorganize and revitalize the system to better meet the needs of the children. The administration's and the school board's pointed resistance to the court's authority reflected the community's ignorance of its past record of discrimination against minority children and its disdain for the federal court official who insisted that the school system fulfill its constitutional obligation to its minority children. The community's and the school system's ability to thwart Judge Battisti's effort to bring about compliance with the law exemplified the weakness of the third branch of government in the face of political, or community, resistance.

Despite the long history of blatant resistance followed by continual foot dragging, the district eventually had complied with enough of the components of the remedial order that Judge Battisti became amenable to releasing the district under specified conditions, and in 1994 a negotiated agreement was reached. However, Judge Battisti died a few months later, and Judge Robert Krupansky took over the case. In 1995, citing internal dissension, financial mismanagement, administrative incompetence, and a leadership vacuum following the recent resignations of two top administrators and the superintendent of schools, Judge Krupansky stripped the local board of education of its authority. The judge transferred responsibility for district operations to the state superintendent of schools, acting on behalf of the state board of education.[1]

Following an energetic grassroots campaign, the voters of Cleveland passed a tax levy November 5, 1996 to provide increased funding for schools. This was the first levy to pass since 1983. However, by every measure, the performance of Cleveland students was abysmal and *declining*. Cleveland's school population was 70 percent black and 70 percent of the students lived in poverty. Virtually any family that could afford to do so had either placed their children in private schools or moved to the suburbs. The system was foundering, devoid of management or pedagogical expertise and lacking leadership by people whose foremost commitment was to the educational needs of Cleveland's children. Having rejected parental attempts at participation for decades, the district succeeded in insulating itself from public scrutiny. The district's deplorable performance had driven most of the middle class away, leaving it to squander the futures of the disadvantaged children whose parents were least capable of holding the system accountable.

During the summer of 1997, the state legislature, against the wishes of Cleveland's representatives, voted to transfer governance of the school district to Cleveland's mayor, Michael White. White would appoint a chief executive officer to oversee the daily operations of the

---

[1] Reed v. Rhodes, No. C73-1300 (N.D. Ohio 3 March 1995) (order).

school district. The voters of Cleveland would have no voice in the transfer until four years later.

Perhaps one of the most tragic aspects of the mismanagement of the Cleveland Public School System was the lost opportunity in the remedial order. Judge Battisti's order was widely viewed as one of the most comprehensive of its time. The directive to improve reading scores and the directive that the state establishes a "positive action program" to fulfill its constitutional obligations to ensure that minimum standards were met illustrated the ultimate goal of improving the quality of the education service provided by the district. Yet, during the two decades of federal court supervision, district and public attention to the transportation aspect had eclipsed the other thirteen components of the remedial order, directives that, had they been followed, would have improved the educational service to *all* of Cleveland's public school children. Dr. Aileen Kassen reflected:

> It was just sad. . . . (T)he order was great. It could have been done if the political will had been there. But neither the school board nor the city council nor the media helped the public understand what this could have been. . . . The public never did understand. They didn't understand what had happened before (the segregative acts by the school district) and they didn't understand the potential benefits that Battisti was offering.[2]

By 1997, thirteen secondary schools and thirty-seven elementary schools had become virtually all black,[3] the parties having stipulated in May 1995 to a revision of the student assignment which allowed for more parent and student choice. Many people who had supported the objectives of the remedial order felt discouraged that so little of what was envisioned had been realized. They feared that with resegregation, the inequities among the schools would increase, and that without court supervision, the school system would decline further. As Juanita Dalton-Robinson observed, "When Battisti died, the whole commitment died with him at that level, I think. . . . Battisti

---

[2] Dr. Aileen Kassen, former deputy director of the Office on School Monitoring and Community Relations, telephone interview by author, 10 July 1997.
[3] Enrollment Data provided by the Office on School Monitoring and Community Relations (OSMCR) 30 May 1997.

envisioned the district taking full responsibility for making this work."[4]

A March 9, 1997 editorial in Cleveland's *The Plain Dealer* declared, "Cleveland is losing another generation of children to ignorance and poverty while adults fight about money and power. Poisoned politics has dominated the schools debate in this town for so long--so tragically, heartbreakingly long--that civic life seems not to know another way."[5] And Blanche Wallace, a long time activist in the community, lamented, "These children, I feel so strongly that they're being cheated. . . ."[6]

The Move Toward Release

The parties to the suit began negotiating a settlement of the case in the spring of 1992, and on March 15, 1994, they signed a comprehensive settlement agreement and filed it with the court.   Judge Battisti scheduled a "Fairness Hearing" on April 13, during which the court would examine the "overall fairness and adequacy of the settlement in light of the likely outcome and costs of continued litigation," as well as plaintiff class and public concerns.[7]

The settlement agreement called for the implementation of Vision 21, a seven-year educational improvement and desegregation plan, to be financed in part ($295 million over six years) by the state and in part by the district ($275 million). In approving the settlement agreement, the court noted that the agreement would ensure state participation in the funding of Vision 21 (for seven years), without which the district could not operate the program. The agreement provided that the district would place a general operating levy on a ballot in May 1994 and at least once a year thereafter until Cleveland voters approved the mill rate sufficient to fund the district's obligations under the Vision

---

[4]Juanita Dalton-Robinson, retired social worker and former member of the advisory commission to the Office on School Monitoring and Community Relations, telephone interview by author, 9 July 1997
[5]Editorial, *Cleveland Plain Dealer*, 9 March 1997, 1(A)
[6]Blanche Wallace, community schools activist, telephone interview by author, 21 July 1997.
[7]Reed v. Rhodes, 869 F. Supp. 1274, 1279 (N.D. Ohio 1994).
Judge Battisti explained that the court was not required to reach conclusions of fact or law regarding compliance with the remedial order in the settlement of a class action suit.

21 program. The agreement required that the district maintain racial compositions in its schools within $\pm$ 15 percent of the district-wide ratio of blacks and whites until the year 2000. However, the agreement allowed for the exemption of eleven schools from that requirement during the 1994-'95 school year, and the exemption of two of those schools the following year.

The settlement agreement included several provisions for improving the education service delivered by the district. It required that the district implement new programs "to ensure that by the end of the first grade all children will read;" that the district "undertake substantial efforts" to assist students in passing the state proficiency tests, focusing on mathematics and science courses; that the district improve the learning environment in the schools; and that it implement intervention strategies for students performing poorly on standardized tests. The plaintiffs, the state defendants, the court, and OSMCR pledged to monitor school district performance on these obligations, and the court required the school district to establish desired outcomes and a timetable for achieving those outcomes.[8]

The settlement agreement explicitly acknowledged "the defendants' obligation to demonstrate that they (had) eliminated the vestiges of segregation to the extent practicable" before the court would relinquish jurisdiction. Furthermore, noted Judge Battisti, it offered monetary and non-monetary relief which was possibly greater than what the plaintiffs could obtain through further litigation. In light of these factors, Judge Battisti deemed the agreement "fair and reasonable." He observed that notice of the settlement had been well publicized and comments solicited, and that very little opposition to the settlement agreement had been expressed.[9]

On or before July 1, 1997, the court was to hold an evidentiary hearing to determine whether the defendants had complied with the settlement agreement and all parts of the remedial order and whether "all vestiges of past discrimination and segregation (had) been eliminated to the extent practicable." The court's granting of unitary status and releasing the school district from the court's jurisdiction, except to enforce the settlement agreement, would depend on proof of compliance with agreement and remedial order. Judge Battisti's

---

[8]Ibid., 1283.
[9]Ibid., 1280-82.

approval of the settlement agreement rendered it a consent decree, legally binding on the parties.

Crisis

On October 19, 1994, Judge Frank Battisti, the judge who had presided over the Cleveland desegregation case for over twenty years, died unexpectedly. Judge Robert Krupansky, an appellate judge, volunteered to take over the case. In early 1995, the school district, perhaps anticipating that Judge Krupansky, a Nixon appointee, would be more amenable than Judge Battisti had been to ending the court's jurisdiction, asked the court for a partial declaration of unitary status with regard to student assignment. If the court granted the district's motion, it would no longer have been required to transport students for purposes of desegregation.

On February 21, 1995, following receipt of information from the Office on School Monitoring and Community Relations (OSMCR) of the financial crisis plaguing the district, Judge Krupansky scheduled a hearing to address the Cleveland board of education's request for grant of partial unitary status, the financial status of the district, the current status of Superintendent Sammie Campbell Parrish, and the board's decision to submit another levy to the electorate.

Subsequently, on March 3, 1995, citing a "leadership and management void" and expressing skepticism that the board of education could "administer its educational agenda" and continue to implement the remedial order, Judge Krupansky abruptly transferred authority over the Cleveland school district to State Superintendent of Schools Ted Sanders. He noted that internal dissension within the administration had culminated in the resignation of Superintendent Sammie Campbell Parrish that day, following the resignation of two other top administrators within the previous two months. Judge Krupansky also cited the district's "critical financial condition," its $29.5 million budget shortfall, and its failure to secure an emergency loan to meet its operational costs through the end of the fiscal year. Owing to the large number of dilapidated and/or under utilized schools which were creating a significant drain on the financial resources of the district, Judge Krupansky ordered the state superintendent to recommend fourteen schools for closing by May 1, 1995.[10] The order

---

[10]Reed v. Rhodes, *supra* note 1.

amounted to much more than financial receivership; it transferred authority over all aspects of school district operations

Three days later, Judge Krupansky appointed Daniel McMullen, former director of OSMCR, special master for the purpose of exploring with the parties to the suit alternatives to the current student assignment plan. On May 16, 1995, the district withdrew its motion for partial unitary status, and the plaintiffs, the district, and the state board of education jointly stipulated to modify the consent decree of March 1994 to allow for greater flexibility in student assignment. The district was to aim for at least 33 percent African-American enrollment in all schools, but some schools would be allowed to exceed 90 percent African-American enrollments, if that ratio resulted from parental choice. The purpose of the joint stipulation was to reduce long bus rides, increase student and parent choice in school assignments, and reduce busing costs. This agreement was to remain in effect for the 1995-'96 school year only, after which student assignment would be reassessed.[11]

A report issued in April of 1995 by the Citizens League of Cleveland's Public School Reform Task Force shed light on many of the shortcomings within the district which had led to the administrative and financial crisis culminating in the transfer of authority over the school district to the state. The report detailed the progress and shortcomings of the district with respect to a 1991 reform agenda that had been established by the League. The agenda included, among other things, developing a strategic vision for the district and negotiating a settlement of the desegregation case. The task force reported that some progress had been made, including formulation of the Vision 21 plan, but that no implementation plan had been formulated for Vision 21.[12]

The task force report stated that Vision 21 was a "detailed vision statement," rather than a strategic plan. It lacked "strategic clarity and coherency" in terms of implementation and represented instead a series of short-term survival tactics.[13] Thus, the reform plan that had formed

---

[11]Joint Stipulation, Reed v. Rhodes, (N.D. Ohio 16 May 1995) (No. C73-1300).
[12]*Using the Power of Collaboration to Help Cleveland's Children: Community Priorities for Reform of the Cleveland Public Schools During State Takeover* (Cleveland: The Citizens League of Greater Cleveland, 1995), 4.
[13]Ibid., 23.

the basis of the settlement agreement had been doomed from the start. It established goals without providing plan for meeting those goals.

According to the report, Superintendent Sammie Campbell Parrish had the vision to design the plan, but she lacked the management skills to mobilize an administration to implement the program. Lack of trust and communication between the board of education and Campbell Parrish further hindered the superintendent's effectiveness. Acknowledging the long history of political interference with the goals of educating Cleveland's children, the task force concluded, "The Board-superintendent dynamic highlights the Cleveland community's easy willingness to 'change people rather than politics'--to ignore the inherent problem of allowing political interference in the business of educating children in the first place--and to unrealistically rely on individuals to come in and single-handedly lead us out of problem situations."[14]

In addition to its failure to implement Vision 21, the district returned to litigation after failing to implement the student assignment component of the consent agreement. The Citizens League Task Force suggested that the district had never been satisfied with the student assignment component of the consent agreement and had never intended to implement it, but signed the agreement to improve the chances of passage of the school levy that year. These actions by the district suggested bad faith on its part, claimed the task force. The task force urged the district to "ignore the political implications of the student assignment plan" and adhere to the guidelines agreed to or set by the court. It beseeched the district, "Vigorously avoid the divisive Cleveland tradition of using the desegregation case as a political expedient, whether to gain public support for another tax levy attempt or for the reelection of Board members. Base the decision only on what's best for the education of Cleveland's students."[15]   Such references to the school board's and administration's misplaced motives, breach of the public trust, and political maneuverings pervaded the report, suggesting that little if anything had changed in terms of district priorities nearly two decades after court supervision of the district had begun.

---

[14]Ibid., 33.
[15]Ibid., 22.

District Performance

When Richard Boyd was appointed superintendent of schools following the resignation of Superintendent Parrish and the court's placement of the district under state supervision, he set two priorities for the district: improved student achievement and accountability to the community. He ordered each school in the district to develop a strategic plan that included targets for test scores, attendance, and school climate. Attendance improved in more than 80 percent of the schools, discipline problems declined, and proficiency scores improved in grades four, six, and nine through twelve.[16] Serious problems still plagued the district however, as seen in standardized tests, drop out rates, promotion rates, and state proficiency tests. Despite the administration's talk of accountability, 98 percent of the district's principals won new contracts in 1997.[17]

Eighty-five percent of fourth graders failed at least one section of the state proficiency tests in 1997, a decline of 3 percent from the year before. Nintey-five percent of sixth graders failed, an improvement of 1 percent from 1996. Educators were pleased with the test results, considering that the passing threshold had been raised from 52 percent to 62 percent.[18]

On the 1997 ninth grade proficiency tests, which seniors were required to pass to graduate from public schools in Ohio, 16.4 percent of Cleveland's ninth graders passed the test, a drop of .7 percent from the previous year. Statewide, over 61 percent of ninth graders passed all four parts of the test. Of Cleveland's tenth graders, 35 percent had passed the exam, an improvement of 3 percent from the previous year. Nearly 80 percent of Cleveland's seniors had passed, up 3 percent from the year before. Students repeated the ninth grade test each year until they passed all four portions.[19]

The state department of education reported that the dropout rate for the district was 32.5 percent in 1996, whereas the average for the state's

---

[16] Robert Rawson, Jr. "Cleveland public schools are improving—but it's an uphill run," *Cleveland Plain Dealer*, 8 October 1997, 11(B).
[17] Chris Sheridan. "The principal proficiency test," *Cleveland Plain Dealer*, 27 July 1997, 2(E).
[18] Mario G. Ortiz, "Gains on standard tests please educators," *Cleveland Plain Dealer*, 15 July 1997, 1(B) and 4(B).
[19] Scott Stephens, "Proficiency test results show gains," *Cleveland Plain Dealer*, 31 May 1997, 1(B) and 6(B).

eight largest districts was 5.36 percent. The percentage of seniors graduating was 32.46, whereas the average for the state's eight largest districts was 74.29 percent.[20]

The Ohio Board of Regents reported that for the Cleveland Public Schools class of 1991, 60.7 percent who enrolled in Ohio state-assisted colleges and universities enrolled in a remedial mathematics course and 58.5 percent enrolled in a remedial English class. The expected rates based on statewide patterns were 43.6 percent and 37.1 percent respectively.[21]

Particularly frustrating to many Clevelanders was the fact that so much of the district's energies and finances, which could and should have gone toward educating children, were diverted to fighting the remedial order. Stanley Tolliver, a jurist and long time board of education member, noted with disgust, "(T)his law firm, Squire, Sanders, and Dempsey squandered three million dollars fighting this case. I've often said, I'm a lawyer and I like lawyers to make money, but I don't like lawyers to make money at the expense of kids."[22]

Rashidah Abdulhaaq, an African-American parent who was a court-appointed plaintiff class representative in the desegregation case, also expressed dismay at the district and community resources and energy that went into fighting implementation of the remedial order, rather than improving the educational system. While it was the constitutional rights of the African-American children that were being denied, she observed that the benefits of the remedial order would have reached all school children. Yet the issue was always perceived as an "us against them" or "black against white" zero sum game. It was ironic and disheartening that the African-American children won the case but they never saw the benefits of the remedial order. "It's almost like you were misused. And it hurts, because you look at the dismal effects of Cleveland's school system . . . . They haven't done anything for these kids . . . Kids can't read. They can't get jobs. I mean, it's

---

[20] "FY1996 Vital Statistics on Ohio School Districts," Columbus: Ohio State Department of Education.

[21] Ibid., 21.

[22] Stanley Tolliver, attorney at law, former member of the Cleveland board of education and original member of the advisory board to the Office on School Monitoring and Community Relations, telephone interview by author, 15 July 1997.

ridiculous. But (the district) got money. People got paid. They got tons of money."[23]

As for where to place blame for the dismal condition of the school system, while Abdulhaaq expressed strong resentment toward the school system that had squandered funds fighting the court order, she also placed responsibility squarely on the shoulders of an ambivalent community:

> I think the community is most at fault, because the kids belong to the people who live in this community. That's the parents. Parents have got to understand that public education is not free, and you cannot sit back because the federal court has demanded that the district do something. You can't sit back and just leave this to happenstance. It doesn't happen that way. You have to get up. You must ask questions. You have to keep plodding and researching . . . and to me, we should have pushed for more information from the very day Judge Battisti said "you're guilty."[24]

Abdulhaaq observed that such vigilance was often difficult for minority parents, who besides struggling with survival issues, were less knowledgeable of how to navigate a bureaucracy such as the Cleveland Public Schools. Furthermore, she noted, the system, sometimes intentionally and sometimes inadvertently, established barriers to parental participation. She mentioned barriers of class--the mere image of the administrator in designer clothes could be a barrier if no effort were made to break down that barrier--and educational background. Sometimes parents feared that their vigilance or demands for accountability might work against their children. Furthermore, explained Abdulhaaq, minority parents rarely felt efficacious in a society that in myriad ways accorded them second class status.

Daniel Elliott blamed the collapse of the Cleveland school system not on desegregation, but on the effects of the negative reaction from "very powerful people, including the media," which drove the middle class from the Cleveland Public Schools. "And it wasn't that it was

---

[23]Rashidah Abdulhaaq, parent activist and named plaintiff class representative in Reed v. Rhodes, telephone interview by author, 10 July 1997.
[24]Ibid.

white flight. It was middle class flight. Anybody who could run ran, and that included a lot of black middle class who are now living in Shaker Heights and Cleveland Heights (and attending) well-integrated public suburban school systems." The effect of the opposition from many quarters of the community proved to make reform of the school system through the remedial order, which Elliott termed a "masterpiece of desegregation history," impossible.[25]

Clearly the grinding poverty of inner city Cleveland provided a tremendous challenge to the education system. A late 1990s report by the Annie E. Casey Foundation on child-welfare statistics for the nation's fifty largest cities entitled City Kids Count, painted a grim picture of the lives of Cleveland's children. Cleveland ranked forty-nine (with fifty being worst) in the proportion of children living in distressed neighborhoods (46 percent). Distressed neighborhoods were defined as those with high rates of poverty and male unemployment, a high percentage of families headed by single females and receiving public assistance. Cleveland ranked forty-sixth in terms of the percentage of children living in poverty (43 percent). It ranked forty-fourth in terms of children born to single-parent families (50 percent). The proportion of Cleveland's children living in poverty had increased from 22 percent in 1969 to 43 percent by 1989.[26]

Reform

In 1990, a Cleveland group headed by Virginia Lindseth founded The Institute for Educational Renewal to bring about substantive reform in the Cleveland Public Schools. Dr. Aileen Kassen served as the first director of the organization and secured financing from various sources including Title I funds, various philanthropic foundations, and individual donors. John Caroll University, a Jesuit institution with a strong commitment to solving urban problems, and Urseline University, a Catholic institution, were the original sponsors. Initially consultants with PhDs in education or clinical psychology from northeastern Ohio universities were brought in to provide professional development for teachers in one elementary school. By 1997 the

---

[25]Daniel Elliott, first co-chairman of the steering committee for the Greater Cleveland Project, telephone interview by author, 30 July 1997.
[26]Jean Dubail, "The awful truth about Cleveland's kids," *Cleveland Plain Dealer*, 13 April 1997, 1(H).

project operated in nine Cleveland schools. Dr. Kassen said that two-thirds staff participation in a school was essential to program viability. She said five to eight years were required to achieve the reform envisioned by the Institute. The program funded professional development, including travel to weeklong national workshops.[27]

Juanita Dalton-Robinson, who had served on the advisory commission to OSMCR in the early 1980s, served on the district's strategy council, whose function was to investigate avenues for reforming the troubled school system in the late 1990s. The superintendent of schools and the mayor created the strategy council because they both recognized that unless the schools were doing well, the city would not thrive. The irony in the strategy council's mission, observed Dalton-Robinson, was that the administrative reform the council pursued in the late 1990s had been outlined by the court in the early 1980s when OSMCR and Judge Battisti had recognized that fundamental restructuring of the district administration would be necessary to realize the objectives of the remedial order. OSMCR had been available to assist in modernizing many of the district's antiquated systems, however, resistance to court supervision, and to change had been so pervasive that the district had completely rejected the assistance and expertise that could have allowed it to serve its clientele immeasurably better. "Things that should have been done back in the '80s are just now being done," said Dalton-Robinson, "and it's very discouraging to people like myself who (have followed the case and supported the court-ordered reforms) . . ., 'it's like *déjà vu* all over again' . . ." Despite her frustration over the district's intransigence, Dalton-Robinson saw great potential in the strategy council's reform plan, and viewed the passage of the $13.6 million levy in 1996 as a sign of public confidence in the reform effort.[28]

As a reform experiment, the Ohio Department of Education initiated a school voucher program in Cleveland during the 1996-97 school year, issuing 1,996 Cleveland students from low-income families vouchers to cover up to 90 percent of the cost of private or parochial school tuition. The maximum allotment of $2,250 was just over a third of the per pupil cost of public education. After one year in operation, a Harvard University study found that parents were very pleased with the program, viewing the private schools as safer, more

---

[27]Kassen, *supra* note2, on 4 December 1997.
[28]Dalton-Robinson, *supra* note 4.

focused on academics, and more able to offer individual attention to students.   Most of the students used the vouchers to attend Catholic schools, while about 25 percent enrolled in Hope schools, which were founded by voucher system advocates.   Students tested at the beginning and the end of the school year made gains of 15 percent in math and 5 percent in reading.   Language scores declined by 5 percent overall, however, and by 19 percent among first graders.   Owing to the positive response, the state expanded the program to include three thousand students for the 1997-'98 academic year.[29]

In May of 1997, an Ohio appeals court declared the voucher system unconstitutional, because the vouchers were approved for religious schools.   The Ohio Supreme Court permitted the continuation of the program for one more year pending resolution of the constitutionality issue, which would likely be decided by the U.S. Supreme Court.

In August of 1997, Cleveland Public Schools Superintendent Richard Boyd announced that two elementary schools, Waverly and Revere, would be reconstituted (substantially overhauled) because of declining student achievement, poor attendance, and low ratings in a spring survey completed by staff, parents, and students of the schools. The principals were replaced, and all teachers would be required to reapply for their positions.   Those not hired would be placed in other schools.[30]   Intervention teams would be established in ten other schools that had shown significant declines in test scores and attendance.   Those schools were being considered for reconstitution the following year, depending on their 1997-98 performance.[31]   In 1997, the district also expanded its magnet school program, which was a part of the desegregation plan, to include two new programs (a year 'round school and a secondary level technical academy), bringing the total number of magnet schools to twenty-eight.   In addition, the district offered three vocational magnet high school programs and nine thematic high school programs, which operated within comprehensive high schools.   The district also reinstituted all-day kindergarten in the fall of 1997, after a four-year absence.   This had been one of the

[29]Tamar Lewin, "School Voucher Study Finds Satisfaction," *New York Times,* 18 September 1997, 12(A).
[30]Stephens, "Union against schools' overhaul," *Cleveland Plain Dealer,* 7 August 1997, 1(B).
[31]Scott Stephens and Mario G. Ortiz, "Two schools face staff overhaul," *Cleveland Plain Dealer,* 8 August 1997, 1(B).

promises of the successful levy campaign. Research had shown a correlation between all-day kindergarten and later success in school.[32]

Don Freeman, director of the League Park Center,[33] expressed skepticism at the prospect of substantive reform within the school system. He noted that despite the state takeover, little had changed; the state had not been willing to "clean house administratively," and the result was a continuation of the mismanagement and unaccountability that had characterized the system for so long. "There's been no significant change in terms of the people who have the primary responsibility for administration of the district. And as a consequence of that, on a systematic scale, it's just impossible to initiate, let alone sustain, substantive educational reform."[34]

Freeman said that the remedial order had merely exacerbated a problem that long existed in the Cleveland school system and in other urban areas of the country, the racist/class nature of American society. The remedial plan accelerated the exodus of not just middle class residents of European descent, but that of residents of African descent as well. The net result was a district comprised of predominantly poor, minority children. Given the nature of society, according to Freeman, "it takes no brilliance to . . . be able to observe compulsory non education being institutionalized, and Cleveland's just a microcosm of a macrocosm in that regard."[35]

To illustrate his assessment of organizational incompetence and unaccountability within the central administration, Freeman noted with frustration that reforms had been tried in the district, and some had succeeded. However, owing to poor administration and follow-through, such progress was often lost. For instance, the Primary Achievement Program (PAP) was initiated in the early 1990s in two elementary schools, Anton Gradina and Alfred Benesch. Grades K-3 in the schools were reorganized into a non-graded system wherein students received individualized instruction and progressed as they mastered various skills. The district expanded the program to six to eight other schools, but, owing to inadequate professional development of the staff and other shortcuts taken in replicating the program, it did not produce

---

[32]"All-day kindergarten will start in the fall," *Cleveland West Side Sun News*, 17 April 1997, 3(A).
[33]The League Park Center was the Hough area neighborhood center.
[34]Don Freeman, director of the League Park Center, telephone interview by author, 31 July 1997.
[35]Ibid.

the anticipated results. The PAP concept was therefore "delegitimized," which Freeman termed "tragic and unfortunate," because it had great promise if implemented correctly with the proper staff and building administration training. The lack of central administrative planning and follow-through that doomed the PAP program typified the pervasive incompetence within the central administration, according to Freeman, who described the district's problems as "tantamount to a cancer in its terminal stage."[36]

Freeman observed the tragic irony in the political circumstances that doomed the Cleveland Public Schools, that is, the lack of an "enlightened and vigilant public." The flight of the middle class from the school system had resulted in a situation wherein "the people . . . who are less able to collectively engender accountability of the district are the people who are left with the collective responsibility to do so."[37] This was the crux of the problem throughout the decades-long era of court supervision. Neither the remedial order that many considered a masterpiece in educational reform, nor the most valiant efforts of the judge who crafted the order, could compensate for the lack of an enlightened and vigilant public.

The Governance Issue

In 1996 following two years of state supervision of the troubled Cleveland Public Schools a "Cleveland Summit on Education" was held to search for a solution to the district's problems. The Summit created an advisory committee, which examined struggling urban school systems and found that elected boards of education often consisted of unqualified individuals and experienced high rates of turnover. Based on its findings, the advisory committee recommended to Ohio's general assembly that the Cleveland system be governed by an appointed, rather than an elected, board.[38] The Republican-led general assembly acted upon that recommendation, and in an attempt to instill a measure of accountability in the system, passed House Bill No. 269, which would transfer authority over the school district to the

---

[36] Ibid.

[37] Ibid.

[38] Spivey v. State of Ohio and Mixon v. State of Ohio, Nos. 1:97CV2308 and 1:97CV2309 slip op. at 4-5 (N.D. Ohio 6 March 1998). These cases were consolidated.

mayor of Cleveland. Republican Governor Voinovich wholeheartedly supported H.B.269 and signed it shortly thereafter. The bill abolished the elected school board, which had no authority while the district was under state supervision. It called for Mayor White to appoint a chief executive officer to manage the district with the help of a nine member board which White would appoint from a list of eighteen nominees submitted by a panel of parents, educators, and business leaders.[39]

The mayoral governance issue sharply divided the residents of Cleveland. Those who supported the mayoral governance drive felt that the board of education had not done enough to rid the administration of incompetent people. They anticipated that Mayor Michael White, who had a reputation for being tough, would streamline the system and improve accountability. The act's call for the mayor's appointing a chief executive officer, rather than a superintendent of schools, was clearly an attempt to supplant bureaucratic unresponsiveness with market style efficiency. The Greater Cleveland Roundtable, a group of seventy community members from civic, community, and private organizations and companies, were among those endorsing the mayoral governance plan. The NAACP opposed it, while the east side, predominantly black, United Pastors in Mission, approved of the plan.[40] The Cleveland branch of the League of Women Voters overwhelmingly opposed the mayoral takeover, because "it erodes the principles of participatory government," said league co-president Shirley Babitt.[41]

Juanita Dalton-Robinson, former member of the advisory commission to OSMCR, suggested that dismay over the board of education's ineptitude over the years led to the proposal for the mayoral governance plan. "There is so much disgust with the board that they assume that the board members are not capable of making sound decisions. The reality is that the problems with the district are so pervasive and so tied to how the district has been managed over time that no group of people (elected board) can make the change." She expressed skepticism, however, at the mayoral governance solution. "I'm always amazed at how there's such a romantic notion about

[39] Beth Reinhard, "Mayor to Get School Control in Cleveland," *Education Week*, 9 July 1997, 1, 28-29.

[40] Mario Ortiz, "Roundtable backs White's control of schools, *Cleveland Plain Dealer*, 3 April 1997, 1(A).

[41] "League of Women Voters opposes schools proposal," *Cleveland Plain Dealer*, 15 March 1997.

corporations and how they function, . . . The mayor has his own bureaucracy to manage, and it's not going very well. I think he does not need to take on (anything more)."[42]

While Mayor White established the Summit on Education, demonstrating his commitment to improving the city's schools, not all Cleveland residents were impressed with his involvement in Cleveland public schools. Following the state take over of the Cleveland school district in March of 1995, Mayor White had said that he hoped the judge would agree to end the transportation element of the remedial order and expressed eagerness for complete release from the court's jurisdiction.[43]

Former school board member Stanley Tolliver strongly opposed the mayoral takeover. Tolliver felt that the movement to transfer authority to Mayor White was instigated by the business power structure, which was also aligned with *The Plain Dealer*, Cleveland's primary daily newspaper. Tolliver, who was a member of the team of attorneys preparing to fight the mayoral governance plan, recalled that the board was historically divided between those who backed the business establishment and the status quo with the school system, and those who focused on the educational needs of the children. He noted the strong antiunion element in the measure and was particularly affronted that the voters were given no opportunity to voice their opinions. "It's the epitome of dictatorship, because we're saying taxation without representation is tyranny. And that's what we call it - - tyranny."[44]

Cleveland board of education member Gerald Henley declared, "I think (the bill) is a blatant slap at democracy. It completely ignores the rights of the people of the city of Cleveland." Retired appeals court Judge Sarah Harper, one of the team of attorneys who was prepared to challenge the constitutionality of the measure, felt that the residents of Cleveland were overwhelmingly opposed the mayor's running the schools. The team of attorneys planned to attack the plan based on the fact that it unlawfully withdrew the Cleveland voters' right to select school board members. Lawyers planned to attack that aspect of the

---

[42]Dalton-Robinson, *supra* note 4.
[43]Patrice Jones and Scott Stephens, "Hard work ahead for schools: White urges all to cooperate with order, blames Parrish," *Cleveland Plain Dealer*, 5 March 1995, 8(A).
[44]Tolliver, *supra* note 22.

plan because it represented an unlawful delegation of power to the nominating committee.[45]

James Hardiman, counsel for the NAACP since the inception of the case, expressed concern that removal of the Cleveland superintendent of schools and the Cleveland board of education's authority over the school district could alter their obligations under the remedial order. "Now, the fact that we've got some real knuckle heads that serve on this board of education makes the attempt to put the schools under the mayor's control a lot more palatable than would otherwise be the case." He stressed, however, that the NAACP was concerned that the defendants not be allowed to renege on their responsibilities and commitments through the mayoral takeover.[46]

The Cleveland Teachers Union and other unions which contracted with the district vehemently opposed transferring authority to the mayor, who had incurred the wrath of the teachers union during the August 1996 teachers union strike, when Mayor White declared from the City Club podium that unless changes were made in the school system to diffuse the power of the unions, "the inmates (would) be running the asylum." White later apologized for his choice of words, but many union and political leaders remained convinced that his combative style was counterproductive in his business and political dealings. Union members were especially wary of White's gaining control of the school system, owing to his cost saving initiatives that favored contracting out city services rather using union employees.[47]

Dr. Frances Hunter, professor in the Cleveland State University College of Urban Affairs and former director of the Greater Cleveland Project questioned whether it was appropriate for the mayor, regardless of who he was, to administer the school district. Hunter observed that the business community, with which Mayor White was closely aligned, had a vested interest in the improvement of the school system, to provide a more qualified labor force and to project a more positive image to corporate executives considering moving their families to Cleveland and establishing offices there. The city had made strides recently in rehabilitating its image under the slogan *The Comeback*

---

[45]Tom Corrigan, "Mayoral Takeover Drawing Criticism," *Cleveland West Side Sun News*, 10 July 1997, 1-2(A).
[46]James Hardiman, counsel for plaintiffs in Reed v. Rhodes, telephone interview by author, 18 July 1997
[47]Sandra Livingston and Evelyn Theiss, "White's trouble with the unions," *Cleveland Plain Dealer*, 6 October 1997, 1(A).

City.   Dr. Hunter acknowledged that Mayor White had good organizational skills, was very bright, and that his no-nonsense approach rendered him effective in certain arenas, but, referring to his statement during the teachers' strike which had so offended teachers, she suggested that diplomacy and conciliation were more appropriate in a bureaucracy such as the school system.   Furthermore, she said, the mayor's loyalties would be divided between the school district and the city, as was evidenced in the recent tax abatement election.[48]

As a part of the *Come Back City* campaign to revitalize Cleveland, the city offered tax abatement to corporations to entice them into establishing offices there, rather than in the suburbs.   The city council reasoned that it gained more benefits in the form of jobs for its residents than it lost in corporate income taxes through the abatement. However, because the school system received about 60 percent of the city's tax revenues,[49] it experienced a substantial loss in revenue as a result of the tax abatement policy.   Losses were estimated at $20 million annually from its $500 million budget.[50]   In the summer of 1997, the Cleveland Teachers Union (CTU) organized an initiative to have the question placed on the ballot whether the city, or the businesses themselves, should be required to reimburse to the school system the loss from the abatement.   Following a bitter campaign, which pitted the business community, the mayor, and the media against the CTU,[51] the initiative lost, and the abatement policy remained intact.

Martha Smith, former board of education member, expressed skepticism at Mayor White's ability to revitalize the school system. His interests were aligned with those of big business, and Smith expected that White would cater to business concerns.

> (W)hat's the difference between corrupt board members getting the plums and business getting the plums? And I don't care who gets the plums if kids get educated in the bargain. . . . If

---

[48]Dr. Frances Hunter, former director of the Greater Cleveland Project and later professor at Cleveland State University in the College of Urban Affairs, telephone interview by author, 23 July 1997.

[49]Scott Stephens, Robert J. Vickers, and Mario G. Ortiz, "Voters turn down limits on abatement," *Cleveland Plain Dealer*, 6 August 1997, 1(A).

[50]Paulette Thomas, "Cleveland Schools Are Playing Catch-Up," *Cleveland Plain Dealer*, 20 May 1997, 2(A).

[51]Editorial, "Defeat Issue 1" *Cleveland Plain Dealer*, 3 August 1997, 2(E).

somebody makes some bucks and kids still (get) educated, that would not concern me, but as the plums get taken and kids still (go) down the tube, and huge numbers of them . . ."[52]

Case Western Reserve University Law School Professor Edward Mearns expressed cautious optimism at the mayoral takeover. "We're not talking about an ideal world. We're talking about a conditioned situation. . . . And the conditioned situation here is splattered, no responsibility, (with) everybody blaming everybody else." Mearns pointed to the long history of corrupt politics within the school board, of unreasonable union contracts, and of disorganization within the administration. "It seems healthy to me to focus the responsibility." Mearns felt that the mayor, freed from some contractual and legal obligations, would be able to reform educational policies and increase financial responsibility.[53]

Rashidah Abdulhaaq also alluded to the pervasiveness of the problems of the school system, but she stressed the notion that parental and community vigilance was of utmost importance in revitalizing the school system:

I do think that Mayor White cares about the kids. And he knows that if the school system doesn't prosper, the city is going to die. . . . But see, unless a school district is doing its job, Jesus Christ could run the district and its not gonna help. . . . If he doesn't have the support of the community, that means the parents, [whether they like him or not], . . . Mayor White is going to be just like Judge Battisti; he's going to be blamed. . . . He can only look at the situation and roll up his sleeves and try to make it better. That's what Judge Battisti did. He looked at the situation. It was wrong. It needed something done. He tried to do it. But as parents, caregivers, foster parents, whoever's responsible for these

[52]Martha Smith, former member of the advisory commission to the Office on School Monitoring and Community Relations and former member of the Cleveland board of education, telephone interview by author, 14 July 1997.
[53]Edward Mearns, Jr., court-appointed expert who reviewed the school district's desegregation proposals for the court, telephone interview by author, 11 July 1997.

children, if they don't get up [and do their part] you're not going to have anything any different. . . .

I've told parents and I'm still telling the community [that] if [the mayor] takes the district over, you've got to still get up and go see about your kids. These are not his children. . . . You've got to turn of that T.V. and get your butt up to the school. If they don't do that, like I say, he'll be just like poor Judge Battisti. He really cared."[54]

Three groups, the Cleveland Teachers' Union, the schools' service employees, and the NAACP filed separate lawsuits challenging the mayoral governance plan. They all raised constitutional issues, centering on the fact that the residents of Cleveland were not permitted to vote on the issue for four years. The suits were later consolidated.

On March 6, 1998, Judge White upheld H.B. 269, the mayoral governance measure, given its "readily apparent" rational basis. The judge observed, "There is no dispute that the Cleveland City School District has been financially and operationally troubled."[55] In response to the plaintiffs' charges that the measure violated the Equal Protection Clause of the Fourteenth Amendment of the United States Constitution, as well as Article I, Section 2 of the Ohio Constitution, which provided for equal protection of the laws, Judge White held that because the right to vote, *per se*, was not a constitutionally protected right,[56] and because a suspect class was not involved, the rational basis test was appropriate. He observed that appointed school boards had been held constitutional by the Supreme Court, as long as appointments were not made in a manner that systematically excluded any element of the population. While some areas of the school district were not within the city of Cleveland, and residents of those areas therefore had no influence over the election of the mayor of Cleveland, they were represented in the general assembly and they elected the governor, both of which entities had approved H.B. 269.[57]

To the plaintiffs' claim of an inherent conflict of interest between the mayor's duties as mayor and head of the school system, Judge White responded that H.B. 269 called for the mayor's appointment of a

---

[54]Abdulhaaq, *supra* note 23.
[55]Spivey v. State of Ohio and Mixon v. State of Ohio, *supra* note 38, at 4.
[56]Citing San Antonio Independent School District v. Rodriguez, 411 U.S. 1, 35 (1973)
[57]Spivey v. State of Ohio and Mixon v. State of Ohio, *supra* note 38, at 12.

chief executive officer and a nine member board of education whose members were to be chosen from a diverse local nominating committee, so the measure gave the mayor appointment authority, rather than direct governing authority, over the school system.[58] Thus, Judge White upheld the constitutionality of H.B. 269, moving the district a step closer to local control.

Later that month, on March 27, Judge White declared the Cleveland City School District unitary. The consent decree under which the district had been operating since 1994, allowed for release upon the court's finding that the defendants had: 1)implemented all the provisions of the consent decree, 2) eliminated all vestiges of past discrimination to the extent practicable, and 3) demonstrated good faith commitment to their constitutional obligations.[59] Listing extensive findings of fact and conclusions of law, Judge White found that the defendants had complied with the outstanding remedial obligations under the consent decree. The judge also found, based on the findings of fact and conclusions of law, that the defendants had eliminated the vestiges of prior discrimination and segregation. He stressed that the defendants had shown through extensive testimony and evidence that any disparities in achievement did not result from unconstitutional conduct on the part of the defendants. He observed that no credible or factually supported evidence of any vestiges of past discrimination were presented during the trial. Finally, based on the defendants' compliance and on the absence of vestiges of past discrimination, Judge White held that the defendants had shown good faith.[60]

On June 5, 1998, Judge White signaled his willingness to lift the March 1995 order that placed the district under state control, and he urged state officials to move quickly to ensure that the mayoral governance plan would be in place in time for the start of school in the fall. State schools Superintendent John Goff would appoint a committee which would nominate eighteen candidates from the Cleveland school district, from which the mayor would appoint nine school board members. The mayor would also appoint a chief executive officer to head the school district, according to the provisions

---

[58] Ibid., 23-24.
[59] Reed v. Rhodes, No. C73-1300 (N.D. Ohio 27 March 1998) (memorandum and order at 6). The district had been released from the student assignment component of the remedial order since May 1996, based on compliance.
[60] Ibid., 82-83.

of H.B. 269. A hearing was scheduled for July 17, 1998, when the judge was expected to lift the March 3, 1995 order.[61]

Thus, twenty years of federal court supervision of the Cleveland Public Schools was about to end. The district had, after years of resistance, sufficiently complied with the remedial plan, and in the view of the court, the vestiges of discrimination had been eliminated. Yet, no one could argue that the remedial order had produced the results its proponents had sought. The abysmal test scores of the students and the significant achievement gap, along with high drop out rates demonstrated the inability of the court system to ensure children the education that Chief Justice Earl Warren, in *Brown v. Board of Education*, acknowledged they needed in order to succeed in life. The mayoral governance plan offered hope of substantive change and increased accountability, but any such change for the better would require vigilance and commitment on the part of many, if not all, sectors of Cleveland's population.

Retrospective Assessment

As the hearing on whether to release the district from court supervision began, Boston University Professor Christine Rossell, a desegregation expert, testified that given the demographics of the Cleveland Public Schools, the district had been remarkably and successfully integrated. The desegregation effort had been more successful than several districts that had already been released from court supervision. Yet, after twenty years of court supervision, the outlook for the children of Cleveland was bleak. This dichotomy between the apparently successful legal/technical outcome of the case and the educational results provided compelling evidence of the fallacy of the strategy of using the federal court system to equalize (which was understood to mean improve) the educational opportunity offered minority children. An editorial published in *The Plain Dealer* shortly after the start of the hearing regarding release of the district stated the problem succinctly:

> For all his federal power, Battisti could not control intransigent local politicians, job hungry Board of Education workers, or money-grubbing consultants and attorneys. He

---

[61]Stephens, "Judge OKs mayoral control of schools," *Cleveland Plain Dealer*, 5 June 1998, 1(B) and 4(B).

could not mandate bias-free instruction, quality teachers or involved parents. And he could not keep thousands of parents from dodging his busing system by moving from the city, or removing their children from the public schools. . . . The staff and the enrollment are integrated. Equal opportunities abound. The magnet school programs are among the best in the country. And yet, this system remains among the worst in all of Ohio. Test scores and graduation numbers are atrocious. The racial count works, but little else, and nothing a court can do will make it better.[62]

One of the factors that hindered the successful implementation of the remedial order was the "good ol' days" sentimentality that distorted memories of the district prior to the implementation of the remedial order. Following the civil rights unrest in the early 1960s, the charismatic Superintendent Paul Briggs, with the full support of the media, had played up his ambitious building program and launched a remarkably successful public relations campaign centered on raising the quality of the educational program for all Cleveland Public Schools students. This tact successfully shifted attention from the marked segregation within the system and the gross disparities between the education offered black and white children in the district. The positive image conveyed by Briggs and the media, coupled with the district's traditional policy of eschewing parental participation, served to insulate the school system from accountability for student achievement and the expenditure of funds. The suit, followed by the remedial order and two decades of court supervision, opened the school system to public scrutiny and disclosure of the inequities, the corruption, the incompetence, and the mismanagement that had plagued the system for decades. Yet, because the previous positive image of the district, and especially that of Superintendent Briggs, had been so well entrenched, Judge Battisti and forced busing became the villains and, in the minds of much of the public, the sources of the deterioration of a once great school district.

Former Director of OSMCR, Leonard Stevens, reflected that when the court intervened, the district was so plagued with incompetence that it was incapable of designing and implementing an effective desegregation plan, even if the will had been there. Stevens recalled

---

[62]"A success, they tell us," *Cleveland Plain Dealer*, 9 November 1997, 2(E).

that initially he fully expected that the district would implement all of the education elements of the remedial order, but that the district would flatly refuse to desegregate. The exact opposite occurred. "I was dead wrong," Stevens said. The district deliberately refused to implement the educational elements of the remedial order that would have benefited all district students. Refusal to implement the educational elements was calculated, in Stevens' estimation. The greater the decline in school district performance, if the failure could be ascribed to the judge, the greater would be the political victory. "I think there was the equivalent of a scorched earth policy," said Stevens. The board and administration would have preferred to let the system burn, rather than implement the remedial order, as long as the community would blame the judge, and they did.[63]

Dr. Aileen Kassen believed that the district was particularly remiss in not recognizing and utilizing the invaluable resource it had in the parents of the students. The remedial order called for the training of parents so that they could participate effectively on school community councils, yet the training never took place. "(The parents) never got the backing they needed. ... (T)here were so many good ideas that could have been implemented and would have made such a difference, but there was such resistance, just absolute resistance."[64] Resistance to the court's interference, to the remedial order, and to public scrutiny led the district administration to thwart the objectives of the remedial order at every turn, and in so doing, not just overlook, but actually reject the assistance that parents could have provided.

Dr. Kassen also blamed the business community for abdicating its responsibility to the children of Cleveland. When the will was there, the business community of Cleveland had achieved many positive objectives, but when leadership was needed for smooth implementation of the remedial order, the business community fell through.

Martha Smith, former OSMCR advisory commission member and later a member of the Cleveland board of education, reflected on the years of struggle to improve the school system, "(Y)ou're only human, and can only do so much, and it was always up hill. There was never a time when the pro-integration position was the popular one. And people just got tired and weary . . . there's something so fatiguing and

---

[63]Leonard Stevens, former director of the Office on School Monitoring and Community Relations, telephone interview by author, 18 July 1997.
[64]Kassen, *supra* note 2.

demoralizing about always being on the side that is not popular."[65] Rashidah Abdulhaaq also remarked that many members of the "old guard" had moved on to other endeavors, leaving a void in the community of activists who were still willing to fight for quality education for all children. She felt that many people had been discouraged by the fact that the objective of equal access to quality had been lost in the obsession with busing. She suggested that few people in Cleveland in the late 1990s even understood that the remedial order included educational components. "Desegregation" implied cross-town busing, rather than transportation as one of numerous methods of ridding the system of inequalities and of according all children an equal educational opportunity.[66]

Recalling the extent of the segregation, of the tracking of students, and of the institutionalized subordination of the needs of black students in the years prior to desegregation, Mrs. Charles Green observed:

Even when I think about this now years later, I just can't . . . it brings back certain feelings of -- how on earth could that have happened -- and people who felt that they were acting in the best interests of the children. That's the other thing. I don't feel that there was necessarily a viciousness there on the part of the school board and the school administrators. I think it was just this business of the historical paternalism of knowing what is best for minorities and for people who are poor.[67]

Conclusion

One of the greatest ironies of the history of school desegregation in America was that federal courts and judges were vilified as tyrannical, oppressive, and draconian, when in fact they attempted to accommodate local educational policy makers in every instance. Taking direction from the Supreme Court, the federal district courts deferred to the long-standing tradition of local control in educational policy making. Following findings of decades-long policies which violated the

---

[65]Smith, *supra* note 52.

[66]Abdulhaaq, *supra* note 23.

[67]Mrs. Charles Green, (Dr. Mareyjoice Greene), professor of sociology at Cleveland State University, telephone interview by author, 12 July 1997.

constitutional rights of minority children, federal district court judges invited school boards to develop plans for desegregation which would bring them into compliance with the Constitution. When school boards and administrators failed to do so, the courts were forced to step in and fashion desegregation plans themselves. Time and again, local opposition to desegregation, as reflected in the intransigence of the school boards, pitted communities against courts in battles that intensified racial disharmony, cost taxpayers millions of dollars, and perhaps most tragically, diverted school system and public attention from the educational needs of the children. These battles, which usually produced no winners, clearly produced victims, whose futures, in the case of Cleveland and other deteriorating urban systems, had been sacrificed as adults waged ideological battles and attorneys made millions of dollars.

Law professor Edward Mearns suggested that the seeds of failure in the Cleveland and other desegregation cases may have been planted in 1955 in *Brown v. Board of Education II*, when, in order to achieve consensus (when there was none) the Supreme Court left primary responsibility for implementation of desegregation plans to the defendants in the cases, local school boards and administrators, and placed federal district judges in charge of overseeing the implementation, because they would be more knowledgeable of local conditions. To further accommodate particular circumstances such as administrative inconvenience, the Supreme Court, rather than demanding that all schools be desegregated immediately, said that the process should take place "with all deliberate speed." School boards, of course, chose to emphasize deliberation, rather than haste, in formulating desegregation plans.

The ensuing resistance, which constituted defiance in many cases, could have been anticipated, given the political constraints of local school boards, observed Mearns:

> [The defendant school boards and administrators] are elected or they are appointed [and] they respond to the public. And every school administrator in the United States who has any substantial percentage of minorities in his district cannot say that he does not operate in light of that knowledge. That is, no school administrator can ever draw a school line without an interdependent judgment of what his community will tolerate. Race is in there all the time. The notion that you do things

by accident versus intent doesn't take account of the fact that the people who are running the schools are not stupid. They have a political constraint; that is, the will of their community is going to guide them in many ways.[68]

Thus, the courts sought the cooperation of the school boards, a virtually impossible objective, given the fact that the school board members represented and were a reflection of their communities. They could not afford to be perceived as being cooperative with the judges who first accused the school system (and community) of racial discrimination and then sought to wreak havoc with their children's lives. In the face of school board recalcitrance, then, observed Mearns, judges reluctantly "tightened the ratchet," which only served to confirm the communities' images of the draconian activist judges who gleefully pursued cases which involved social engineering, rather than interpreting the Constitution.

Therein lay the irony and the source of the failure of so many desegregation cases to achieve what the plaintiffs sought, equal opportunity to a quality education through which minority children could hope to attain the comforts of middle class life. The same institutions and forces that for so long denied minority children an equal educational opportunity by relegating them to separate and unequal schools controlled the ultimate success of the court ordered remedy. The Supreme Court understood the public resistance that desegregation orders would engender and the threat that defiance would pose to the prestige and the very integrity of the institution. Courts themselves do not have the authority to implement their own decisions. By allowing the school districts reasonable time and by allowing them to fashion their own desegregation plans, the Supreme Court sought to dissipate resentment and resistance and to encourage the cooperation of the school districts in restructuring their systems. Instead, communities, through their elected school boards and appointed administrators, resisted the courts' authority, ignored the courts' directives, and thwarted the successful implementation of the remedial plans at every turn. In the Cleveland case, the business community and the media capitalized on the fears and the prejudices of the public and effectively sabotaged a remedial plan that could have

---

[68]Mearns, *supra* note 53.

revitalized an unaccountable, highly discriminatory, and moribund inner city school district.

Epilogue

In the spring of 2002, the Cleveland school district was still under the control of the mayor, Jane Campbell at the time, with a CEO, Barbara Byrd-Bennett overseeing day to day operations. Cleveland had an appointed school board. Voters were to be asked in a November 5 referendum whether they approved of the district's remaining under this private-sector style leadership.[69]

Despite several years under the direction of the mayor and CEO, the Cleveland schools were still foundering. The schools report card released in January 2002 placed Cleveland in the Academic Emergency category. Cleveland students had met the academic standards in only four of twenty-seven categories. The standards included tests of fourth, sixth, ninth, tenth and twelfth graders in citizenship, math, reading, writing, and science, as well as each school's overall attendance and graduation rates. Cleveland students met the standards only in ninth, tenth, and twelfth grade writing and in tenth grade reading. This was the third year that Ohio had issued the school report cards, and Cleveland had qualified in one more category in 2000-2001 over the previous year. CEO Barbara Byrd-Bennett said that the gain reflected slow overall improvement. "We're reversing, I believe, decades of failure in the district."[70] Clearly much more was needed to raise student performance to an acceptable level.

---

[69] Janet Okoben, "Campbell wants to keep mayor in charge of schools," *Cleveland Plain Dealer*, (Cleveland.com) 19 March 2002.
[70] Janet Okoben and Scott Stephens, "Cuyahoga's top-ranked schools," *Cleveland Plain Dealer* (cleveland.com), 8 January 2002.

CHAPTER 12

Trends in School Desegregation at the Turn of the Century

Introduction

At the close of the desegregation era in Wilmington, Prince George's County, San Diego, and Cleveland, school systems had technically met their constitutional obligations to offer minority children an equal educational opportunity. They had sufficiently complied with the courts' directives to be declared unitary. Yet, frustration and disillusionment among plaintiffs and their supporters abounded. The achievement gap was a constant reminder of the inability of the school systems to meet the educational needs of minority children. When all was said and done, what had been accomplished by the decades of litigation and court-ordered remedies?

In Wilmington, the showcase of successful metropolitan desegregation, where near perfect racial balance had been effected, minority achievement had not improved, and the plaintiffs complained that meaningful integration had not taken place. Academic tracking had placed minorities disproportionately in low level classes where they were effectively segregated from whites and subjected t   less rigorous curricula and expectations. In Wilmington, the school system and state had been relatively compliant with the court, and the court had remained quite unobtrusive throughout the desegregation era. Thus, once the remedial order was rendered, Wilmington avoided much of the emotional upheaval and combative interaction among the parties and the court that other communities experienced. Yet, minority students in Wilmington continued to struggle and fail academically, and the plaintiffs continued to feel that the school systems were discriminatory in their treatment of students. They feared that with the inevitable return to neighborhood schools, which would result in high levels of racial isolation, the inequities between predominantly white and predominantly nonwhite schools would increase.

In Prince George's County, the desegregation plan had outlived its usefulness as the school district became overwhelmingly black. Minority parents in Prince George's County had long abandoned the goal of meaningful integration, and they generally supported the district's initiative to return to neighborhood schools with renewed focus on quality issues. Yet, even as the parties to the suit worked out the details of a settlement agreement that would release the district from court supervision and end the futile busing plan, the NAACP was reticent to relinquish court supervision because early resistance to the court's authority and legal appeals by the district had built distrust between blacks and whites in the district. Despite an extensive court-ordered magnet school program, minority achievement lagged far behind that of white students in Prince George's County. Desegregation expert Gary Orfield critiqued the district's desegregation plan, because while it called for *Milliken II* relief, it set no standard for success. Yet, where standards had been set by courts in other districts, they had not been met.

In San Diego, continued and increasingly high levels of racial isolation in the district, frustration over unsatisfactory achievement levels among minorities, and according to many close observers of the system, bureaucratic intransigence and indifference belied the outward appearance of a successful and popular desegregation plan. San Diego had avoided the turmoil of forced busing by convincing Judge Welsh that a mandatory desegregation plan would be counterproductive because of the white flight that would likely ensue. Because participation was voluntary by those who transferred, the plan was well received and grew increasingly popular following its implementation in 1977. However, many San Diegans charged that meaningful integration had never taken place. They claimed that throughout the desegregation era, the school district had gone through the motions of complying with court orders, but it had remained unreceptive to substantive change that would have improved the quality of education in the district, particularly for minority students. Parental and community frustration with the school district surfaced during a very contentious teachers' strike in 1996. Though the turmoil surrounding the strike was distressing for all involved, the airing of grievances resulted in the forging of a more collaborative relationship among parents and the school district. The 1998 contract negotiations between the school district and teachers reflected the district's and the teachers' greater receptivity to parental concerns and sensitivity to students' needs. Thus, in San Diego, political pressure on the school district, appeared to have produced a recognition of shortcomings on the part of the district and an openness to change that twenty years of litigation had not achieved.

In Cleveland, twenty years of litigation had produced no winners, but clear losers, the children. Residents of Cleveland who had recognized the potential for educational reform in Judge Battisti's remedial order expressed anger over the opportunity lost. As the court released the school district from supervision in 1998, the overwhelming majority of Cleveland students attended schools that were racially isolated, district achievement levels were abysmal, and dropout rates were shockingly high. The remedial order had included educational components that could have improved the education of all Cleveland's students. However, community and school system resentment toward the court and resistance against its authority prompted the district to fight the remedial order, rather than embrace the opportunity to overhaul the system and make it effective.

Numerous conditions in Cleveland rendered it the most complex and troublesome of the cases studied. Poverty levels were exceedingly high, and racial isolation was especially marked. Historic tensions among Cleveland's white ethnic and black communities made conciliation among them difficult. Responsible leadership in the business community was almost completely lacking, and the media was, in the assessment of many observers, particularly negligent in promoting the widespread myth of an equitable and high quality school system that had been unfairly maligned by the court. Attorneys exploited the situation, mocking the court and inflaming the community as they pocketed millions of dollars in fees. The school board historically consisted of "political hacks" and "knuckle-heads" who used the board as a stepping stone to more prestigious political posts and a position from which to offer friends and relatives lucrative employment or contracts. Petty bickering among school board members and steadfast resistance to the courts' authority consumed virtually all the board members' energies, eclipsing attention to the educational needs of the students. Administrative incompetence and fiscal mismanagement reached such heights in 1995 that the judge placed responsibility for management of the school district with the state. By virtually any measure, the district was foundering. The corrupt practices of the school board, the incompetence of the school district administration, and public complacence which abruptly changed to hostility toward the judge and the court's authority when the court found it guilty of constitutional violations combined to sabotage the best intentions of Judge Battisti, thereby sacrificing the promise of the remedial order.

Thus, these four case studies offer compelling evidence of the limitations of the judicial system in ridding public education systems of the inequities that reflect deep divisions within American society. *Brown* and its progeny eliminated dual school systems, but they were powerless to eradicate racial isolation in schools which was a function of America's increasingly segregated cities and neighborhoods. The courts were even less successful in accomplishing what many perceived as the ultimate goal of the litigation, to raise the *quality* of the educational programs typically offered minority children, thereby offering them a truly equal educational opportunity.

It was clear that minority children in racially isolated school settings received an inferior education. Some argued that the segregation itself, regardless of the cause, resulted in an inferior education. One implication of this position was that conscious and/or unconscious societal racism, which pervaded school systems, precluded the acquisition of an equal educational opportunity by minority children, unless they attended schools with white children. Another implication was that minority children, who tended to be socioeconomically disadvantaged and whose parents tended to be educationally disadvantaged, benefited from exposure to the middle class values of white children in integrated school settings.

Others argued that the stigma of *de jure* or purposeful segregation, rather than racial isolation *per se,* was what caused the injury, and that school systems had fulfilled their constitutional obligations if they eliminated *de jure* segregation. School systems could not be expected to eliminate the consequences of centuries of laws and deeply ingrained mores which resulted in quite pronounced residential segregation in some areas of the country. Nor could school systems be expected to compensate for the educational disadvantages with which minority children tended to enter school or the social pathologies that plagued their neighborhoods and homes and which hindered their ability to progress in school.

Some courts addressed the achievement gap, sometimes incorporating specific educational goals such as closing the achievement gap by a specific year or achieving equity in passage rates on standardized tests. In San Diego, the final order of 1985 set a goal that 50 percent of the students in racially isolated schools should achieve at or above the national norm on standardized tests in reading, math, and language. Yet, test scores dropped in the late 1980s and through the 1990s. Courts could set achievement goals and even order reduction of the achievement gap, but they could not effect a reduction of the gap. Furthermore, such components of the desegregation orders were unenforceable. In *Missouri v. Jenkins* (1995), the Supreme Court held that the school systems could not be held responsible for eliminating the achievement gap. Its causes apparently lay in socioeconomic disparities and societal racism, factors and forces beyond the control of school systems. Thus, in the late 1990s, after decades of litigation, when the courts were releasing school districts based on years of good faith compliance, many of those who had strongly supported principles of equity and quality for all children and who had applauded the courts' efforts to rectify historical and continuing discriminatory practices in public education felt frustrated and disillusioned. They questioned what had been gained by the decades of court-supervised desegregation.

The litigation process was bound to create adversaries, rather than partners in common cause. In the early years of litigation, school boards and administrators had stubbornly denied any wrong doing, despite the overwhelming evidence to the contrary, thereby insulting and alienating their minority constituencies. Repeated appeals of the liability findings and the desegregation orders wasted scarce resources that could have been applied to improving the quality of educational programs, and they served to further alienate minority parents and students. In the case of Cleveland, resistance to the court's authority had been so great, that, as former OSMCR director Len Stevens put it, the school board had adopted a scorched earth policy. The greater the deterioration of the school district, if it could be ascribed to the court's intervention, the greater the political victory for the school system.[1] In short, the adversarial nature of the litigation process ripped communities apart, pitting whites against nonwhites, when they could have been working together to achieve the ultimate and innocuous goal

---

[1]See page 258.

of improving the education system for all children. When the issue of the achievement gap became more prominent in the litigation, the adversarial nature of the legal system led the parties to place blame, rather than to look for solutions.

Judges could not force bureaucratic school systems to be sensitive, receptive, or responsive to the needs and concerns of minority parents and children. In Cleveland, resistance to the courts' authority was so thorough and determined that the district successfully thwarted the implementation of almost all the educational components of the remedial order, including the community involvement component; the district systematically shunned parental input.[2]   As noted by community members in each of the case studies, the school systems were especially effective in shutting out the input of minority parents who had less political leverage, who oftentimes had had negative experiences in school themselves and were therefore easily intimidated, and who tended to be less knowledgeable of effective ways in which to navigate bureaucracies and make their voices heard.

Courts could incorporate racial and human relations components in the desegregation orders, but they could not make the receiving school environments less intimidating for minority students. Courts could not eliminate the conscious and unconscious racism on the part of administrators, teachers, and students in receiving schools. As Pat Meredith of San Diego observed, the children knew when their teachers did not like them. In San Diego, participation in the desegregation plan was voluntary on the part of the transfer students, but it was not voluntary for the receiving administrators, teachers, and students.

Legal remedies were bound to meet with community resentment and resistance. In finding communities guilty of discrimination, judges condemned community members and their ways of life, thereby forfeiting their own status as valued members of the community. Judges were accused of making up law and of social engineering. Ironically, with the Supreme Court setting the standard in *Brown II*, the courts typically made painstaking efforts to remain unobtrusive, to allow as much discretion as possible to local policy makers. It was only when school boards and administrators dragged their feet and sometimes blatantly defied the court's authority, that judges became increasingly dictatorial, imposing more and more specific requirements

---

[2]See comments of Dr. Aileen Kassen and Martha Smith, pages 258.

on school officials.[3] School officials and other community members who were unwilling or unable to admit their complicity in unconstitutional discrimination against minority children vilified judges.

Another irony of the desegregation process was that those who resisted the court's authority and adamantly claimed to have done nothing wrong clearly recognized the inferiority of the overwhelmingly minority schools. Once the desegregation orders were in place, crash programs were often initiated to "spruce up" the schools in minority neighborhoods to make them more acceptable to the white children transferred there and to their parents. The concept of magnet schools, which were designed to entice white children into minority neighborhoods, rankled many minority parents because the old schools had been deemed adequate for their children, but they were clearly unsatisfactory for white children.

As legal battles ensued, business and political leaders typically offered no moral leadership. Once the litigation began and at least until the remedial orders were issued, school boards, other political leaders, and business leaders often focused on fighting the inevitable desegregation orders, rather than constructing workable plans for desegregation. Politicians and the media vilified the judges and exploited people's fears and prejudices, effectively equating the specter of cross-town busing with leading lambs to slaughter. In the cases of Wilmington and San Diego, and eventually Prince George's County, political leaders changed their tone and urged peaceful compliance after the courts issued the remedial orders. In Cleveland, however, elected officials continued to thwart the court's directives at every turn, with the support of the business community, almost throughout the era of desegregation. These elected officials reflected the values and social structures of their communities, and political leaders could hardly have been expected to support the judges who had found their constituents guilty of unconstitutional acts. So strong was the pressure on elected officials and appointees of those officials, that school board members and superintendents sometimes openly declared that they would do nothing to integrate until forced to do so by the courts.[4]

---

[3]See comments by Professor Edward Mearns on 261.
[4]Superintendent Goodman of San Diego made such a declaration in 1974 in response to a call to take action against increasing racial isolation in the system's schools. See page 146. In Prince George's County, a board

In his book *The Burden of Brown: Thirty Years of School Desegregation*, Raymond Wolters argued that beginning with *Green v. New Kent County* (1968), the Supreme Court and lower courts overstepped their authority by expanding the *Brown II* mandate and ordering districts with a history of unconstitutional discrimination to take positive steps toward *integration*. He placed much of the blame for a perceived decline in the quality of education in "*Brown* districts" squarely on the shoulders of overzealous courts. "In the *Brown* districts, education has suffered grievously from naively liberal court orders, from the influence of progressive education, and from the defiant and irresponsible behavior of some students. The Constitution has also suffered as judges have arrogated the right to make social policy." He acknowledged that "segregation was anachronistic in the middle of the twentieth century," but countered that "in a democracy social reform should be undertaken by the people's elected representatives, not by unelected judges."

Judges' naiveté regarding the courts' efficacy, shortcomings of progressive education, and students' defiant and irresponsible behavior may very well have contributed to a decline in public education in the *Brown* districts. However, Wolter's narrow focus ignores other crucial factors, particularly the indifference of majorities to the subtle and not-so-subtle discriminatory practices of school systems and the intransigence of school boards. This intransigence led to their squandering enormous sums on legal fees, to their forfeiting many of the benefits of remedial orders, and to their alienating much of their constituencies. Furthermore, Wolters' position that social reform should be undertaken by elected officials rather than unelected judges is legitimate, except when the social policy in question denies people their constitutional rights.

In the decade following *Brown* many school districts took only the most tentative steps to dismantle their unconstitutional dual schools systems, and the popular "freedom of choice plans," besides placing the burden of desegregation on minority students, resulted in very little change. Minorities faced with recalcitrant school boards had no choice but to seek further intervention by the courts. Judges, in turn, acted appropriately in requiring school systems to take positive actions to

---

member said he would rather have the court tell him to desegregate than have to justify a desegregation plan to the community. See page 95.

restore the victims of segregation to the position they likely would have held absent the constitutional violation.

Nevertheless, near complete reliance on the courts to rid school systems of inequalities, of racism, and of bureaucratic intransigence and incompetence was misguided. Legal action had been necessary to bring an end to officially sanctioned segregation in public schools at a time when minorities were effectively excluded from the political process. Legal action arguably remained a necessary component of the effort to achieve equal educational opportunity well into the 1970s, owing to racial disharmony and indifference on the part of middle class whites to the educational needs of poor and minority children. However, advocates for the educational rights of minorities were doomed to fail when they directed virtually all of their efforts towards litigation, rather than attempting to build political consensus to improve educational opportunities for minorities.

The Challenges of Poverty and Racial Isolation

The decades of court supervision of school districts to eliminate constitutional violations and provide minority children an equal educational opportunity had produced very limited gains. While dual school systems had been eradicated, inequities related to race, ethnicity, and particularly poverty within and among school systems abounded. Courts had forced school systems to mix children of different races, requiring busing when necessary, and they had ordered enhanced educational programs to try to eliminate the vestiges of prior discrimination, but the courts were relatively powerless to solve the myriad problems of poor and minority school systems.

A strong correlation existed between racial isolation and socioeconomic isolation, as did a very strong correlation between poverty rates and low achievement in school. In the 1994-95 school year, students in racially isolated minority schools were 16.3 times as likely to be in a high poverty school as students in overwhelmingly white schools. In areas with high concentrations of poverty, parents were far less educated, children were much more likely to live in single parent homes with multiple problems, children were much more likely to have serious and untreatable health problems, and families moved much more often during the school year. Schools with high concentrations of students below the poverty level had to devote more resources to family and health crises, security, children who did not begin school speaking English, seriously disturbed children, children with no education-related materials in their homes, and children with inadequate preparation for school. These schools tended to have less qualified teachers and high teacher turnover. In states that had instituted qualifying exams for graduation, high poverty schools had much higher failure rates.[5] The school systems in Wilmington, Prince George's County, San Diego, and Cleveland devoted considerable resources to meeting the challenges of virtually all of these poverty-related socioeconomic conditions.

Whether school systems were well integrated, as in Wilmington, or highly racially identifiable, as in Cleveland, a significant achievement gap between white and nonwhite students persisted throughout the nation. The achievement gap tended to be self-perpetuating in that it often led to segregation within schools through ability tracking. In his profoundly moving work on the continual and pervasive discrimination experienced by African-Americans in America, *Two Nations: Black and White, Separate, Hostile, and Unequal*, political scientist Andrew Hacker of City University of New York pointed out that race was never mentioned in this common practice of separating children by ability level, but black children were disproportionately placed in lower level classes, and once labeled as "slow," regardless of the potential they later demonstrated, they rarely escaped from that academic track.[6] While the pedagogical merits of such tracking systems were debatable, the fact was that children who were placed on the slower tracks were rarely challenged to the degree that those on the "fast" track were.

An unpublished 1986 Elementary and Secondary Civil Rights Survey conducted by the Office of Civil Rights of the U.S. Department of Education found that black students were classified as "educably" mentally retarded, "trainably" mentally retarded, or seriously emotionally disturbed 2.3 times as often as white students, and all minority students were so classified 1.6 times as often as whites.[7] Minority students were suspended from school nearly twice as often as whites, and black students were suspended three times as often as

[5]Gary Orfield, et al., *Deepening Segregation in American Public Schools* (Boston: Harvard Project on School Desegregation, 1997), 17-19.
[6]Andrew Hacker, *Two Nations: Black and White, Separate, Hostile, and Unequal* (New York: Charles Scribner's Sons, 1992) 164.
[7]Cited in Percy Bates, "Desegregation: Can We Get There From Here?" *Phi Delta Kappan* 72 (September 1990): 10.

whites. These figures supported the growing evidence of segregation within schools.[8]   Racially segregated classes offered very little opportunity for meaningful interaction among children of different ethnic backgrounds.

Scholars remained divided as to whether African-American students had benefited by exposure to white children within the school environment. One study concluded that black children did benefit, that they had more friends of other races, that they eventually worked in high-status jobs, that they tended to attend and graduate from multiracial colleges and universities, and that they tended to live in integrated neighborhoods.[9]

Other researchers found that integration in schools actually had been debilitating to black children. They found that there was "little meaningful contact" between blacks and whites, and that the self-esteem of black children was diminished by integration.   These findings led Andrew Hacker to conclude that black-white proportions were critical to successful integration, and that 20 percent black was optimal, because that mixture provided a sufficient group for friends and support for minority students, while still providing sufficient benefits that arose from attending a racially balanced school.   This "optimal level" of integration cited by Hacker highlighted a major factor in the futility of continuing busing plans that had long outlived their usefulness, such as those in Prince George's County and Cleveland, because the school districts had become overwhelmingly minority. The minority ratios often exceeded eighty to twenty, where it was highly questionable whether any measurable benefits could be realized.

One of the ironies surrounding the desegregation and busing controversy was that most people assumed that African-Americans were supportive of the decision.   It was thought that they fully endorsed racial integration of schools and the eventual busing mandates, because they believed that their children would receive important educational advantages.   However, as Yale Law School professor and Solicitor General for President Clinton, Drew Days observed, black children and families had paid a high price.   For instance, the closing of black schools resulted in the loss of gathering places that had served not only

---

[8]Percy Bates, "Desegregation: Can We Get There From Here?" *Phi Delta Kappan* 72 (September 1990): 10.
[9]Hacker, 166.

as educational facilities, but as community centers. Secondly, black students bore the brunt of the burden of busing. Thirdly, black teachers and administrators were dismissed and demoted in disproportionate numbers. Finally, black students faced increased disciplinary action in new schools.[10]

Despite the shameful physical conditions of many of the former all-black schools, their loss and the departure of the children to strange and distant neighborhoods deprived African-American parents of their former influence on their children's education. Dempsey and Noblit described the decrease, after desegregation took place, in the "closeness and family atmosphere" that had existed in small black community schools. The schools had been the focal points for the communities, teachers were revered, and families and extended families alike could be counted on for promoting the children's education.[11] The increasing call in the 1990s for a return to neighborhood or community schools was based on the desire for a return to the educational community Dempsey and Noblit described.

Recognizing the critical role of parents in the educational process, New York University law professor Derrick Bell wrote in 1983:

> [F]rom the beginning many black parents and their community leaders realized what some civil rights lawyers have not yet acknowledged. There can be no effective schooling for black children without both parental involvement in the educational process and meaningful participation in school policy making. Experience, often painful, has taught these parents and communities that neither object is brought closer merely by enrolling their children in predominantly white schools -- especially if those schools are located a long bus ride from their homes and neighborhoods.[12]

Similarly, Drew Days asserted that blacks had long questioned the advisability of pushing racial integration to the limits of the Supreme

---

[10]Drew S. Days, III, "Brown Blues: Rethinking the Integrative Ideal," *William and Mary Law Review* 34 (Fall 1992): 55.

[11]Van Dempsey and George Noblit, "The Demise of Caring in an African-American Community: One Consequence of School Desegregation," *The Urban Review* 25 (1993): 53-74 (*passim*).

[12]Derrick Bell, "Learning from Our Losses: Is School Desegregation Still Feasible in the 1980s?" *Phi Delta Kappan* 64 (April 1983): 575.

Court's jurisdiction, especially when extensive busing had been involved. Their voices went unheeded for some time, because they coincided with what "untrustworthy" white school boards were arguing. Major civil rights organizations representing the plaintiffs in desegregation had vehemently rejected any notion of stopping short of the constitutional limit for remedies.[13]

In the 1990s, the debate continued with regard to the Court's constitutional justification for requiring busing to achieve desegregation, as well as its practical soundness. Forty years after *Brown*, segregated schools no longer resulted from *de jure* discriminatory pupil assignment. Increasing residential segregation, had fundamentally changed America's demographic landscape, and many whole school districts were predominantly one race.

Residential segregation had been much more intractable than school segregation. Congress finally addressed housing discrimination in the 1968 Civil Rights Act, but in contrast to the (judicially prompted) aggressive efforts to desegregate schools, until the 1990s, administrative branches of the federal, state, and local governments had been much less assertive in fighting housing segregation.[14] Early in his first term, President Clinton called for stronger enforcement of anti-housing discrimination legislation. George C. Galster, a research associate at the Urban Institute, a Washington think tank, called the Clinton move "the most significant initiative we have seen in more than a generation." The Justice Department had increased its staff assigned to enforcing fair housing legislation by about one third and had filed and settled several cases against banks that allegedly discriminated in their lending practices.[15]

Notwithstanding the Clinton Administration's efforts, for the previous few decades, residential segregation had steadily advanced in many areas. Some analysts blamed the "white flight" from the inner cities to the suburbs, which left core areas virtually 100 percent minority, on court-ordered busing for desegregation. The trend began in the 1940s, however, and would undoubtedly have occurred without busing orders, though perhaps at a slower pace. White exodus had occurred at vastly different rates, but research showed that as blacks and

---

[13]Days, 58.

[14]Karl Tabor, "Desegregation of Public School Districts: Persistence and Change," *Phi Delta Kappan* 72 (September 1990): 23.

[15]Peter Schmidt, "Administration Falls Short, Right Report Says," *Education Week*, 25 January 1995, 15.

other minorities moved into neighborhoods, especially after the percentage surpassed the "comfort zone" for whites (10 to 20 percent minority), whites began to leave, seeking homes in suburbs, where they were surrounded by other whites. This occurred even when the blacks who moved in were of the same socioeconomic status as the whites.[16]

Regardless of the causes of increased segregation in housing patterns, the demographic trend necessitated a reassessment of the evolved *Brown* mandate. If the constitutional requirement had been to achieve racial balance for its own sake, then further comprehensive inter-district integrative efforts would have been obligatory. The Court rejected racial balance, however. In *Swann* (1971), the Court said that racial balance was an appropriate "starting point" which the courts could use to design a remedy for *de jure* segregation. The Court restated its position that racial imbalance alone was not a constitutional violation in *Milliken I* (1974) and in *Pasadena City Board of Education v. Spangler* (1976).

If the *Brown* mandate was, on the other hand, to remove the vestiges of past *de jure* segregation and to offer equal educational opportunities to students of all colors and ethnicities, then the first part of that goal had, for all practical purposes, been accomplished. The second half of the mandate, on the other hand, had tested the courts' resources and authority, and in the end had proven impossible for the judicial system to effect. By the late 1990s, as the courts relinquished jurisdiction over desegregation cases, despite increasing racial isolation and a persistent achievement gap, the limitation of the courts' power was evident. As the preceding case studies demonstrated, the effects of a history of troubled race relations, poverty, and racial isolation had proven too onerous for the courts to remedy.

The Court's Retreat

The Supreme Court signaled its willingness to begin releasing school districts from court supervision in the early 1990s with *Board of Education of Oklahoma City Public Schools v. Dowell* (1991) and *Freeman v. Pitts* (1992). In *Oklahoma v. Dowell*, the school district had desegregated under a court-ordered plan implemented in 1972. After five years of compliance, the district court released the school

---

[16]Hacker, 37-38.

district from formal supervision, declaring that it had achieved unitary status.   The district later abandoned busing and reintroduced a neighborhood school program for grades K-4, which included a transfer option from schools in which a student was in the majority to one in which he or she was in the minority.

The Supreme Court held that a school system could achieve unitary status and thereby be released from court supervision, despite the fact that some schools had overwhelmingly black or white student bodies if 1) it had complied with a desegregation order within a reasonable time period, 2) it was deemed unlikely to revert to its discriminatory practices, and 3) it had eliminated, to the extent practicable, vestiges of prior discrimination in its school policies. Chief Justice Rehnquist noted that school districts which had come under the courts' supervision did not have a *perpetual* obligation to correct racial imbalance which occurred due to changing housing patterns. Writing for the five to three majority (the newly appointed Justice Souter did not participate), the Chief Justice stressed the temporary nature of the judicial supervision and the ideal of returning school districts to local control after they had complied with the desegregation decree for a "reasonable" period of time.   The Chief Justice emphasized that the federal courts' control over school systems was limited to the time required to relieve the effects of past intentional discrimination.   In determining whether vestiges of past *de jure* segregation had been eliminated, the Chief Justice advised that the court should consider "every facet of school operations," student assignment, faculty, staff, transportation, extra-curricular activities, and facilities; this is, the *Green* factors.

Justice Marshall, joined by Justices Blackmun and Stevens, strongly dissented, noting that the Court's jurisprudence held current school boards accountable for the effects of past discrimination. Marshall declared that racially identifiable schools perpetuated a message of racial inferiority and that their existence in school districts with a history of state-sponsored segregation constituted evidence of noncompliance with desegregation orders. He said, "In my view, a standard for dissolution of a desegregation decree must take into account the unique harm associated with a system of racially identifiable schools and must expressly demand the elimination of such schools." Marshall further proclaimed, "I believe a desegregation decree cannot be lifted so long as conditions likely to inflict the stigmatic injury condemned in *Brown I* persist and there remain feasible methods of eliminating such conditions."

However, in 1992, *Freeman v. Pitts* reemphasized the majority's understanding of the temporal nature of federal court supervision of local school districts. Specifically, the Court addressed the question of whether a district court could incrementally release a school system from a desegregation order after the district had met some, but not all, of the court's demands for achieving a unitary system under *Green*. The district court had released the DeKalb County (Georgia) School System from supervision with regard to two of the six "*Green* factors," holding that the school system had achieved unitary status with respect to student assignment and facilities. The court ordered further efforts in teacher and principal assignments, resource allocations, and equalizing the quality of education in different areas of the county.

The DeKalb County School System, like those of Oklahoma City, Prince George's County, San Diego, and Cleveland, had experienced significant demographic changes while it underwent court-ordered desegregation. The school district's population grew from 70,000 to 450,000, and the percentage of black students increased from 5 percent to 47 percent. Racially identifiable schools resulted from this population growth and from the migration of whites and blacks to the suburbs.

The Court of Appeals for the 11th Circuit reversed the district court, rejecting the incremental approach to ending desegregation orders, and holding that the *Green* factors were not severable. The appellate court ordered the school district to initiate aggressive measures, such as pairing and clustering of schools, busing, and gerrymandering of school zones to achieve integration.

In a unanimous decision, the Supreme Court reversed the appellate court and affirmed the district court's holding. The Court upheld the incremental release of school districts from court supervision. The Court rejected the appellate court's apparent assessment that until complete compliance with the court's mandate had been achieved, "heroic measures" were required to achieve racial balance throughout the school district.

The Court unequivocally stated that racial balance was not to be pursued for its own sake, but only when racial imbalance resulted from a constitutional violation. The Court further declared that once racial imbalance resulting from *de jure* segregation had been corrected, the school district was not obligated to remedy racial imbalance resulting from demographic factors. "Where resegregation is a product not of state action but of private choices, it does not have constitutional implications. It is beyond the authority and beyond the practical ability of the federal courts to try to counteract [continuous] and massive demographic shifts." In June 1995, DeKalb County was released from federal judicial oversight following more than two decades of court supervision.

Thus, with *Oklahoma v. Dowell* and *Freeman v. Pitts*, the Court entered a new phase in the history of school desegregation, wherein it signaled lower courts to withdraw from supervision of school districts when they had demonstrated compliance with court orders. In doing so, the Court acknowledged the limited mandate of *Brown* and its progeny, which was to eliminate *de jure* racial segregation and its "vestiges" from public schools. Determination of the point at which the vestiges of past segregation had been eradicated proved difficult and controversial, but the Court made it clear that no constitutional authority existed for court-ordered racial balancing in schools to counteract residential segregation resulting from private choices. Furthermore, the Court implicitly acknowledged its limited authority in the oversight of traditionally locally controlled school systems.

Freeman v. Pitts did not signal an abrupt judicial turnabout, however. Individual circumstances, especially the courts' perceptions of the school districts' "good faith," would affect the courts' willingness to release individual districts.[17] In *Freeman v. Pitts*, the justices all agreed with the concept of incremental relinquishment of judicial supervision; they all agreed that good faith on the part of the schools district was an important factor in relinquishment; and they all agreed that the judicial remedy should be limited to alleviation of the original constitutional violation. However, the various concurring opinions (Scalia's, Souter's, and Blackmun's) revealed that the justices were not in complete agreement on the appropriate role for the Court in the 1990s with respect to school desegregation. Thus, the requests of

---

[17]The concept of good faith compliance was quite nebulous, of course. Many school districts had resisted the courts' authority for years or decades, before finally giving in and at least superficially complying with the court's orders. In Cleveland, after years of outright defiance, the school board adopted a more cooperative stance with the court, but to say that it had ever complied in good faith would have required a very loose interpretation of the term. Nevertheless, the district was released from supervision in 1998.

school districts to be released from court supervision would be evaluated on an individual basis.

In 1995, the Supreme Court, in *Missouri v. Jenkins*, sent an even stronger message that judicial authority in desegregation cases was limited and that judicial oversight of school districts for the purposes of desegregation was a temporary measure. The Court made it clear that good faith compliance and removal of the vestiges of past desegregation were the criteria for release, rather than attainment of academic goals such as eliminating the achievement gap. The remedial order in Kansas City had been the most far-reaching and expensive in the nation, having mandated an ambitious building program in the city along with a wide range of "quality education programs." The Kansas City, Missouri School District (KCMSD) was transformed into a super-magnet in the hope that the extraordinary facilities and academic offerings in the city would attract white children from the suburbs. The idea was that white children would not only integrate the school system, but that they would bring with them middle class values which would further improve the academic atmosphere. The results were disappointing, however. Neither the impressive array of educational programs nor the extravagant facilities attracted a large enough number of suburban children to render the district "integrated." Even more disappointing, achievement levels among minorities in the district remained unacceptably low.

In 1994, the State of Missouri requested release from court supervision and from their financial responsibility for the desegregation programs, arguing that it had complied in good faith with the courts' orders. The defendants argued for continued oversight based on the low achievement levels of minority students, which the lower court had earlier determined were a vestige of past discrimination. The Supreme Court held that the lower court exceeded its broad remedial powers in attempting to create a magnet school district of the KCMSD to serve the inter-district goal of attracting suburban students. The Court rejected the argument that judicial supervision should continue as long as the achievement gap persisted, noting that the district was entitled to know rather precisely what its obligations were under the desegregation decree. The Court held that many factors beyond the control of the school system and the state affected student achievement and that requiring the attainment of academic goals unrelated to the effects *de jure* segregation would unjustifiably delay the KCMSD's return to local control.

With *Oklahoma v. Dowell, Freeman v. Pitts,* and finally *Missouri v. Jenkins,* the Supreme Court unequivocally reaffirmed its view of the judicial system's limited authority in public education and the temporal nature of judicial oversight in desegregation cases. The courts' duty was to demand compliance with plans that would render school systems unitary and free from constitutional violations. They had neither the authority nor the practical ability to compel districts or states to take extraordinary measures indefinitely to fulfill diversity or quality educational goals, however meritorious those goals were.

Following the Supreme Court's seminal ruling in *Missouri v. Jenkins,* U.S. District Judge Russel G. Clark took steps to return the district to local control as soon as possible. The parties reached an agreement under which the state would pay the district $314 million over a period of three years, until June 1999, after which the state would be released from its obligations.[18]

In 1998 the school district was restructuring with the approval of Judge Clark. At school's opening in the fall of 1998, well over half of the district's sixty magnet school programs were to be abolished and the schools would return to regular neighborhood schools. Those magnet schools that were deemed successful in terms of student achievement would continue to operate as magnets, at least for a time. These changes would save the district about $eleven million, mostly in transportation costs.[19]

Kansas City's strategy of developing an "irresistible" magnet program to draw in white students from the suburbs never came close to reaching its goals of desegregation or improving achievement levels among minorities in the inner city schools. Most desegregation experts, even those who agreed on little else, agreed that the Kansas City program was simply too extravagant, without including measures to ensure that funds were allocated efficiently or effectively. David Armor, a research professor at the Institute of Public Policy at George Mason University, observed, "There were never enough white students to justify making all those schools magnets. They got too much money, and they spent some of it on facilities that will never have the demand to justify them." Armor noted that the difficult cutbacks the district faced as the court-mandated programs ended could have been

---

[18]Caroline Hendrie, "Falling Stars," *Education Week,* 25 February 1998, 36-37.
[19]Ibid., 35-37.

predicted. The district had been operating under artificial, temporary circumstances, and it would be very difficult to return to normal funding.[20]

Gary Orfield, professor of education and social policy at Harvard University and director of the Harvard Project on School Desegregation, as well as a strong proponent of traditional desegregation remedies and a skeptic about magnet and other compensatory educational programs, agreed that much of the money in Kansas City was misspent. "You dumped this tremendous amount of money into a school district that did not have the will or the capacity to spend it very effectively or monitor itself. Then all of a sudden the plug was pulled."[21] This lack of accountability requirements attached to *Milliken II* type funds engendered criticism in Prince George's County, as well as in San Diego, where millions of dollars were spent on magnet programs, with little or no measurable achievement gains.

Other cases reflected the trend of a judicial retreat. Denver was declared unitary and released from court supervision in 1995. Once the desegregation order was lifted, a 1974 state constitutional amendment prohibiting busing for integration applied to the district. Furthermore, by the 1990s, political and popular opinion supported an end to busing. Nevertheless, many residents felt uneasy about the prospect of returning to neighborhood schools, many of which would be racially imbalanced.[22]

Elsewhere, in Mobile, Alabama, following a remarkable turn of events, Judge W. Brevard Hand ended the over three-decade-old desegregation case in April 1997. At the fairness hearing regarding the district's request for release, the Mobile County Public School System's counsel was joined by Gregory Stein, former lead counsel for the plaintiffs, Norman Chachkin, head of the NAACP's Legal Defense Fund, and Julietta Kayyem of the Department of Justice, all of whom supported the district's position that it had complied in good faith with the desegregation orders.[23]

In Rockford, Illinois, where the school district had been found guilty of systematic discrimination against African-Americans and

---

[20] Ibid., 39.

[21] Ibid.

[22] Hendrie, "A Denver High School Reaches Out to the Neighborhood it Lost to Busing," *Education Week*, seventeen June 1998, 1, 22.

[23] Steven Giardini, legal counsel for the Mobile County Public School System, telephone interview by author, 9 July 1998.

Hispanics in 1993, the U.S. Court of Appeals for the 7th Circuit unanimously rejected the lower court's call for reducing the achievement gap by one-half by the year 2000-2001, eliminating academic tracking, and meeting quotas in virtually all classes, teacher assignments, student disciplinary actions, and cheerleading.[24]   The appeals court clearly reflected the signals sent by the Supreme Court, especially in *Missouri v. Jenkins.*

In April 1998, Judge Susan Webber Wright approved a consent decree in the Little Rock case which allowed the district more flexibility in student assignments and set the stage for a 2001 release of the school system from court supervision. The consent decree allowed for greater use of neighborhood schools, as long as no school became more than 80 percent white. The new consent decree eliminated a requirement included in a 1989 decree calling for reducing the achievement gap. Experts had testified that that goal might never be met, regardless of the effort expended by the district.[25]

Hartford, Connecticut was a notable exception to the trend of judicial releases in desegregation cases in the 1990s, but the Hartford case remained within the state court system, as the San Diego case had. In Hartford, a desegregation case filed in 1989 culminated in a Connecticut Supreme Court ruling in 1996 that the state was responsible for taking steps to desegregate the school district, regardless of the cause of the segregation.[26]   The Connecticut high court decision was the first in nearly twenty years wherein a state supreme court had ruled against *de facto* segregation.   Hartford's twenty-five thousand-student school system was 95 percent black or Hispanic; thus a remedy would necessarily involve inter-district transfers or redrawing of district lines.[27]   As an initial response to the court's ruling, the Connecticut legislature devised a school choice plan that provided monetary incentives for school districts to accept students from other districts if their enrollment would reduce racial or ethnic imbalance. The state also ordered the state department of education to

---

[24]People Who Care v. Rockford Board of Education, 111 F.3d 528 (7th Cir. 1997).

[25]Little Rock School District v. Pulaski County Special School District No. 1, LR-C-82-866, slip op. (E.D. Ark. 10 Apr. 1998).

[26]Sheff v. O'Neill, 678 A.2d 1267 (Conn. 1996).

[27]Jeff Archer, "Conn. Supreme Court Orders Desegregation for Hartford," *Education Week*, 7 August 1996, 6.

undertake an assessment of inequities among districts and recommend a five-year plan for further desegregation.[28]

Missouri lost its bid in 1997 to end the inter-district St. Louis desegregation plan, the largest in the country, when the federal district judge overseeing the case rejected the state's effort, and the U.S. Court of Appeals for the 8th Circuit upheld the ruling in September 1997. The St. Louis plan transferred thirteen thousand inner city black students to suburban schools and fifteen hundred suburban white students into the city, at a cost of $100 million a year to the state. The appeals court said that it would be premature to end the suit, because settlement negotiations were ongoing.[29] The Supreme Court denied cert. in March 1998.

In May 1998, along with approving continued funding for Kansas City, the Missouri legislature approved funding for continuing St. Louis' desegregation program for at least six years. A portion of the funding would be contingent on voter passage of a local tax increase. Lawmakers hoped that the funding package would expedite resolution of the twenty-six year old St. Louis case.[30]

As more school systems were being released from judicial oversight, it was unclear what types of policies would be permissible to promote racial integration. Legal disputes over race-conscious policies had produced differing results. Most experts agreed that a crucial question would be whether a goal of diversity within a public school system would be considered a compelling interest that would justify distinctions based on race or ethnicity. Opponents of such policies argued they would only be permissible to correct actual past wrongs. The Civil Rights Project, a Harvard based organization founded by Harvard law professor Christopher Edley Jr. and desegregation expert Gary Orfield, were constructing a legal principle that the desire for racial diversity was a sufficiently compelling reason for schools to use race-based classifications.[31]

As the number of school districts returning to neighborhood assignment plans increased, Orfield expressed concern that racial segregation would become even more marked than it had been prior to

---

[28] Archer, "State Policy Update," *Education Week: Quality Counts '98*, 8 January 1998, 120.

[29] Missouri v. Liddell, 126 F.3d 1049 (8th Cir. 1997).

[30] "News in Brief," 17.

[31] Hendrie, "Without Court Orders, Schools Ponder How to Pursue Diversity," *Education Week*, 30 April 1998, 36.

the era of court-ordered desegregation. These were exactly the concerns raised in Wilmington and Cleveland as the schools became increasingly racially isolated. Given the demographic trends, many argued that school systems should focus on quality academic programs, rather than integration. However, integration advocates argued against having to make that choice.[32]

Numerous school systems whose desegregation orders had been lifted, including Cleveland; Wilmington; Austin; Broward County, Florida; Denver; Norfolk, Virginia; and Oklahoma had reverted to some version of a neighborhood school system. Others whose orders had not been lifted yet had returned to neighborhood schools or planned to do so. These included Duval County, Florida; Kansas City; Nashville; San Jose; and Prince George's County. Seattle was replacing a busing program it voluntarily adopted for a neighborhood plan that offered parents the choice of enrolling their children anywhere in the district.[33] Numerous districts that were returning to neighborhood school plans offered families such options. Delaware had passed school choice legislation that gave children throughout the state that option.

As the era of court-ordered desegregation drew to a close, school districts and states increasingly looked toward other means to equalize disparities among and within school districts and to provide an equal educational opportunity. The achievement gap was the most conclusive evidence of the public education system's failure to prepare minority children equally well for success in life. Each solution spawned its own set of controversies, however. Many school districts planned to retain or enhance their magnet school programs to promote diversity, but such schools engendered complaints and even lawsuits in several instances because many admissions policies relied on race or ethnicity, among other criteria. Issues of school finances became increasingly pertinent as resegregation heightened awareness of financial disparities among predominantly white and predominantly nonwhite districts. School funding formulas in many states came under fire and required revision to meet state constitutional obligations. A drastic measure to which some states were turning in an effort to overhaul foundering school systems was the state takeover. Some states resorted to this measure in response to the "academic bankruptcy" of a school

---

[32] Ibid.
[33] Ibid.

district, while others tended to do so in response to financial crises. In Cleveland, both conditions existed when Judge Krupansky transferred authority over the district to the state and later when the state legislature transferred authority to the mayor of Cleveland. The vast majority of takeovers were in overwhelmingly minority school districts. The following section addresses these equity-related issues of the post-*Brown* era.

Intractable Problems and Innovations

The Achievement Gap

A study released in late 1996 by the Education Trust, a Washington-based nonprofit organization, showed that after decades of progress, the achievement gap between whites and nonwhites was widening again. Between 1970 and 1988, minorities had made significant gains in academic performance, while the performance of white students had stagnated. During that period, the gap between African-Americans and Caucasians had narrowed by one-half and the gap between Hispanics and Caucasians had narrowed by one-third. However, in the late 1990s, African-American, Hispanic, and Native American students performed well below others in every subject and at all grade levels tested. In some cases minority scores had declined, whereas in others the scores of white students had increased, leaving minorities behind. The Education Trust reported that while almost all minority students mastered basic skills by age seventeen, they failed, in disproportionate numbers to master the higher-level skills necessary for assuming productive roles in society. The researchers attributed the earlier gains of minorities to changes in family characteristics and demographics. More black parents were better educated, had fewer children, and were less likely to live in poverty than previously, all of which characteristics correlated with better performance in school. David Grissmer, a research scientist with the RAND Corporation countered that family alone did not explain the dramatic gains of minorities during the 1970s and 1980s. He pointed to desegregation programs, compensatory education programs that boosted reading and math skills, and increased public funding of schools. The Education Trust report attributed the loss of these gains to public complacence. "In fact, we have constructed an educational system so full of inequities that it actually exacerbates the challenges of race and poverty, rather than ameliorates them.   Simply put, we take students who have less to begin with and give them less in school, too.[34]

The Education Trust found the following inequities: 1) poor and minority children were more likely to be in classes taught by teachers who did not at least minor in the relevant subject matter, 2) poor and minority students were more likely to be in classrooms that lacked adequate books and other teaching materials, 3) poor and minority students were more likely to be placed in low level classes.   The study found significant disparities among states with regard to minority achievement.   For instance, 44 percent of Hispanic fourth graders in disadvantaged urban settings in Texas performed at grade level or above in math, whereas only 27 percent of California's similarly situated Hispanic students performed as well.   In Tennessee, 23 percent of the public K-twelve students were black and 24 percent of students in Advanced Placement math and science classes were black, whereas in Virginia, 26 percent of K-12 students were black, but only 7 percent of the students in AP math and science were black.   In New York, where twenty percent of the public K-12 students were black, 20 percent of the students in the gifted and talented program were black, whereas in Mississippi, where 51 percent of the public K-twelve students were black, only 7 percent of the students in the gifted and talented program were black.[35]

Besides being a member of a minority group, being poor and living in an urban area were heavy strikes against a student.   Poor students in urban schools performed worse on tests than did poor students in high-poverty schools outside of cities.   On the National Assessment of Educational Testing Progress, a federal testing program that provides state-by-state data, urban students performed much worse than their non-urban counterparts.   Most urban students were not exposed to challenging curricula, well-prepared teachers, or high expectations.[36]

Furthermore,   urban   districts   tended   to   have   less   parent involvement than other districts.   Truancy was a serious problem in urban schools, as well.   The Consortium on Chicago School Research

---

[34]*Education Watch: The 1996 Trust State and National Data Book*; quoted in Lynn Olson, "Examining Race and Demography,"_*Education Week: Quality Counts '97*, 22 January 1997, 10-11.
[35]Ibid, 11.
[36] Lynn Olson and Craig D. Jerald, "The Achievement Gap," *Education Week: Quality Counts '98*, 8 January 1998, 10-12.

wrote about inner city schools, "In these schools, norms have disintegrated to the point that class attendance appears optional." School systems were simply unequipped to address the myriad problems that children brought with them to school. "Many of the intractable problems that plague city schools are deeply rooted in the poverty, unemployment, crime, racism, and human despair that pervade the neighborhoods around them. Too often, teachers and administrators are asked to solve problems that the public and its leaders in state houses and city halls have lacked the will and courage to tackle."[37]

Educators stressed the need for establishing uniform state academic standards that specified what students were expected to know at each grade level and before graduating from high school, in order to improve overall achievement. By January 1998, thirty-eight states had adopted academic standards in all four core subject areas, and Iowa was the only state that was not working on developing statewide standards.[38] The rigor of the state standards varied markedly, however.[39] A 1997 study done by the American Federation of Teachers found that only Virginia had exemplary standards in all four subject areas. California and Florida had exemplary standards in two subject areas. Despite the progress in setting standards, few states required that students meet them before being promoted to the next grade or graduating.[40]

Ironically, while the purpose of high stakes competency or exit exams was to increase student performance and school system and student accountability, such exams were encountering legal challenges because of the disproportionate failure of minority students. Complaints were filed with the U.S. Department of Education's Office for Civil Rights in Ohio in 1994 and in Texas in 1996, charging bias in the tests. The Ohio dispute dragged on for years, with the OCR and the state finally reaching agreement that the test could stand, but that state officials had to make sure that students were adequately prepared

---

[37]Editorial, "The Urban Challenge," *Education Week: Quality Counts '98*, 8 January 1998, 6.

[38] Craig D. Jerald, Bridget K. Curren, and Lynn Olson, "The State of the States," *Education Week: Quality Counts '98*, 8 January 1998, 76.

[39] Editorial, "The Urban Challenge," 6.

[40] Matthew Gandal, "Making Standards Matter 1997," (Washington, D.C.: American Federation of Teachers 1997): quoted in Millicent Lawton's, "AFT, Foundation Find Good and Bad in States' Standards," *Education Week*, 6 August 1997, 13.

for the tests.[41] With the disproportionate placement of white students in honors classes and the disproportionate placement of minority students in lower level and remedial classes, there was no question that white students were better prepared for such competency tests.

<u>Magnets</u>
As courts released school systems from the obligation to bus children for integration, many sought to continue operating their magnet schools to promote diversity and raise achievement levels in a less objectionable manner than "forced busing." In the four Wilmington area school districts, administrators operated magnet programs in predominantly black Wilmington schools that were losing suburban students as they chose to attend schools closer to their homes. In San Diego, the comprehensive array of magnet programs remained popular, as they had been throughout the era of desegregation. Yet the magnet concept had long engendered controversy as well.

In Jonathan Kozol's searing critique of the funding inequities among public school districts, *Savage Inequalities: Children in America's Schools*, he noted that the magnet school system in Chicago provided a private school atmosphere for those children who won admission. Moreover, the magnet programs retained the allegiance of families that otherwise likely would have opted for private schools. On the other hand, the magnet programs left the children who did not attend those schools, usually the very poor, even more isolated, with their more successful peers having transferred. Kozol wrote, "The magnet system is, not surprisingly, highly attractive to the more sophisticated parents, disproportionately white and middle class, who have the ingenuity and, now and then, political connections to obtain admission for their children."[42] Children who had attended preschool and those who attended one of the better elementary schools were advantaged as they applied to the magnet high schools. An even greater advantage, wrote Kozol, was the social class and education of parents.

---

[41] Lonnie Harp, "OCR Probes Bias Complaint against Texas Exit Test," *Education Week*, 7 February 1996, 11.
[42] Jonathan Kozol, *Savage Inequalities: Children in America's Schools* (New York: Harper Perennial, 1991), 59.

This is the case because the system rests on the initiative of parents. The poorest parents, often the products of inferior education, lack the information access and the skills of navigation in an often hostile and intimidating situation to channel their children to the better schools, obtain the applications, and (perhaps a little more important) help them to get ready for the necessary tests and then persuade their elementary schools to recommend them. So even in poor black neighborhoods, it tends to be children of the less poor and the better educated who are likely to break through the obstacles and win admission.[43]

While the proponents of such programs stressed that they were based on merit, merit in such cases was strongly predetermined by issues related to class and race.[44]

As court ordered desegregation plans ended, legal challenges to race conscious admissions procedures in magnet schools arose. Lawsuits and other complaints of discrimination arose in Arlington, Virginia; Boston; Buffalo; Charlotte-Mecklenburg, North Carolina; DeKalb County, Georgia; Houston; Louisville; New Orleans; and San Francisco. Usually it was Caucasian or Asian-American families who protested the exclusion of their children from popular programs based on their race. Sometimes advocates for black children complained that the use of academic criteria unfairly disadvantaged blacks. At the heart of the controversy was just how much admissions panels could structure the racial or ethnic makeup of the schools when they were not under a court order to do so. Would the educational value of racial diversity qualify as a compelling state interest? Many districts were reassessing their admissions policies to their magnet schools in order to avoid legal challenges.[45]

Boston's prestigious Latin School withstood a legal challenge when a federal judge in May 1998 upheld the district's use of race as an admissions factor. The judge held that the importance of integrated programs justified the use of race as a criterion. The judge noted that

---

[43]Ibid, 60.

[44] Ibid.

[45] Hendrie, "New Magnet School Policies Sidestep an Old Issue: race," *Education Week*, 10 June 1998, 10-11.

when the court had lifted the district's desegregation decree, it had restricted the district from resegregating.[46]

In Arlington, Virginia, U.S. District Judge Albert Bryan, Jr. rejected the Arlington County school system's use of racial preferences to admit students to magnet schools. The school district used a lottery system for admissions, but passed over some white students with higher lottery numbers to ensure that an adequate number of nonwhite students would be accepted. The judge ordered the district to use the unmanipulated lottery system only. Subsequently, the school system developed a weighted lottery system that took into account income, first language, and race in admissions. This system, too, was challenged and rejected by the district court, as well as by the Court of Appeals for the 4th Circuit.[47] That decision was under appeal.[48]

In early 1998, the Education Department's Magnet Schools Assistance Program issued new rules for the $300 million in grants to be paid out over the following three years. The program's purpose, among other things, was to reduce racial isolation of minority groups in schools. However the new regulations, which reflected an attempt to comply with a 1995 Supreme Court decision that restricted the use of race or ethnicity in government programs, advised those seeking grants for magnet schools to seriously consider race-neutral admissions policies unless they were under court supervision to desegregate. Jeanette Lim of the Education Department's office for civil rights said that the new rules had created "a trend toward less set-asides and more lotteries" in admissions.

School Financing

In 1973, the Supreme Court ruled in *San Antonio Independent School District v. Rodriguez* that Texas' school funding formula, which, like that of most states, was based primarily on property taxes and which resulted in vastly different per pupil expenditures did not violate the Equal Protection Clause of the Fourteenth Amendment. Without recourse in the federal court system, parents in several states subsequently filed suits charging that their states' funding formulas violated their state constitutions, which typically specified the states'

---

[46]Wessmann v. Gittens, No. 97-11923JLT (D.Mass. 1998).

[47]Tuttle v. Arlington School Board, No. 98-418-A, (E.D. Va. 14 Apr. 1998).

[48]Lisa Farbstein, Director of Community Services, Arlington Public Schools, telephone interview by author, 15 July 1998.

obligations regarding public education. Numerous state supreme courts ruled their funding formulas unconstitutional, which required state legislatures to devise new formulas balancing the demands of the poorer districts with those of the wealthier ones. In 1989, the Texas Supreme Court struck down the state's education funding formula, finding that it did not provide for the "efficient system of public free schools" that the Texas Constitution required.

As segregation grew in the 1980s and 1990s, issues of funding equity became increasingly salient. Jonathan Kozol's *Savage Inequalities: Children in America's Schools* graphically depicted the gross inequities between city and suburban school districts. Kozol crisscrossed the country in the late 1980s, examining conditions in inner city schools and comparing them with their suburban counterparts. He described dilapidated, sewage flooded schools in East St. Louis without adequate heating, books, or science lab equipment. He spoke with children there, virtually all of whom were black, and who understood very well the differences between their schools and those of other American children. He visited schools in poverty-ridden North Lawndale on the South Side of Chicago where conditions were so deplorable that as one city alderman put it, "Nobody in his right mind would send [his] kids to public school."[49] Yet, nearby Winnetka boasted of New Trier High School, with its preppy atmosphere that was showcased in *Town and Country*. In North Lawndale, students were assigned to multiple study halls to save funds on teacher salaries, and high teacher absenteeism coupled with an inadequate pool of substitutes resulted in many classrooms being completely unsupervised. Kozol described the strikingly different conditions of the schools in Camden, New Jersey and nearby upscale Cherry Hill, and the even more affluent Princeton. He found that the average per pupil expenditures in New York City public schools were half that of the more wealthy suburbs. Among New York City's thirty-two districts there were gross disparities, and disparities existed even within districts, depending on the affluence or poverty of the neighborhoods. Kozol visited schools with no windows or ventilation systems, gymnasiums that served as classroom space to four classes of children simultaneously, and ceilings with gaping holes and plaster falling like snow on the students. In New York City, it was not only disparities in property tax revenues that impoverished certain schools while

---

[49] Kozol, 53.

generously funding others. A report by the nonprofit Community Service Society disclosed that owing to disparities in allocations made by state legislators, the poorest schools in the district received approximately ninety cents per pupil in legislative grants, whereas the richest districts received as much as fourteen dollars per pupil.[50]

When questioned about the inequities in funding, educational programs, and general conditions between the city and suburban schools, suburban residents responded to Kozol with such comments as "urban children would not know how to make use of the special programs provided at New Trier" and "equalizing the funding would merely result in mediocrity for all." Yet, as many urban observers pointed out in the cities Kozol visited, no suburban parents would accept their children's being subjected to the conditions in many urban school settings.

By the late 1990s, most states had been sued over education funding inequities and many education funding formulas had been declared unconstitutional. Almost every state constitution directed the state legislature to provide a uniform, general, or common education. Sixteen constitutions specified that the education systems were to be thorough or efficient.[51] In early 1997, funding formulas in thirteen states violated their state constitutions and lawsuits were pending in twelve more.[52]

Despite the numerous successful challenges to state education funding systems, there was little consensus among policy experts with regard to developing systems that would survive constitutional challenges. Some critics noted with frustration that despite all the legal action and efforts at reforming funding formulas, achievement had not improved.

Consultants Lewis Solomon and Michael Fox who observed and participated in numerous efforts to revise school funding formulas noted that concepts of "thorough" and "efficient" were largely overlooked in funding discussions. "Virtually every funding model under consideration defines equity and adequacy solely as a function of how much more money will be funneled to schools." Solomon and Fox argued that funding formulas as a whole were fatally flawed,

---

[50] Ibid., 98.
[51] Lewis C. Solomon and Michael Fox, "Fatally Flawed School Funding Formulas," *Education Week*, 17 June 1998, 60.
[52] "Resources," *Education Week: Quality Counts '97*, 22 January 1997, 54.

because "they push more money into a system that produces far too much failure and promotes far too little change where it really counts-- student learning."[53]

Solomon and Fox proposed seven guidelines for policymakers as they revised funding formulas:

1. Adequacy--a *student-centered* formula should include the basic elements of a quality education, considering environmental and other factors that affect learning;

2. Equity--funding should flow to the *child and school*, rather than the district, to ensure that the monies are applied as directly as possible to the needs of the child;

3. Efficiency--formulas should include market incentives and disincentives with consequences for failures and rewards for success, rather than merely maintaining or increasing old spending patterns;

4. Performance--formulas should incorporate incentives for high achievement and disincentives for poor performance; they should promote flexibility and innovation in poorly performing schools;

5. Stewardship--formulas should require that funds be set aside for regular maintenance of buildings, with penalties for irresponsibility;

6. Accountability--formulas should require districts to maintain accurate data on achievement, expenditures, program components, student demographics, resource allocation, etc.;

7. Tax effort--formulas should reflect the tax efforts of communities so taxpayers in one district do not have to compensate for the lesser efforts of other communities.

Solomon and Fox observed that few funding formulas took these factors into consideration and they therefore "miss[ed] a strategic opportunity to build funding formulas that actually work[ed] to promote learning."[54]

State Takeovers

In some instances of exceedingly poorly performing districts, states took over the administration of the districts, either through the actions of legislatures or through court orders. By 1998, twenty-three states had passed laws authorizing states or municipalities to seize control of

---

[53]Solomon and Fox, 60.
[54]Ibid., 60, 48-49.

school districts in crisis, and twenty-one school systems had been taken over, including the District of Columbia.[55]   New Jersey pioneered this remedy in Jersey City (1989), followed by Paterson (1991), and then Newark (1985).   New Jersey law called for radical house cleaning in such cases, including removal of the superintendent, the school board, the business administrator, the personnel director, the legal counsel, and the heads of curriculum and instruction.   A state-appointed superintendent assumed the day-to-day administration of the district with input from an advisory board which had no decision-making authority.   Saul Cooperman, the former state education commissioner who designed the takeover law explained, "You have to absolutely, absolutely get rid of the people who brought you the problem. If a person has brought you pestilence and famine, you don't say, 'Gee, I'd like to work with you for another two or three years.'"[56]

In Jersey City and Paterson, impressive achievements were made in terms of administrative efficiency following the state takeovers.   In 1997 it was still unclear what the results of the takeover in Newark would be or whether the state's administration of the districts would improve test scores.[57]

In April 1997, responding to long term concerns about achievement levels and district mismanagement in Hartford, the Connecticut legislature transferred authority over the school system to the state.   In June 1997, the legislature dissolved the locally elected school board and appointed a board of trustees to oversee the district.[58]

The state of Illinois appointed a three-member panel to sort out the chaotic fiscal affairs of the destitute East St. Louis school system in October 1994.   The elected school board and the appointed board clashed continuously, and in March 1996, the state panel dissolved the board.   However, a state judge reinstated the members holding that they had not been given due process and that the voters of East St. Louis had effectively been disenfranchised.   Battles between the appointed and the elected boards severely hampered reform in the district.   Richard Mark, head of the appointed panel remarked:

---

[55] Beth Reinhard, "Racial Issues Cloud State Takeovers: Interventions Often Face Legal Challenges," *Education Week*, 14 January 1998, 1, 18.

[56] Charles Mahtesian, "School takeover reactions mixed," *Cleveland Plain Dealer*, 5 October 1997, 17(A).

[57] Ibid.

[58] Archer, "State Policy Update," 120.

This process could have worked a lot quicker and we could have had a lot more success if there had been cooperation by the board and superintendent. But without that cooperation, it's a battle every day to get the most minor issue resolved. If you want to see results quickly, you just have to remove the board and superintendent.[59]

In 1995, the state of Illinois dissolved Chicago's elected school board and placed Mayor Richard Daley in charge of the schools. Many observers felt the action was relatively well received in Chicago because the legislature took care to enlist the support of the affected parties in Chicago before finalizing the transfer of authority. Parents continued to have a strong voice in decision-making through local school councils, which were created under a 1988 reform law.[60]

West Virginia returned control of the Logan County school district to local authorities in 1995 following a three year state takeover. During those three years, test scores improved, drop out rates declined, and management improved. Henry Marockie, state superintendent of public instruction observed that the key to success in West Virginia's experience had been cooperation. "It started out hostile. It was a partnership before it was over, and that is why, in my judgment, it was successful."[61]

In 1995, after years of mismanagement and poor student achievement, Congress and President Clinton created a "control board" which selected a board of trustees to run the Washington, D.C. public schools. The control board took over the system in November 1996. A retired army general, Julius W. Becton, Jr. was appointed superintendent of schools. Of the district's nearly eighty thousand student population, 96 percent was minority and 88 percent was African-American. According to the 1990 U.S. census, one fourth of the district's children lived in poverty.[62]

Achievement levels reflected the demographic conditions. In 1994, only 22 percent of the district's fourth graders were reading at

---

[59]Hendrie, "Ill will comes with Territory in Takeovers," *Education Week*, 12 June 1996, 12-13.

[60]Lynn Olson, "Veterans of State Takeover Battles Tell a Cautionary Tale," *Education Week*, 12 February 1997, 25.

[61]Ibid.

[62] David Hoff, "A Question of Authority," *Education Week: Quality Counts '98*, 8 January 1998, 126.

grade level on standardized tests, and in 1996, only 20 percent of the district's eighth graders were performing math at grade level. This figure compared with 61 percent nationwide. In 1996 only urban students in Maryland performed worse than Washington, D.C. students in math and science.[63]

The dismal performance did not result from under funding; the district spent $7,327 per student in 1993-94. However, much of the money was misdirected; the district employed only sixteen teachers for every administrator, whereas the average urban district had forty-two teachers for every administrator.[64] The district received tens of millions of dollars a year in federal grants for various programs, but much was wasted or misallocated. In 1996 the National Science Foundation rescinded a $13.5 million grant to the Washington schools, citing a management void and other problems. The district received $25 to $30 million per year in Title I funds between 1986 and 1996 and was required to develop "aggressive programs" to help disadvantaged children learn. Yet programs were never developed and achievement never improved.[65]

In the summer of 1998, Mayor Michael White of Cleveland stood poised to take over responsibility for the Cleveland public schools, the initiative having survived a court challenge in early 1998 and the court having lifted the March 1995 order that placed authority over the district with the state superintendent of schools. Given the school system's very troubled history, residents of Cleveland seemed eager to see what Mayor White could accomplish. Even the teachers' union had stopped fighting the initiative and was willing to work with White.

Takeovers engendered very bitter feelings, and by early 1998, at least eight lawsuits had been filed in response to government takeovers of elected school boards. The actions provoked accusations that minority districts were singled out and that voter rights were being violated. Proponents of the takeovers noted that they were necessitated by the abysmal performance of students, massive debt, and gross mismanagement. Oftentimes states intervened following years or even decades of inaction or incompetence by local school boards. However to others, the moves were insulting and driven by a lack of confidence

---

[63]Ibid.
[64]Ibid.
[65]Valerie Strauss and Sari Horwitz, "As Students Fail, U.S. Aid Goes to Waste," *Washington Post*, 16 February 1997, 24(A).

in the ability of members of minority groups to manage school systems. Of the twenty-one districts that had been overtaken by early 1998, eighteen had predominantly minority enrollments and most were at least 80 percent nonwhite. Of eight additional systems that had been threatened with takeovers, six were predominantly minority and three were at least 93 percent nonwhite.[66]

Many educators responded that districts with large minority populations were vulnerable to takeovers because they were often beset by problems such as poverty, broken families, and crime, factors that undermined student achievement. Williard Murray, a former California legislator who wrote California's takeover law, said that school boards in some poor minority communities had become the centers of patronage systems because the school systems were the only large employers in the area. "Unfortunately, the focus becomes political, not educational."[67] Peter B. Contini, an assistant education commissioner in New Jersey, stressed that the key to enduring reform was teaching communities to prioritize the education of children over employment opportunities for adults.[68]   Cleveland's school system politics exemplified the conditions described by Murray and Contini. Numerous residents of Cleveland who were interviewed for this project complained of the improper political maneuverings and the self-interested motives of board members. The school district was the largest employer in the city, and was viewed by too many as a source of employment, rather than a provider of education to the city's youth.

The voting rights issue with respect to takeovers was particularly salient in the eight southern states with a history of voting rights violations. The Justice Department demanded that states with such histories gain clearance with the Department before taking action that removed locally elected boards of education. This requirement resulted in a protracted investigation by the Justice Department in Texas in 1997 and a three-month delay in the state's effort to intervene in the debt-ridden Wilmer Hutchins district outside of Dallas. In the meantime, the IRS and the FBI both stepped in and raided district offices looking for evidence of financial misdeeds. Subsequently, Texas filed suit in federal district court in Washington to be granted permission to forego the Justice Department's pre-approval in future

---

[66]Reinhard, "Racial Issues," 1, 18.
[67]Ibid., 18.
[68]Hendrie, "Ill Will;" 13.

takeover cases. The court dismissed the action as not ripe for adjudication, however, and the U.S. Supreme Court affirmed that holding in March 1998. The Court did not rule on the merits of the state's argument.[69]

Whether legal battles ensued or not, state officials who stepped in to take over foundering districts were virtually always met with resentment, anger, and resistance from local administrators, teachers, parents, and the media. Clearly, state takeovers were not a panacea. Ohio State Superintendent of Public Instruction John Goff and Ohio State Representative Michael Fox, chairman of the House education committee agreed that the Ohio experience with the takeover of the Cleveland district suggested that school systems could not be run effectively from a distance. Veterans of takeovers tended to agree that state governments should consider carefully their goals and strategies before forging ahead with takeovers. They should have plans for academic improvement, along with systems for measuring success. They also should have plans for gaining the support and cooperation of the teachers, principals, and the public. Finally, they should have plans for the resumption of local control, lest they be saddled with running the district indefinitely.[70]

Thus issues of financial, programmatic, and academic equity continued to dog school districts and states in America in the post-*Brown* era. *Brown* and its progeny had essentially eliminated dual school systems, but courts could not rid schools of the inequities that pervaded American society. The socioeconomic disadvantages that rendered minority children less ready to begin kindergarten than their white counterparts were often compounded during their school years. Shortcomings within the school system, such as inadequate funding, poor administration, and lack of teacher training, were often exacerbated by environmental problems such as inadequate parent and community support, high crime rates, and other social pathologies. Together, these factors drastically reduced minority children's access to an equal educational opportunity, and no judge or court could eliminate these barriers.

---

[69]*Texas v. U.S.,* 66 U.S.L.W.4234 (U.S. March 31, 1998).
[70] Olson, "Veterans of State Takeover Battles," 25.

Conclusion

In a September 1997 address at Little Rock's Central High School on the fortieth anniversary of the dramatic showdown there between the Arkansas National Guard and the 101st Airborne Division, President Clinton decried the growing rate of racial segregation in America. He lamented the increasing segregation in schools and the fact that Americans rarely associated with people of other races:

> Segregation is no longer the law, but separation is still the rule. . . . Today, children of every race walk through the same door, but then they often walk down different halls. Not only in this school, but across America, they sit in different classrooms, they eat at different tables. They even sit in different parts of the bleachers at the football game. Far too many communities are all white, all black, all Latino, all Asian. Indeed, too many Americans of all races have actually begun to give up on the idea of integration and the search for common ground.[71]

Indeed, on the eve of the twenty-first century, America was a nation characterized by relatively high levels of racial segregation. The idealism of the 1950s and 1960s had waned, and much of America seemed resigned to the *de facto* separation of the races. Many educators and activists who had followed the course of school desegregation closely now prioritized raising achievement levels over continued efforts at integration. Blacks who had chafed at the notion that black children needed the presence of white children in order to learn looked forward to rebuilding a sense of community in their neighborhood schools.

Yet experience showed that school systems and schools with overwhelmingly minority populations had inferior facilities, less experienced teachers, less rigorous courses, lower achievement levels, higher rates of disciplinary problems, higher dropout rates, and lower parental participation. Usually these school systems were comparatively under funded, although sometimes they were generously funded, but poorly managed. In other words, these school systems and

---

[71]Kevin Sack, "In Little Rock, Clinton Warns of Racial Split," *New York Times,* 26 September 1997, 1(A) and 27(A).

schools suffered from public neglect. Thus, public schools, which many Americans viewed as the great bastion of equality, often reinforced, rather than eradicated, socioeconomic inequalities.

With federal legal remedies for all practical purposes exhausted, states and communities would have to look inward, demanding accountability from school systems, school administrators, and teachers. The experience of San Diego in the wake of the contentious teachers' strike showed that school systems could be made to respond to community and parental pressure. San Diego had the advantage of having a truly diverse student population, however, with many middle class parents who were comfortable navigating the bureaucracy of a public school system. In too many cities across America, public school systems had deteriorated to such a degree that most families with sufficient resources had either abandoned the city for the suburbs or abandoned the public school system for private schools, leaving those less capable of demanding accountability from a school system with the responsibility of doing so.

The achievement gap between white and nonwhite students in America testified to the different educational experiences of the groups. Whether the cause was related to home and socioeconomic factors or whether it resulted from institutionalized racism as reflected in funding and facility disparities, lower expectations, and lower teacher experience, or a combination of these factors, minority students were leaving school disproportionately unprepared to take on the responsibilities of adulthood. Furthermore, racial isolation itself would arguably disadvantage all children, but particularly minority children, who would be less prepared to thrive in integrated college and work settings. Magnet schools continued to offer a diverse learning environment for some youngsters. Funding formula revisions would eliminate the extreme disparities within states among school districts. For the most desperate of situations, the state takeover was a viable, but only temporary solution, for grossly mismanaged or "academically bankrupt" districts.

However, none of these remedies would substitute for either parental and community support for the school system or constant demands for accountability from the school system by parents and community members who, along with the students, were directly affected by the quality of school systems. It was this combination of cooperation and political pressure that produced quality schools in the school districts adjacent to Cleveland, Chicago, Kansas City, and other underachieving inner city districts.   Rashidah Abdulhaaq and Don Freeman of Cleveland, Ebrima Ellzy-Sey of Wilmington, and Jonathan Kozol echoed the words of countless other experienced advocates of quality public education programs when they expressed the notion that the *sine qua non* of a responsive, quality educational program was an enlightened and vigilant public.

Bibliography

Interviews

Abdulhaaq, Rashidah, parent activist and named plaintiff class representative in *Reed v. Rhodes*. Telephone interview by author, 10 July 1997.

Ames, Gail, administrator, School Choice, Red Clay Consolidated School District. Telephone interview by author, 5 May 1998.

Aron, Gloria, community activist with children in the Cleveland school system. Telephone interview by author, 12 July 1997.

Brown, Harold, professor of business administration, San Diego State University and founding member of the Integration Task Force for the San Diego City Schools. Telephone interview by author, 21 August 1996.

Castro, Irma, director, Latina Advocacy Program, San Diego City Schools. Telephone interview by author, 19 March 1996.

Charney, Michael, founder of West Side East Side Let's Come Together (Welcome). Telephone interview by author, 20 August 1997.

Chrispeels, Janet, assistant professor at the University of California Santa Barbara and former member of the Citizens Advisory Committee on Racial Integration. Telephone interview by author, 2 September 1996.

Dalton-Robinson, Juanita, retired social worker and former member of the advisory commission to the Office on School Monitoring and Community Relations. Telephone interview by author, 9 July 1997.

Dyer, Christina, legal counsel for the San Diego City Schools. Interview by author, 9 November 1995, San Diego.

Elliott, Daniel, first co-chairman of the steering committee for the Greater Cleveland Project. Telephone interview by author, 30 July 1997.

Ellzy-Sey, Ebrima, founding member of the Coalition To Save Our Children, chairman of the Education Committee of the Wilmington NAACP, retired Red Clay District school teacher. Interview by author, 5 June 1995, Wilmington, and telephone interviews by author, 27 October 1995, 1 December 1995, and 30 April 1998.

Emerson, Diane, administrative secretary, superintendent's office, Brandywine School District. Telephone interview by author, 30 April 1998.

Freeman, Don, director of the League Park Center. Telephone interview by author, 31 July 1997.

Gonzales, Jose, acting general counsel for the San Diego City Schools. Telephone interview by author 8 May 1998.

Gourley, Ann, test development specialist, Prince George's County Public Schools. Telephone interview by author, 26 April 1995.

Green, Mareyjoice (Mrs. Charles), professor of sociology at Cleveland State University. Telephone interview by author, 12 July 1997.

Hardiman, James, counsel for plaintiffs in *Reed v. Rhodes*. Telephone interview by author, 18 July 1997.

Hunter, Frances, former director of the Greater Cleveland Project and later professor at Cleveland State University in the Urban Affairs Program. Telephone interview by author, 23 July 1997.

Ima, Kenji, professor of sociology, San Diego State University. Telephone interview by author, 29 September 1996.

Jenkins-Bundy, Bonnie, director of public affairs, Prince George's County Public Schools. Telephone interviews by author, 14 September 1994, 6 March 1995, 3 April 1995, and 6 April 1995.

Kassen, Aileen, former deputy director of the Office on School Monitoring and Community Relations. Telephone interviews by author, 10 July 1997 and 4 December 1997.

Klumpp, Katie, parent activist in the San Diego City Schools. Telephone interview by author, 31 August 1996.

Krumholz, Norman, former director of Cleveland city planning and later professor at Cleveland State University in the Urban Affairs Program. Telephone interview by author, 25 July 1997.

Kudumu, Walter, director of the Center for Parent Involvement in Education. Telephone interview by author, 22 March 1996.

Lawrence-Wallace, Cynthia, retired instructor with the Teacher Education Program at the University of California San Diego. Telephone interview by author, 23 August, 1996.

Lindsley, Byron F., retired judge and chairman of the Citizens Committee on Equal Educational Opportunities. Telephone interview by author, 19 August 1996.

McDonald, Judy, former member of the Integration Task Force, San Diego City Schools. Telephone interview by author, 2 September 1996.

McWilson, Jimma, member of We the Collective. Telephone interview by author, 22 March 1996.

Mearns, Jr., Edward A., professor of law at Case Western Reserve University Law School and court-appointed expert who reviewed the school district's desegregation proposals for the court. Telephone interview by author 11 July 1997.

Meredith, Pat, assistant principal at Balboa Park Elementary School, San Diego. Telephone interview by author, 2 September 1996.

Murphy, Denise, administrative secretary in the Office of Information and Support, Colonial School District. Telephone interview by author, 6 May 1998.

Nichols, Jack, assistant state superintendent for administrative services, Delaware Department of Public Instruction. Interview by author, 6 June 1995, Dover, and telephone interviews by author, 18 October 1995 and 4 May 1998.

Payzant, Thomas, former superintendent of the San Diego City Schools. Telephone interview by author, 21 October 1996.

Preston, Jeanna, director of the San Diego City Schools Parent Involvement and Support Program. Telephone interview by author, 22 March 1996.

Reilly, James. Interview by author, 4 June 1995, Wilmington.

Rishel, Frank, deputy superintendent of schools, Christina School District. Telephone interview by author, 5 May 1998.

Smith, George Walker, former president of the San Diego Board of Education. Telephone interview by author, 26 August 1996.

Smith, Martha, former member of the advisory commission to the Office on School Monitoring and Community Relations and former member of the Cleveland board of education. Telephone interview by author, 14 July 1997.

Stevens, Leonard, former director of the Office on School Monitoring and Community Relations. Telephone interview by author, 18 July 1997.

Swift, Shuford, researcher for plaintiffs in *Carlin*. Telephone interviews by author, 18 May 1996 and 8 June 1998.

Thorton, Alvin, member of the Prince George's County board of education and professor of political science at Howard University. Telephone interview by author, 17 March 1995.

Tolliver, Stanley, attorney at law, former member of the Cleveland board of education and original member of the advisory board to the Office on School Monitoring and Community Relations. Telephone interview by author, 15 July 1997.

Wallace, Blanche, community schools activist, Cleveland. Telephone interview by author, 21 July 1997.

Williams, Francine, director of the Race and Human Relations Program, San Diego City Schools. Telephone interview by author, 28 March 1996.

Williams, Judith, president of the San Diego Council of PTAs (Parent Teacher Associations) 1995-1996. Telephone interviews by author, 22 March 1996 and 13 June 1998.

Court Cases

Belton v. Gebhart (and Bulah v. Gebhart), 87 A. 2d 862 (Del. Ch. 1952); 347 U.S. 483 (1954).

Board of Education v. The Superior Court (Carlin), 71 Cal.Rptr.2d 562 (Cal.App. 4 Dist. 1998).

Board of Education of Oklahoma City Public Schools v. Dowell, 498 U.S. 237 (1991).

Bolling v. Sharpe, 347 U.S. 497 (1954).

Briggs v. Elliott, 347 U.S. 483 (1954).

Brown v. Board of Education of Topeka, Kansas (I), 347 U.S. 483 (1954).

Brown v. Board of Education of Topeka, Kansas (II), 349 U.S. 294 (1955).

Butchers' Benevolent Association v. Crescent City Livestock Landing & Slaughterhouse Co. (The Slaughterhouse Cases) 16 Wall. (83 U.S.) 36 (1873).

Carlin v. Board of Education, slip op. (San Diego Super. Ct., 9 March 1977) (No. 303800).

_____. Final Order for 1977-1978 School Year (San Diego Super. Ct., 8 Aug. 1977).

_____. Final Order (San Diego Super. Ct., 21 May 1985).

_____. Final Order As Amended May 1989 (San Diego Super. Ct., 4 May 1989).

_____. Final Order Terminating Court Jurisdiction (San Diego Super. Ct., 16 Aug. 1996).

Civil Rights Cases, 109 U.S. 3 (1883).

Coalition to Save Our Children v. State Board of Education, slip op. (D.Del. 2 March 1994).

_____. 901 F. Supp. 784 (D.Del. 1995).

Cooper v. Aaron, 358 U.S. 1 (1958).

Craggett v. Board of Education, No. C64-369 (N.D. Ohio 1964)

Crawford v. Board of Education of City of Los Angeles, 120 Cal. Rptr. 334(1975); Sup., 130 Cal. Rptr. 724, seventeen Cal. 3d 280 (1976).

Davis v. County School Board of Prince Edward County, 347 U.S. 483 (1954).

Dayton Board of Education v. Brinkman, 433 U.S. 526 (1979).

Dred Scott v. Sandford, 60 U.S. 393 (1857).

Evans v. Buchanan, 256 F.2d 688 (3d Cir. 1958).

_____. Plaintiffs' Findings of Fact and Conclusions of Law (D.Del. 25 Feb. 1974).

_____. Slip op. (D.Del. 27 Nov. 1974).

_____. Brief of Intervening Defendants (D.Del. 27 Nov. 1974).

_____. 379 F. Supp. 1218 (D. Del 1974), 423 U.S. 963 (1975).

_____. 393 F. Supp. 428 (D.Del. 1975).

_____. 416 F. Supp.328 Order (D.Del. 27 Dec. 1976).

_____. 435 F. Supp. 832 (D.Del. 1977).

_____. 555 F. 2d 373 (3d Cir. 1977), *cert. denied*, 434 U.S. 880 (1977).

_____. 447 F. Supp. 982 (D.Del. 1978), *aff'd*, 582 F.2d 750 (3d Cir. 1978).

_____. Order (D.Del. 9 Jan. 1978).

Freeman v. Pitts, 887 F.2d 1438 (1989), 503 U.S. 467 (1992).

Gong Lum v. Rice, 275 U.S. 78 (1927).

Green v. County School Board of New Kent County, 391 U.S. 430 (1968).

Jackson v. Pasadena City School District, 59 Cal. 2d 876 (1963).

Keyes v. Denver School District No. 1, 413 U.S. 189 (1973).

Little Rock School District v. Pulaski County Special School District No. 1, 921 F.2d 1371 (8th Cir. 1990).

_____. LR-C-82-866, slip op. (E.D. Ark. 10 Apr. 1998).

Marbury v. Madison, 1 Cr. (5 U.S.) 1 (1803).

McLaurin v. Oklahoma State Regents for Higher Education, 339 U.S. 637 (1950).

Milliken v. Bradley (I), 418 U.S. 717 (1974).

Milliken v. Bradley (II), 433 U.S. 267 (1977).

Missouri v. Jenkins, 115 S. Ct. 2038 (1995).

Missouri v. Liddell, 126 F.3d 1049 (8th Cir. 1997).

Morgan v. Hennigan 379 F. Supp. 410 (D. Mass. 1974); Morgan v. Kerrigan, 401 F. Supp. 216 (D. Mass. 1975); 509 F. 2d 580 (CA1 1974); cert denied 421 U.S. 963 (1965).

NAACP v. Board of Education of Prince George's County, (D. Md. 1981) (No. K-81-2597).

_____. Memorandum in Support of Motion to Dismiss for Lack of Jurisdiction and in Opposition to Plaintiffs' Motion for Consolidation, (D. Md. 1981) (No. K-81-2597).

_____. Memorandum of Understanding, (D. Md. 1972) (No. 72-325-K) and (D. Md. 1981) (No. K-81-2597).

Pasadena City Board of Education v. Spangler, 427 U.S. 424 (1976).

People Who Care v. Rockford Board of Education, 111 F.3d 528 (7th Cir. 1997).

Plessy v. Ferguson, 163 U.S. 537 (1896).

Reed v. Rhodes, 422 F. Supp. 708 (N.D. Ohio 1976), *remanded* 549 F.2d 1220 (1977), 455 F. Supp 546 (N.D. Ohio 1978) and 455 F. Supp 569 (N.D. Ohio 1978), *aff'd* 607 F.2d 714 (6th Cir. 1979), *cert. denied* 455 U.S. 935 (1980).

_____. No. C73-1300, slip op. (N.D. Ohio 25 August 1979).

_____. No. C73-1300 (N.D. Ohio 27 August 1979) (order).

_____. 869 F. Supp. 1274 (N.D. Ohio 1994).

_____. No. C73-1300 (N.D. Ohio 15 March 1994) (settlement agreement).

_____. No. C73-1300 (N.D. Ohio 21 Feb. 1995) (notice of hearing).

_____. No. C73-1300 (N.D. Ohio 3 March 1995) (order).

_____. No C73-1300 (N.D. Ohio 6 March 1995) (order of reference).

_____. No. C73-1300 (N.D. Ohio 16 May 1995) (joint stipulation).

_____. No. C73-1300 (N.D. Ohio 27 March 1998) (memorandum and order).

San Antonio Independent School District v. Rodriguez, 411 U.S. 1 (1973).

Sheff v. O'Neill, 678 A.2d 1267 (Conn. 1996).

Shelley v. Kraemer, 334 U.S. 1 (1948).

Sipuel v. Board of Regents of the University of Oklahoma, 332 U.S. 631 (1948).

Spivey v. State of Ohio and Mixon v. State of Ohio, Nos. 1:97CV2308 and 1:97CV2309, slip op. (N.D. Ohio 6 March 1998).

Swann v. Charlotte-Mecklenberg Board of Education, 402 U.S. 1 (1971).

Sweatt v. Painter, 339 U.S. 629 (1950).

United States v. Cruikshank, 92 U.S. 542 (1875).

Vaughns v. Board of Education of Prince George's County, 355 F. Supp. 1051 (D. Md. 1972).

_____. Complaint (D. Md. 1972) (No. 72-325-K).

_____. Memorandum of Understanding (D. Md. 1972) (No. 72-325-K) and (D. Md.) (K-81-2597).

Texas v. U.S., (Case No. 97-29).

Newspaper and Magazine Articles and other Primary Sources

"All-day kindergarten will start in the fall." Cleveland West Side Sun News, 17 April 1997, 3(A).

Archer, Jeff. "Conn. Supreme Court Orders Desegregation for Hartford." *Education Week*, 7 August 1996, 6.

_____. "State Policy Update." *Education Week: Quality Counts '98,* 8 January 1998, 120.

Brown, DeNeen L. "Schools Accord Pushes Changes." *Washington Post*, 21 March 1998, 1(B).

_____. "Defining the Problem in Pr. George's." *Washington Post*, 26 March 1998, 5(D).

Brown, DeNeen L. and Robert Pierre. "Md. Agrees to Terms in Pr. George's Busing Suit." *Washington Post*, 19 March 1998, 1(A).

Brown, DeNeen L. and Jackie Spinner. "Judge Backs Pact to End Desegregation Lawsuit." *Washington Post*, 13 March 1998, 8(B).

Carper, Thomas R. "Desegregation settlement will benefit Delaware children." *Wilmington News Journal*, 5 December 1993, 3(F).

"Civil Rights Act of 1964." *Congressional Quarterly Almanac*, 1964, 338-80.

"Congress Looks to Chapter 1 Rewrite." *Congressional Quarterly Almanac*, 1993, 407-8.

Corrigan, Tom. "Mayoral Takeover Drawing Criticism." *West Side Sun News*, 10 July 1997, 1(A).

"Delaware Districts Lose Busing Appeal." *New York Times*, 25 July 1978, 10(A).

Dennison, Sandy. "Panel hopes to end '78 busing order." *Wilmington News Journal*, 31 October 1991, 1(B).

_____. "Del. board oks school deseg plan." *Wilmington News Journal*, 17 December 1993, 1(A).

_____. "Crafting a Settlement." *Wilmington News Journal*, 30 January 1994, 1(A).

Denton, Herbert H. "NAACP Sues County, Asks More Integration." *Washington Post*, 30 March 1972, 1(A) and 9(A).

_____. "Desegregation Deadline Set." *Washington Post*, 30 December 1972, 1(A).

Dubail, Jean. "The awful truth about Cleveland's kids." *Cleveland Plain Dealer*, 13 April 1997, 1(H).

Editorial. "New Castle County Schools: Outcome of deseg case will not solve achievement problems." *Wilmington News Journal*, 30 December 1994.

_____. *Cleveland Plain Dealer*. 9 March 1997, 1(A).

_____. "Defeat Issue 1." *Cleveland Plain Dealer*, 3 August 1997, 2(E).

_____. "The Urban Challenge." *Education Week Quality_Counts '98*, 8 January 1998, 6.

"Education Bill Provisions." *Congressional Quarterly Weekly Report, 1965* 52 (17 December): 3572-77.

Frazier, Lisa. "Prince George's School Plan Hurt by Tax Revolt." *Washington Post*, 1 December 1996, 1(B).

_____. "Prince George's School Board Votes to End Busing." *Washington Post*, 25 October 1997, 7(H).

_____. "Debate on Busing Lacks Passion." *The Washington Post*, 28 November 1997, 3(D).

_____. "Final Accord Reached on Ending Pr. George's Busing." *Washington Post*, 20 March 1998, 1(C).

"First General School Aid Bill Enacted." *Congressional Quarterly Almanac*, 1965, 275-93.

Frazier, Lisa and Robert E. Pierre. "Schools Did All They Could, Superintendent Testifies." *Washington Post*, 19 November 1997, 1(B).

Frazier, Lisa and Michael D. Shear. "Extra Money Failed to Raise Scores in twenty-one County Schools." *Washington Post,* 26 October 1997, 1(A).

Gandal, Matthew. "Making Standards Matter 1997." Washington, D.C.: American Federation of Teachers, 1997. Quoted in Millicent Lawton, "AFT, Foundation Find Good and Bad in States' Standards." *Education Week,* 6 August 1997, 13.

"Goodman Testifies at Trial, Suggests Desegregation Solutions." *San Diego Union,* 3 December 1976, 9(B).

Hardy, David W. "Black Fairmont Heights: Fears, Cautious Optimism." *Washington Post,* 30 November 1969, 1(D) and 9(D).

Harp, Lonnie. "OCR Probes Bias Complaint Against Texas Exit Test." *Education Week,* 7 February 1996, 11.

Hendrie, Caroline. "Ill Will Comes with Territory in Takeovers. *Education Week,* 12 June 1996, 1 and 12-13.

_____. "Without Court Orders, Schools Ponder How to Pursue Diversity." *Education Week,* 30 April 1997, 1 and 36.

_____. "Falling Stars." *Education Week,* 25 February 1998, 36-38.

_____. "New Magnet School Policies Sidestep an Old Issue: Race." *Education Week,* 10 June 1998, 11.

_____. "A Denver High School Reaches Out to the Neighborhood it Lost to Busing." *Education Week,* 17 June 1998, 1 and 22.

Hoff, David J. "Tracking Title I." *Education Week,* 22 October 1997, 16-17.

_____. "A Question of Authority, *Education Week: Quality Counts '98,* 8 January 1998, 126.

Huth, Tom. "Kids Were Ready Before Today." *Washington Post,* 30 January 1973, 1(C).

Jaynes, Gregory. "Wilmington Teachers End Strike With Approval of Three-year Pact." *New York Times,* 22 November 1978, 14(A).

Jensen, Christopher. "Battisti names twenty-one to panel to monitor desegregation." *Cleveland Plain Dealer,* 24 June 1978, 12(A).

Jerald, Craig D. Bridget K. Curren, and Lynn Olson. "The State of the States." *Education Week: Quality Counts '98,* 8 January 1998, 76.

Jones, Patrice and Scott Stephens. "Hard work ahead for schools: White urges all to cooperate with order, blames Parrish." *Cleveland Plain Dealer,* 5 March 1995, 8(A).

"Judge Battisti Must Sift Mountain of Evidence to Render His Verdict." *Cleveland Plain Dealer,* 14 February 1976, 1(A).

Keller, Bess. "San Diego's New Chief an Unlikely Pick." *Education Week,* 18 March 1998, 1 and 18.

Krause, Charles A. "'I'd Rather Be With Blacks.'" *Washington Post,* 30 January 1973, 1(C) and 3(C).

Kuznik, Frank. "The Politics of Desegregation." *Cleveland Magazine,* September 1978, 82-88 and 200-202.

"League of Women Voters opposes schools proposal," *Cleveland Plain Dealer,* 15 March 1997, 1(A).

Leff, Lisa. "Demographics Foil P.G. Schools' Efforts to Achieve Racial Balance." *Washington Post,* 12 September 1993, 1(A) and 24-25(A).

_____. "For Schools, Court Order Provided No Shortcut to Excellence." *Washington Post,* 13 September 1993, 1(A) and 10(A).

_____. "Mistrust, High Costs Conspire Against Alternatives." *Washington Post,* 14 September 1993, 1(A) and 6(A).

Lewin, Tamar. "School Voucher Study Finds Satisfaction." New York Times, 18 September 1997, 12(A).

Lipton, Eric. "The Struggle of a County's Schools." *Washington Post,* 21 June 1998, 1(A).

_____. "Building Better Schools." *Washington Post,* 21 June 1998, 1(A).

Lipton, Eric and Lisa Frazier. "Affluent Parents Seek Wealth of Solutions." *Washington Post,* 24 June 1998, 1(A).

Livingston, Sandra and Evelyn Theiss. "White's trouble with the unions." *Cleveland Plain Dealer,* 6 October 1997, 1(A).

Mahtesian, Charles. "School takeover reactions mixed." *Cleveland Plain Dealer,* 5 October 1997, 17(A).

McCombs, Philip A. "Prince George's Desegregation of Schools Peaceful, Smooth." *Washington Post,* 30 January 1973, 1(A) and 10(A).

_____."Mixing Goal Not Reached." *Washington Post,* 3 February 1973, 1(B).

McGruder, Robert G. and Thomas H. Gaumer. "Board appeals; slow to obey orders, judge says." *Cleveland Plain Dealer,* 28 April 1978, 1(A).

Meyer, Lawrence. "Plan 'Abhorrent' In Pr. George's." *Washington Post,* 14 November 1969, 1(C).

_____. "Top Level Talks Slated on Schools." *Washington Post,* 15 November 1969, 1(B).

_____. "Pr. George's Meets HEW School Order." *Washington Post,* 18 November 1969, 2(C).

_____. "In All-White Cheverly: Apprehension, Protest." *Washington Post*, 30 November 1969, 1(D).

Miller, Beth. "Deseg case officially laid to rest." *Wilmington News Journal*, 20 November 1996, 1(A).

Monroney, Mike. "Prince George's Schools Take Integration Step." *Washington Post*, 10 August 1955, 27(A).

"New Dynamics in Prince George's." *Washington Post*, 2 August 1996, 20(A).

"Obey Battisti, board lawyers advise." *Cleveland Plain Dealer*, 24 April 1978, 1(A) and 10(A).

Olson, Lynn. "Veterans of State Takeover Battles Tell a Cautionary Tale." *Education Week*, 12 February 1997, 25.

Olson, Lynn and Craig D. Jerald. "The Achievement Gap." *Education Week: Quality Counts '98*, 8 January 1998, 10-12.

Olten, Carol. "Reaction to Carlin Ruling On S.D. Integration Mixed." *San Diego Union*, 11 March 1977, 1(A) and 10(A).

Ortiz, Mario G. "Roundtable backs White's control of schools." *Cleveland Plain Dealer*, 3 April 1997, 1(A).

_____. "Gains on standard tests please educators." *Cleveland Plain Dealer*, 15 July 1997, 1(B) and 4(B).

"Parents Wary of Area Desegregation Plan." *Washington Post*, 30 November 1969, 1(D).

Perk, Jr., Ralph J. "Why did school board have to go to court?" *Cleveland Plain Dealer*, 17 February 1988, 13(A).

"Prince George's Busing Realities." *Washington Post*, 4 July 1997, 20(A).

"Pr. George's Saluted on Desegregation." *Washington Post*, 30 January 1973, 10(A).

Raspberry, William. "School Reforms to Nowhere." *Washington Post*, 27 March 1998, 25(A).

Reinhard, Beth. "Mayor to Get School Control in Cleveland." *Education Week*, 9 July 1997, 1, 28-29.

_____. "Racial Issues Cloud State Takeovers: Interventions Often Face Legal Challenges." *Education Week*, 14 January 1998, 1.

Reynolds, Maura. "Integration's failures shake schools' faith: 25 years after Carlin suit." *San Diego Union*, 2 December, 1992, 1(A).

_____. "Path to school integration has been rocky, winding." *San Diego Union*, 3 December 1992, 1(A) and 13(A).

Roberts, Steven V. "Leaders of Wilmington, Del. Seek Smooth Start of Busing." *New York Times*, 2 February 1978, 16(A).

Ruth, Eric. "Deseg trial draws to early close." *Wilmington News Journal*, 7 January 1995, 4(A).

Sack, Kevin. "In Little Rock, Clinton Warns of Racial Split." *New York Times*, 26 September 1997, 1(A) and 27(A).

Schmidt, Peter. "Desegregation Study Spurs Debate Over Equity Remedies." *Education Week*, 12 January 1994, 5.

_____. "Del. Desegregation Case Pivots on Student Statistics." *Education Week*, 1 March 1995, 14.

_____. "Administration Falls Short, Right Report Says." *Education Week*, 25 January 1995, 15.

_____. "Districts View Desegregation Within a New Light." *Education Week*, 13 December 1997, 10.

Scott-Blair, Michael. "L.A. Ruling Felt Here By Schools." *San Diego Union*, 30 June 1976, 1(A).

_____. "Carlin Says City Schools Fail to Keep Integration Promise." *San Diego Union*, 5 November 1976, 3(B).

_____. "School Chief Hits Integration Move." *San Diego Union*, 14 December 1976, 1(B).

_____. "Study Shows Whites Move From Busing." *San Diego Union*, 5 January 1977, 1(B) and 4(B).

_____. "Carlin Case Indifference is Assailed." *San Diego Union*, 23 January 1977, 1(A) and 9(A).

_____. "S.D. Leaders Assailed on Integration." *San Diego Union*, 16 February 1977, 1(B) and 4(B).

_____. "Imbalance found in twenty-three schools." *San Diego Union*, 10 March 1977, 1(A) and 4(A).

_____. "Welsh Order Only Beginning of Long Road." *San Diego Union*, 10 March, 1977, 5(A).

_____. "Parents Reject Forced Busing." *San Diego Union*, 20 May 1977, 1(A) and 21(A).

_____. "School Integration Proposal Fails to Win Approval." *San Diego Union*, 20 May 1977, 1(A) and 20(A).

_____. "Debate on Busing Sought." *San Diego Union*, 19 August 1977, 3(B).

_____. "Bus Mix-Ups Only Hitch Here As School Integration Starts." *San Diego Union*, 13 September 1977, 1(A) and 4(A).

Shapiro, Margaret. "Rehearing Set in '72 School Case." *Washington Post,* 29 September 1981, 1(A) and 11(A).

Shapiro, Margaret and Leon Wynter. "Pr. George's Faces Busing Case Renewal." *Washington Post,* 2 September 1981, 1(A) and 9(A).

Sheridan, Chris. "The principal proficiency test." *Cleveland Plain Dealer,* 27 July 1997, 2(E).

Solomon, Lewis C. and Michael Fox. "Fatally Flawed School Funding Formulas." *Education Week,* 17 June 1998, 60 and 17-18.

Stephens, Scott. "Proficiency test results show gains." *Cleveland Plain Dealer,* 31 May 1997, 1(B) and 6(B).

_____. "Union against schools' overhaul." *Cleveland Plain Dealer,* 7 August 1997, 1(B).

Stephens, Scott and Mario G. Ortiz. "Two schools face staff overhaul." *Cleveland Plain Dealer,* 8 August 1997, 1(B).

Stephens, Scott, Robert J. Vickers, and Mario G. Ortiz. "Voters turn down limits on abatement." *Cleveland Plain Dealer,* 6 August 1997, 1(A).

Stern, Laurence. "Voluntary Integration Approved By County." *Washington Post,* 11 April 1956, 1(A).

Leonard Stevens. "Cleveland shrugs off applause it deserves." *Cleveland Plain Dealer,* 16 February 1988, 3(B).

Strauss, Valerie and Sari Horwitz. "As Students Fail, U.S. Aid Goes to Waste." *Washington Post,* 16 February 1997, 24(A).

Taylor, Jr., John H. "Looking Back on the Long Ride." *Wilmington News Journal,* 5 December 1993, 1(F).

Thomas, Paulette. "Cleveland Schools Are Playing Catch-Up." *Cleveland Plain Dealer,* 20 May 1997, 2(A).

"Thousands of Parents Attend Intense Integration Sessions." *San Diego Union,* 12 May 1977, 1(A) and 10(A).

Trombley, William. "Strike Perils Busing Plan in Delaware." *Los Angeles Times,* 30 October 1978, 3, 22.

Wagner, Joseph L. "Busing jeered by more than 2,000 here." *Cleveland Plain Dealer,* 26 April 1978, 2(A).

Walter, Franklin B. "Only Cleveland can solve Cleveland's problems." *Cleveland Plain Dealer,* 15 February 1988, eleven(A).

Watson, Douglas. "Parents Hit Pr. George's School Plan." *Washington Post,* 16 November 1969, 1(D).

_____. "Integrate or Face Fund Loss, U.S. Orders Prince George's." *Washington Post,* 30 July 1971, 1(A).

Unpublished Sources

Bradford, Jr., William A. (attorney for plaintiff NAACP) Letter to Paul Nussbaum re: *Milliken II* Relief, 21 June 1985. (filed with Memorandum of Understanding, NAACP v. Board of Education of Prince George's County, No. K-81-2587 (D. Md. 1981).

Davis, Donna G. "Empowering the Hispanic Female in the Public School Setting, Part I." San Diego: San Diego City Schools Planning, Research, and Evaluation Division, 1989. Unpublished.

"Delaware School Finances." Dover: Delaware Department of Public Instruction, 1994. Unpublished.

"District Totals." San Diego: San Diego City Schools, Schools Services, 1998. Unpublished.

"Fast Facts and other information about San Diego City Schools." San Diego: San Diego City Schools, Public Support and Engagement, 1995. Unpublished.

"FY1996 Vital Statistics on Ohio School Districts." Columbus: Ohio Department of Education, 1996. Unpublished.

"Proposed Phased Implementation of Neighborhood School Assignments: A Six Year Plan, 1994". Upper Marlboro, Md.: Prince George's County Public Schools, 1994.

"Regulations for the Reorganization of the New Castle County School District -- 1980." Dover: Delaware Department of Public Instruction, 1980. Unpublished.

Riley, Kevin W. "National Integration Conference Symposium: Integration at a Crossroad: From Compliance to Commitment; Investing in our Nation's Future." San Diego: San Diego City Schools Community Relations and Integration Services Division, 1990. Unpublished.

"San Diego Plan for Racial Integration, 1995-1996." San Diego: San Diego City Schools, Schools Services Division, 1996. Unpublished.

"San Diego Plan for Racial Integration, 1997-1998." San Diego: San Diego City Schools, Schools Services Division, 1997. Unpublished.

Santa Cruz, Rafaella M. and Maria Nieto Senour. "Empowering the Hispanic Female in the Public School Setting, Part II." San Diego: San Diego City Schools Planning, Research, and Evaluation Division, 1989. Unpublished.

_____. "Reading Parity in the Cleveland City School District." Cleveland: Office on School Monitoring and Community Relations, 1985. Unpublished.

_____. "Dropouts in the Cleveland Public Schools: OSMCR Report to Judge Frank Battisti." Cleveland: The Office on School Monitoring and Community Relations, 1997. Unpublished.

Swift, Shuford. "History of the Carlin Case." San Diego: By the author, 3910 Alicia Dr., San Diego, CA 92107, November 1994. Unpublished.

"Testing Results for Court-Identified Racially Isolated Schools: Spring 1995." San Diego: San Diego City Schools, Planning, Assessment, and Accountability Division, 1995. Unpublished.

"Using the Power of Collaboration to Help Cleveland's Children: Community Priorities for Reform of the Cleveland Public Schools During State Takeover." Cleveland: The Citizens League of Greater Cleveland, April 1995. Unpublished.

"Vaughns Highlights." (This is a timeline of significant dates in the *Vaughns* case produced and provided by the Prince George's County Public Schools.) Unpublished.

Weiss, Larry. "Summary of Carlin v. Board of Education." Report prepared by law student intern for the San Diego City Schools, 1985. Unpublished.

Secondary Sources

1994 Maryland School Performance Program Report: State, School System, and Schools, Prince George's County Public Schools (MSPP). Upper Marlboro: Prince George's County Public Schools, 1994.

Annual Report to the Community, 1994. Upper Marlboro: Prince George's County Public Schools, 1994.

Bates, Percy. "Desegregation: Can We Get There from Here?" *Phi Delta Kappan* 72 (September 1990): 8-17.

Bell, Derrick. "Learning from Our Losses: Is School Desegregation Still Feasible in the 1980s?" *Phi Delta Kappan* 64 (April 1983): 572-75.

Benjamin, Kay E. "A Case Study of an Urban Superintendent: Paul Briggs, 1964-1978." Ph.D. diss., Cleveland State University, 1995.

Bolner, James and Robert Stanley. *Busing: the Political and Judicial Process*. New York: Praeger Publishers, 1974.

Connell, R. W. "Poverty and Education," *Harvard Educational Review* 62 (Summer 1994): 125-49.

Days, III, Drew S. "Brown Blues: Rethinking the Integrative Ideal." *William and Mary Law Review* 34 (Fall 1992): 53-74.

Dempsey, Van and George Noblit. "The Demise of Caring in an African-American Community: One Consequence of School Desegregation." *Urban Review* 25 (1993): 53-74.

Edsall, Thomas Byrne and Mary D. Edsall. *Chain Reaction: The Impact of Race, Rights, and Taxes on American Politics.* New York: W.W. Norton & Company, 1992.

Education Watch: The 1996 Trust State and National Data Book. Quoted in Lynn Olson. "Examining Race and Demography," *Education Week: Quality Counts '97,* 22 January, 10-11.

"Events Leading to School Order." *Washington Post,* 30 December 1972, 12(A).

Feldman, Joseph, Edward Kirby, Susan E. Eaton, and Alison Morantz. *Still Separate, Still Unequal: The Limits of Milliken II's Educational Compensation Remedies.* Cambridge: The Harvard Project on School Desegregation, 1994.

Hacker, Andrew. *Two Nations: Black and White, Separate, Hostile, and Unequal.* New York: Charles Scribner's Sons, 1992.

Hillson, Jon. *The Battle of Boston.* New York: Pathfinder Press, 1977.

Kluger, Richard. *Simple Justice:__The History of Brown v. Board of Education and Black America's Struggle for Equality.* New York: Alfred A. Knopf, 1976.

Kozol, Jonathan. *Savage Inequalities: Children in America's Schools.* New York: Harper Perennial, 1991.

A Long Day's Journey into Light: School Desegregation in Prince George's County. Washington, D.C.: U.S. Commission on Civil Rights, 1976.

Lukas, J. Anthony. *Common Ground: A Turbulent Decade in the Lives of Three American Families.* New York: Alfred Knopf, 1985.

McLaughlin, Milbrey Wallin. *Evaluation and Reform: The Elementary and Secondary Education Act of 1965, Title I.* Cambridge: Ballinger Publishing Company, 1975.

Mearns, Jr., Edward A. "The city didn't want to believe it," *Cleveland Plain Dealer,* 16 February 1988, 3(B).

O'Brien, David M. *Storm Center: The Supreme Court in American Politics.* 3d ed. New York: W.W. Norton & Company, 1993.

Orfield, Gary. *Must We Bus? Segregated Schools and National Policy.* Washington, D.C.: The Brookings Institution, 1978.

_____. *The Growth of Segregation in American Schools: Changing Patterns of Separation and Poverty Since 1968.* Boston: Harvard Project on School Desegregation, 1993.

_____. Foreword to *Still Separate, Still Unequal: The Limits of Milliken II's Educational Compensation Remedies*, by Joseph Feldman, Edward Kirby, Susan E. Eaton, and Alison Morantz. Cambridge: The Harvard Project on School Desegregation, 1994.

Orfield, Gary, Mark Bachmeier, David R. James, and Tamela Eitle. *Deepening Segregation in American Public Schools.* Cambridge: Harvard Project on School Desegregation, 1997.

Orlich, Donald. *"Brown v. Board of Education:* Time for a Reassessment." *Phi Delta Kappan* 72 (April 1991): 631-32.

Peltason, J.W. *Fifty-eight Lonely Men: Southern Federal Judges and School Desegregation.* New York: Harcourt, Brace & World, Inc., 1961.

Raffel, Jeffrey. *The Politics of School Desegregation: The Metropolitan Remedy in Delaware.* Philadelphia: Temple University Press, 1980.

Report of the Citizens Committee on Equal Educational Opportunities to the Board of Education, San Diego City Schools. By Byron R. Lindsley, Chairman. San Diego: Board of Education of the City of San Diego, 1966.

"Resources." *Education Week: Quality Counts '97*, 22 January 1997, 54.

Richan, Willard C. *Racial Isolation in the Cleveland Public Schools: A Report of a Study Sponsored by the United States Commission on Civil Rights.* Cleveland: Case Western Reserve University, 1967.

Rosenberg, Gerald. *The Hollow Hope: Can Courts Bring About Social Change?* Chicago: University of Chicago Press, 1991.

School System of Choices, 1994. Upper Marlboro: Prince George's County Public Schools, 1994.

Sinclair, Barbara. *The Transformation of the U.S. Senate.* Baltimore: Johns Hopkins University Press, 1989.

Stevens, Leonard. *More Than a Bus Ride: The Desegregation of the Cleveland Public Schools.* Cleveland: Office on School Monitoring and Community Relations, 1985.

Stickney, Benjamin D. and Virginia R. L. Plunkett. "Has Title I Done Its Job?" *Educational Leadership*, February 1982, 378-83.

"Supplementary AP material on busing." *New York Times*, 12 September 1978, 88.

Tabor, Karl. "Desegregation of Public School Districts: Persistence and Change." *Phi Delta Kappan* 72 (September 1990): 18-24.

Trombley, William. "Desegregation in Wilmington a 30-Year fight." *Los Angeles Times*, 30 October 1978, 16.

U.S. Congress. Senate. Committee on Labor and Public Welfare. *Elementary and Secondary Education Act of 1965.* 89th Cong., 1st sess., 1965. Rept. No. 146.

U.S. Congress. Senate. Subcommittee on Education. *Hearings on Elementary and Secondary Education Act of 1965.* 89th Cong., 1st sess., 1965, 529.

Urban League of Cleveland. *The Negro in Cleveland, 1950-1963: An Analysis of the Social and Economic Characteristics of the Negro Population.* Cleveland: The Urban League of Cleveland, 1964.

Whalen, Charles and Barbara Whalen. *The Longest Debate: A legislative history of the 1964 Civil Rights Act.* Cabin John, MD: Seven Locks Press, 1985.

Wilkinson, J. Harvie. *From Brown to Bakke: The Supreme Court and School Integration: 1954--1978.* New York: Oxford University Press, 1979.

Word, Elizabeth, Charles M. Achilles, Helen Pate Bain, Carolyn Breda, John Folger, B. DeWayne Fulton, John Johnston, Martha Nannette Lintz, Jayne Boyd Zaharias. *Student/Teacher Achievement Ratio (STAR) Project: Tennessee's K-3 Class Size Study.* Nashville: Tennessee State Department of Education, 1990.

Index

---

[1] Throughout the text when the term *Brown* is used, it usually refers to both *Brown I* and *Brown II*, that is, both the Court's 1954 ruling that purposely segregated schools were unconstitutional and its 1955 ruling that segregated school systems must be dismantled.

Printed in the United States
45898LVS00001B/28-48

9 781931 202459